Secrets of the Trade

An Esalen Book

The Esalen Publishing Program

is edited by Stuart Miller

Secrets of the Trade

NOTES ON MADNESS, CREATIVITY & IDEOLOGY

Joe Kennedy Adams

NEW YORK / THE VIKING PRESS

An Esalen Book

First published in 1971 by The Viking Press, Inc.
625 Madison Avenue, New York, N.Y. 10022
Published simultaneously in Canada by
The Macmillan Company of Canada Limited

SBN 670-63171-x

Library of Congress catalog card number: 71-149269

Printed in U.S.A.

Acknowledgments:

UNIVERSITY BOOKS, INC.: "Psychosis: 'Experimental'
and Real" from *The Psychedelic Reader.* Published by
University Books, Inc., a subsidiary of Lyle Stuart, Inc.,
New Hyde Park, New York 11040. Copyright © 1963,
1965 by University Books, Inc.

"Differentiation and Dedifferentiation in Healthy Func-
tioning," "Deception and Intrigue in So-Called Mental
Illness," and "The Overemphasis on Sex in Western
Civilization" originally appeared in the *Journal of
Humanistic Psychology.*

TO THOMAS SZASZ

. . . a thing may be true even if nobody believes it, and something else may be false if everybody believes it. Such, it may be remarked, is usually the case.

—*The Philosophy of Mr. B*rtr*nd R*ss*ll*

P. E. B. JOURDAIN

"For nothing is hid that shall not be made manifest, nor anything secret that shall not be known and come to light. Take heed then how you hear. . . ."

—LUKE

Preface

One type of madness that can be particularly intriguing and puzzling is that in which the madman believes he has discovered something of great importance, not only to himself but also to the society in which he lives. For example, about fourteen years ago a man was taken to a mental hospital following an episode during which he sent an urgent telegram to President Eisenhower and also painted the word "LOVE" in boxcar letters on the roof of his fine suburban home, so that the occupants of planes overhead could see the message and spread it as quickly as possible (this was long before the "love generation" made such tactics less unusual).

The above example illustrates that this type of madness, like most types, can be very dangerous to the madman himself, however harmless or loving his attitude may be toward other people, for unless he exercises discretion in telling of his great discovery, he may find himself inside a mental hospital, usually involuntarily. Discretion, however, is perhaps the least likely virtue to coexist with the excitement of discovery; even such a sober, practical, and logical thinker as Archimedes, upon discovering the famous principle that bears his name today, is said (by Vitruvius) to have rushed out of the public baths in Syracuse and run naked down the street shouting "Eureka! Eureka!"

If we classify Archimedes as a creative genius, who had indeed discovered something of great importance and who therefore had every right to become greatly excited and perhaps even to ignore such mundane incidentals as the custom of wearing clothing in public, and at the same time we consider the patient who painted "LOVE" on his roof just another "nut," then we not only do the latter a grave injustice, but we show a great misunderstanding of both creativity and madness. We do not know what the patient had discovered about love and what he was trying to communicate. He may have gained a very great and very sudden understanding which he may have had good reason to believe that Mr. Eisenhower lacked, and even if his insight was not a new one within the society, as was presumably that of Archimedes, it may have been an act of creativity of very high order. Further, it is no insult to Archimedes to say that perhaps he was temporarily mad, as many other brilliantly creative men have been.

For the present author the relation between creativity and madness is not a subject of mere academic or theoretical concern, for the essays in this collection grew in large part out of two episodes of madness experienced by the author himself, in January 1960 and in February 1961.

These episodes fall into the category already mentioned, i.e., during each of them I had the conviction that I had made some important discoveries which I must somehow communicate not only to my colleagues in psychology but also to the entire world. My early efforts at communication, however, were no more discreet than those of most madmen; during the second episode, for example, I attempted to run naked down the street— so that everyone could see that the millennium had arrived—and would have done so had I not been intercepted in the driveway by a psychiatrist.[1] This effort to communicate resulted in a month's residence in a sanitarium, where I had to be kept in physical restraint for several days, during which, among other colorful acts, I managed to gnaw the leather strap which held me to the bed halfway through.

Lest the title mislead the reader, I should emphasize that there are few if any secrets revealed, in the sense of inside information about behind-the-scenes plans and maneuvers, or even in the broader sense of facts, techniques, or ideas usually known only to professionals in the field of "mental health." Instead I have attempted to present a rather complexly interwoven set of ideas, attitudes, and facts (often historical) which I hope will give some readers a new perspective on the social structure in which they

1. Even at the time I thought of Archimedes, and this thought increased the already grandiose delusions of discovery. Later reflections revealed a number of differences.

are embedded, including especially the roles and functions of experts—not just mental-health experts but ideologists of all kinds. Psychologists will not need to be told that I am not an authority (on anything), but others should be warned that they cannot quote me as such. These essays are intended to stimulate the reader to do some reading, thinking, and observing, not to give him well-formulated and fully documented conclusions. Readers with a sense of humor, as well as a toleration for horror, will enjoy this book the most; without both these characteristics I would not be alive today.

There is much hatred in this book, but it is hatred of human sacrifice, not of humans. Nothing that I say should be interpreted as a reflection upon those who were closest to me at the time of my disturbance, especially my wife, my colleagues at the Mental Research Institute, and the two psychiatrists who were unfortunate enough to have me as a patient. I have tried to indicate how fortunate I was in this respect. For those not so close, I cannot make such a blanket statement; with few exceptions, however, there is no lingering animosity on my part, and I hope there is none on the part of those to whom I behaved unreasonably and unintentionally rudely. The important facts are that many thousands of people are incarcerated unnecessarily, that millions are suffering unnecessarily, and that enormous amounts of creative energy are being wasted and destroyed instead of being utilized in a constructive way. If this book contributes in any way, directly or indirectly, to some solutions of the present situation, it is well worth "making a fool of myself," as some critics, with some justification, may maintain. Perhaps I can have a role as the Fool of psychology, though I would prefer to have plenty of strong competition for such a role.

As each essay, except the last, was written to be read separately, there is considerable repetition, but as my writing tends to be compact, perhaps the repetition will serve a useful purpose.

Most of the essays are preceded by prefaces which may help the reader to understand what I am trying to say and why I consider it of any importance, as well as its relationship (in part) to my own experiences. The essays are arranged in the chronological order in which they were written, which is not identical with the order in which some have been previously published. A note on "The Necessity of Phenomenology" is placed in the appendix because of its relatively technical nature.

I have never met Thomas Szasz, but have dedicated this book to him because of my respect and admiration for his work, his integrity, and his courage, as well as because of the great personal debt I owe to his writing, which has been not only a rich and exciting source of information and ideas but also a continuing inspiration and encouragement not to give up in the face of apparently hopeless odds.

I am indebted also to Mike Murphy, Dick Price, Alan Kringel, Sid Jourard, Tony and Evelyn Sutich, Steve and Susie Hughes, and others who have encouraged me over the years, and to Stuart Miller, whose persistent efforts are largely responsible for the publication of this book.

San Francisco   JOE KENNEDY ADAMS
June 1 9 7 0

Contents

Secrets of the Trade

1

Differentiation and Dedifferentiation in Healthy Functioning

PREFACE At the time of my first episode of madness, January
1960, I was investigating the uses of LSD (then a
relatively unknown drug) in a research project located
at the Mental Research Institute of the Palo Alto
Medical Research Foundation and sponsored by the
National Institute of Mental Health. Over a period of
about fourteen months I had taken the drug about ten
or twelve times myself and had conducted dozens of
sessions with others, including a number of psychologists and psychiatrists who volunteered as subjects.
Late in December 1959 I underwent a session using
200 gamma (micrograms) which was immediately
followed by a severe depression, lasting five days, during which I thought suicide was unnecessary because I
was going to die anyway—and should. This state of
depression, which at the time seemed not in the least
"psychotic" to me, declined during the last day and then
was dramatically and abruptly terminated by an intense
and ecstatic *righteous rage,* unlike anything I remem-
bered experiencing before and accompanied by technicolor visions and feelings of omnipotence. This

experience apparently had nothing whatever to do with
the external circumstances at that moment, but was
entirely a function of what was going on within me. I
had just purchased a jacket to wear in the snow (we
planned a weekend trip to the mountains), and it was
while I was walking back to my car that this most strange
and uncanny experience occurred. I had read a brief
description by Carl Jung of the experience of the
magician archetype and this was the only reality I had
to hang onto; although some experts will scoff at the
idea, this "book learning" was a great help in controlling my behavior at the time and in avoiding being
panicked by my strange state. The rage, the pleasure of
which I can describe only as somewhat like an orgasm
in every part of my body, beginning at the top of my
head and spreading quickly to my extremities, lasted
only a few seconds, but the accompanying flight of ideas
and feelings of cleverness and omnipotence continued
for perhaps twenty minutes or so, during which I drove
home. My two-and-a-half-year-old son responded immediately and positively to some subtle kind of change
in my behavior or appearance ("Box with me,
Daddy," he said, playfully putting up his tiny fists),
and it was while I was playing with him that the
magician vanished as suddenly as he had appeared (as
Jung describes). During the next sixty hours, the
magician came and went a number of times, and there
were many other strange experiences, over which I had
no control whatsoever. I found it easy, however, to
control my *behavior,* to drive a car, etc. There are
presumably many "psychotics" who are in this condition: some kind of inner experience is going on and
they are quite aware of being "crazy" in this way, but
their *behavior* is under relatively good control.

When I awoke one morning, about sixty hours after
the episode began, to find that the autonomous inner

process was no longer present, I experienced an elation and sense of physical and mental well-being that persisted for many months. I felt thoroughly rejuvenated, mentally and physically, and thus became much more open, aggressive, spontaneous, and unguarded than I had been before. It was at this point that my behavior changed so markedly that most of the people who knew me were appalled and considered me "disturbed." People *who had not known me before,* however, did not usually see me as pathological or disturbed; some of my new acquaintances thought I was just unusually extroverted and lively. My interest shifted away from drug research to the problem of what is "healthy" existence or behavior and to the ways in which people control each other's behavior by their concepts, perceptions, role behaviors, expectations, etc., a topic in which I had been interested for many years but which now seemed obviously necessary and fundamental to any progress whatsoever in the field of "mental health." I became very aware of the degree of liveliness or deadness in face-to-face interactions, but was often insensitive to the way in which I was being perceived, which was of course usually concealed, especially by those who perceived me unfavorably.

The following essay was dashed off at some time during these months of elation. At the time I fully expected it to be a bombshell in the field—the extent of this delusion is indicated by the fact that I have never seen any reference whatsoever to it. The reader will note the looseness of my writing, both in the sense of abrupt transitions from one topic to another and in the sense of making many assertions without any attempt to justify them. At the time it was written, however, this paper seemed to hang together very well and my sweeping assertions seemed to be largely verifiable by any discerning reader who would take the trouble to consult his own experience and observations. Although I still have the latter conviction, I am no longer so sanguine about such an effort's being made.

Differentiation and Dedifferentiation in Healthy Functioning

Psychologists and other specialists have written at great length about the process of becoming an individual, i.e., of becoming differentiated from the external world—particularly from one's parents—and thereby gaining at least a measure of freedom and of mastery over the environment. While the necessity and desirability of this process has ordinarily been granted (in fact, its achievement is one of the commonest goals of psychotherapy), some disadvantages have also been noted, especially those of isolation, aloneness, or contactlessness which often result. Some theorists take the point of view that these unfortunate results indicate that differentiation has not been sufficiently thorough; others believe that it has proceeded too far already in our culture, and that what is needed is a more symbiotic or undifferentiated way of living, as found in some "primitive" cultures.

Differentiation has often been discussed in terms of character structure, i.e., an individual is placed along a dimension (or group of dimensions) having to do with degree of autonomy or independence. There are, however, a few theoretical discussions of a bipolar dimension along which a given individual moves back and forth from time to time, a process of becoming temporarily more differentiated ("closed," autonomous, or independent) or becoming dedifferentiated ("open" or dependent), depending upon the situation.

The functional value of "closing" and "opening" has also been pointed out. When the individual "closes up" he becomes "cold," "hard," "distant," or "mean." He is protected from intimacy, involvement. An individual in such a state can be formidably aggressive, either actively, as in cold-blooded slashing at one's opponent, or passively, as in politeness, stubbornness, pseudo-kindness, or unintelligibility. The person who is

Reprinted in slightly revised form from the *Journal of Humanistic Psychology*, vol. 1, no. 2 (Fall 1961).

consistently cold-blooded is mistrusted and feared by the average person, for he is difficult to influence and is capable of extraordinary ruthlessness; nevertheless, such a person may be extremely conscientious and "good"; he may, for example, be an idealist who will not allow anyone to get close to him, even temporarily, because no one quite measures up to his standards. Thus, differentiation can be a great asset to an individual as an aid in aggression or defense.

The functional value of dedifferentiation or "opening" has also been discussed. To become "open" is to allow intimacy, and with intimacy comes feeling. With feeling the body seems "alive," without it, "dead." Not all feelings are pleasant however, and the individual who repeatedly experiences fear, anxiety, guilt, horror, sadness, humiliation, or other dysphoric feelings will tend to become more and more "closed" and inaccessible, whereas one who experiences excitement, elation, sexual pleasure, relaxation, self-esteem, release from unpleasantness, or other pleasurable feelings will tend to seek opportunities to be "open." What has just been stated is, of course, a form of hedonistic theory, a theory that has never been adequately tested for several reasons, among them: (1) the lack of an adequate and communicable descriptive phenomenology of feeling, (2) the methodological and ethical difficulties in producing feelings experimentally, and (3) a strong behavioristic bias which is still very much alive.

Differentiation is a well-known principle of ontogenetic and phylogenetic development and is used also in the description of large and complex social systems. In the present discussion I shall limit the term to three ranges of meanings: (1) intrapsychic events, (2) interpersonal relations, and (3) relations between the individual and "the world." For example, the conceptual abstraction of structure from content, as in logic and pure mathematics, is a form of differentiation, as is figure-ground formation in perception. To be aware of differences between oneself and others and to verbalize such differences explicitly are also forms of differentiation. To shoot an animal and to say "I did it" is a form of differentiation; a less differentiated view is expressed by the Hopi hunter, who regards himself, the deer, and other objects or events as acting jointly in such a way that the death of the deer resulted.

The term "dedifferentiation" will be used analogously, to mean the breaking down of a differentiation, though not necessarily completely.

To bring two concepts into relation with one another, when they have previously existed only in separate contexts, is a form of dedifferentiation, though not a complete one. To ignore or devalue distinctions that one has previously made is another example. To feel close to another person, or to be intellectually or physically intimate with another person are forms of dedifferentiation. To dedifferentiate "completely" with another person or with the universe is to lose all consciousness of self. Such an extreme dedifferentiation may be ecstatically gratifying (beatific or erotic "oneness") or incredibly traumatic (the experience or incorporation, of being devoured either against one's will or in a suicidal manner), and in either case can result in psychosis.

In differentiation and dedifferentiation intrapsychic processes tend to co-vary with interpersonal processes, e.g., intrapsychic dedifferentiation tends to make one more "open" to interpersonal dedifferentiation. This co-variation provides some justification for the fear of the "coldly" objective individual, who tends to be interpersonally differentiated at the same time that he is intrapsychically differentiated.

The usual views of character development have included a greater and greater degree of differentiation, both intrapsychically and interpersonally. It has been recognized by all theorists, however, that the healthy person will have close relationships with (i.e., dedifferentiate with) others, and some theorists have recognized the value of intrapsychic dedifferentiation (e.g., "regression in the service of the ego").

I propose that the concept of *flexibility and range in differentiation and dedifferentiation* be substituted for that of differentiated character structure. In the remainder of this paper I shall try to illustrate this proposal by making a number of assertions which, like several already made, cannot be proved at the present time, but which are more or less in accord with a considerable body of observations and widely accepted hypotheses. Though most of these assertions did not originate with me, the way in which they are formulated and combined may be unusual.

It is clear that high degrees of both differentiation and dedifferentiation are necessary for survival and for gratification. The child who is not permitted to dedifferentiate, physically and psychologically, with his parents will die or be warped and stunted. The child who is not allowed to differentiate himself from his parents will be too dependent upon

Mama or Daddy, and later will tend to attach himself in an over-dependent manner to a spouse, a boss, a group, a therapist, an ideology, etc.

The foregoing statements, however, need qualification. A child who is permitted a high degree of dedifferentiation with parents who are capable of differentiation is in a better position to achieve a high degree of differentiation than one who is permitted less dedifferentiation. Conversely, a child who is allowed and encouraged to differentiate from parents capable of dedifferentiation can dedifferentiate more adequately than one who is not allowed and encouraged to differentiate. Similarly, during adolescence the individual who dedifferentiates with peers capable of differentiation is more likely to be capable of differentiation than one who defends consistently against dedifferentiation.

The capacity for intrapsychic differentiation is also dependent in part upon the child's human and nonhuman environment. The child learns both from the consequences of his actions with objects and from human tutelage to differentiate perception, thought, memory, feeling, etc. from each other. Within each of these processes further differentiation is achieved, both in terms of structure and in terms of content. For example, within thought, logical reasoning is differentiated from free association, and relevant content (in a given situation) is differentiated from irrelevant content. Logic and mathematics are subjects par excellence for many such differentiations.

Differentiation of intrapsychic structure and content tend to be associated with clarity, precision, and objectivity. A relatively undifferentiated intrapsychic structure tends to vagueness, ambiguity, and subjectivity. The most outstanding creative scientists in their intrapsychic processes move flexibly and appropriately back and forth along these dimensions. Some great artists, like Léonardo, have had the same flexibility (Leonardo was, of course, also a scientist), but it is perhaps possible to achieve a high order of creativity in art without high degrees of differentiation, whereas a highly original scientific achievement without high degrees of dedifferentiation (as well as differentiation) would clearly be impossible.

Intrapsychic differentiation is typically a necessary condition for objective accomplishment, whereas dedifferentiation is typically necessary for gratifying and "full" experience.

There has been much nonsense written about these two processes, at least much that is half-truth. Certain philosophers, for example, have written that the separation of subject from object is artificial, that there is in reality only one event. To take such statements too literally is to court death or psychosis. Consider the hackneyed example of the individual who encounters a tiger in the wild and who truly believes that separation of subject from object is only a product of an "unrealistic" abstraction process, thus providing a convenient meal for the tiger, who has never been confused by metaphysics.

Statements such as "All is one" and "Everything is connected with everything else" are thrilling or comforting to those who are frightened at being differentiated from the external world, whereas those who are threatened by intrapsychic differentiation find something profound in statements like "Everything both is and is not" and "Nothing important can be proved." Such people, especially the second group, usually dislike and fear mathematics, a subject which not only forces one to be clear, but which also occasionally forces one to conclusions whether one likes those conclusions or not. It seems to me that part of their resistance to mathematics and the "hard" sciences consists of a fear or hostility toward being forced to yield to anything, even rationality (which they sometimes explicitly despise and devalue), or of forcing others to yield by the presentation of a clear-cut proof or argument. This hypothesis is in accord with the greater resistance to these subjects among women and among men who dislike open aggression in any form whatsoever. It is also possible that mathematics, logic, and the "physical" sciences appeal to those who enjoy forcing others to yield or agree, those who enjoy being "safe" in their assertions, or those who want to find a basis for universal agreement and uniformity. To form a reasonable hypothesis about any particular individual one would have to examine that individual's professional orientation and activity.

Current attacks upon "science" arise in part from a misunderstanding of scientific processes, which to a great many people represent consistent and extreme degrees of differentiation (clarity, objectivity, provability, communicability). There is realistic justification for these attacks insofar as scientists themselves subscribe to the same view, and apparently many do subscribe. There are relatively few sources of money for "scientific" research, for example, unless one submits a proposal in which all variables are clearly defined and measurable, and in which an experimental design is presented that will yield some clear-cut evidence about some clearly defined hypotheses; in other words, after what to many scientists is the most difficult, most interesting, and most significant scientific work has already been done. This situation is not by any means confined to psychology. There is little wonder that some students leave graduate school with the feeling that research is one of the dullest and least creative of all occupations, because a too steady insistence upon differentiated states does indeed amount to a desiccated existence.

The defensive value of differentiation should not be underrated, however. Clarity, rationality, and objectivity (e.g., keeping busy with something outside oneself) are functionally valuable in defending against self-doubt, feelings of loneliness or worthlessness, intimacy, or fear of incorporation.

Both differentiation and dedifferentiation play important roles in the maintenance of health (mental, emotional, and physical) as well as in character formation and objective accomplishment. As the child moves into puberty and adolescence he dedifferentiates more and more with peers—if all goes well—finally selecting a mate and dedifferentiating with that person and then with their children.

Any culture places sanctions upon various kinds of differentiation and dedifferentiation, and these sanctions vary with role and status. In view of the functions of these processes, therefore, the topic of mental (or emotional or physical) health is inevitably connected with that of the freedoms and rights of individuals and of groups. For this reason the topic of mental health is inevitably controversial, quite aside from the usual methodological and theoretical problems. The expert, like the layman, cannot help using his own reactions and the reactions of his group of reference as a yardstick, even if he readily admits that he is far from perfect himself. For example, an expert who avoids any open conflict with groups or even with other individuals may regard some actions as pathological or immature, when those same actions might be regarded as healthily independent and aggressive by experts who enjoy some conflict now and then. To stand up for what one believes, openly and aggressively, in the face of individual or group opposition, is a differentiating process which may produce in one person a feeling of freedom and self-respect, whereas another in the same context would feel anxiety, guilt, or shame. To pretend to believe something one doesn't believe produces feelings of cowardice, insignificance, or self-contempt in some, whereas others regard such pretense as what any sensible adult does every day, either from necessity or as courtesy, or sometimes even for the protection of other people.

The reference group's restrictions on differentiation and the ruthlessness with which restrictions are enforced become blatantly apparent during adolescence. During this time the individual is quite vulnerable to the nearly complete loss of self within the group, as in fascist or communist youth movements or in some religious conversions. A large proportion of people never recover from dedifferentiation during adolescence; to challenge the majority of one's reference group becomes from that point on unthinkable, as it cuts the individual off from the life-giving processes on which he is hopelessly dependent, or at least feels that he is. On the other hand, many "outsiders" during adolescence never recover from the paucity of dedifferentiation during this period.

It is only through a cyclical process of differentiation and dedifferentiation that any individual maintains strength, courage, the capacity for feeling, and the capacity for creative work. Those who are lost in a symbiotic interpersonal dedifferentiation, whether in marriage or in other relationships, are unable to enjoy life fully because of the gnawing awareness of the over-dependency upon external objects (and thus the threat of loneliness) and lack of contact with the self. The individual cannot be himself because he lacks not only the courage to threaten the symbiotic attachment but also the knowledge that only by destroying it can he be himself.

Severe cultural and internal restrictions are also placed upon dedifferentiation. In his development the healthy adolescent boy engages in much body contact with his male peers in sports and horsing around, and in frank and intimate discussions, not only in terms of content but also in manner and spontaneity of speaking. A feeling of masculine adequacy and "belongingness" is thus fostered. Among adult males in contemporary American society the only dedifferentiations that are socially acceptable in many middle- and upper-class circles are verbal, and these tend to lack the spontaneity and, therefore, the intimacy of adolescence. Among laborers and athletes body contacts are common, especially of a more or less playfully aggressive nature, as well as spontaneous and uninhibited verbal exchanges. Thus the latter groups maintain more of a sense of closeness and solidarity with other males.

Girls, on the other hand, have had more cultural restrictions on overtly aggressive dedifferentiation with each other and especially with boys. These restrictions contributed to the rise of feminism, when righteous indignation turned some women into battleaxes, and also led to the covertly controlling women who uses seduction, manipulation, chastity, piety, etc. to control men and, if possible, other women. Similar results can be observed among boys and men who have been too "good."

Theorists of character structure have often erred in thinking in terms of too rigid a developmental sequence, the end result being a "genital heterosexual character structure" which, once achieved, supposedly remains fixed. The relatively low degree of dedifferentiations found among middle- and upper-class men can easily lead to a longing and intense need for close contact with males; thus homosexuality flourishes among these classes, as do high degrees of nonsexual dedifferentiation with women. It is not unusual to find among these classes men who prefer to talk over intimate problems with women rather than with other men. Laborers who have homosexual relations are probably bisexual and prefer women to men sexually, though not for companionship in general or for friendly advice.

So strong does the desire for male dedifferentiation and the disgust, fear of, and boredom with dedifferentiation with women become in our culture that many men welcome war as an escape from women and a return to intimate male society. The Army pup tent, for example, is a stroke of genius for male dedifferentiation. On bivouac each soldier carries only a "shelter half"; thus he must pair with a buddy to make a pup tent under which they sleep in close proximity. Wise sergeants and officers are usually not too snoopy about what goes on under pup tents, knowing that a certain amount of homosexuality is to be expected, especially in the prolonged absence of women. This might be called the "blood-and-guts" school of homosexuality (usually bisexuality).

Fighting, competing, disagreeing, and arguing are usually processes of interpersonal differentiation, whereas caressing, cooperation, agreeing, and supporting are usually processes of dedifferentiation, and it seems plausible that being free to engage in the first group can help one to be free to engage in the second, and vice versa. I am referring, of course, to open and honest fighting, with limited objectives, and not to cutthroat, behind-the-back, anonymous, or hypocritical maneuvers. The suppression of open aggression has resulted in great damage to the vitality, intimacy, and honesty of interpersonal relations. One does not need to subscribe to the concept of a huge accumulation of latent hostility, built up through repression, to see the plausibility of this connection; holding hostile impulses in check but leaving the channels open for the spontaneous expression of positive impulses may be too difficult a feat for the human organism to manage. At any rate, one can find numerous instances of relationships that have deteriorated because of the maintenance of too unvarying an attitude—of romantic attachment, of loving kindness, of deference, of superiority, of formality, of friendliness, of dignity, of pleasantness, of toughness, of seriousness, of coolness, etc.

There are semantic pitfalls in this way of speaking; when engaging in open argument, for example, even when one is violent and exasperated, there may be implied in the behavior a dedifferentiation on a higher level—"We can argue because we respect each other's intelligence and right to disagree," "We want to arrive at mutual understanding," "We like each other enough to tolerate disagreement"—thus one might say that such argument is not classifiable as either differentiation or dedifferentiation, but as both. Such an objection raises a question about the precise definitions of these terms and about levels of human interaction rather than about the principle involved.

Psychotherapy can provide a relationship in which flexibility and range in differentiation and dedifferentiation can be increased. In practice, the opposite result is sometimes attained, e.g., a constant guardedness of manner and lack of spontaneity, an inability to be objective in certain content areas, an unwillingness to lose an argument—or even to have one, the loss of the self in adherence to a theoretical system and the perception of others primarily in terms of whether they are or are not members of the same cult. Some therapists have a constricted character structure (in terms of flexibility and range of differentiation and dedifferentiation) which may account for some of these results, because the therapist must necessarily exercise some control upon the course of therapy and must necessarily use himself to some extent as a measuring instrument. This does not mean that the therapist will see that the patient becomes like the therapist in behavior; he may overtly or covertly steer the patient in the "opposite" direction, i.e., toward that aspect of himself which is submerged or undeveloped.

An individual who fails to differentiate himself sufficiently from others is over-dependent and a drain on others. An individual who fails to dedifferentiate sufficiently eventually "dries up," feeling leaves his body and he becomes "cold" and "constricted"; such people can be either harmless, like many patients in mental hospitals, or very destructive, like the joy killers of the world. In some cases they do a great deal of good, because they can be rational when others have yielded to pressures to become irrational.

Jung is one of the few who have emphasized the health-giving function of extremely dedifferentiated states such as those found in "primitive" ceremonies and in mystical or transcendental experiences. It is significant that Jung is also concerned with differentiation (individuation) as the goal of psychotherapy. Only a highly differentiated person can go into one of the extremely dedifferentiated states and emerge fully. The primitives and mystics do not emerge fully—they accept the "mysteries" revealed during the dedifferentiated states as literal truths about the universe. Such extremely dedifferentiated states renew feeling in the body, which can last beyond the period of the session itself; thus they are, in a sense, a fountain of youth. These states can be relatively easily produced by mass meetings, music, chanting, dancing or other rhythmic motion, psychodrama, or drugs. Properly used, they can greatly aid the ability to differentiate, as well as the ability to dedifferentiate.

The writer proposes flexibility and range in differentiating and dedifferentiating as a partial definition of healthy functioning. If our society would accept these as goals in the development of the individual, we could perhaps emerge into an unprecedented era of satisfaction in living. There is the very real danger, however, of severe restrictions upon both flexibility and range, with increasing job specification, standardization of training, centralization of control, definition of role, togetherness, manipulation of motives, conditioning of behavior, etc.

2

A Gymnasium for the Production of Dionysian Rites and Other Health-Giving Rituals

PREFACE   The theory that we use up an enormous amount of energy in "holding ourselves down" is one with which I had been familiar for many years, but had never really believed until my first psychotic episode. The increase in energy which began when I awoke to find the autonomous process gone and which lasted for months was one of the most impressive aspects of my change, and one of the main reasons I insisted that what had happened was not an "unfortunate mishap" but, on the contrary, the best thing that had ever happened to me. I became very sensitive to the loss of energy that occurred whenever I inhibited my impulses. Naturally my behavior was at times overbearing and egocentric, at times even irresponsible, and I can now fully appreciate why others did not share my enthusiasm for my great transformation. Nevertheless, I was partly right and I could see that so many people were "dead" because there was little opportunity for them to be

"alive." After the second episode, which tended to have
the opposite effect from the first—I felt drained and
devoid of energy much of the time—I tried to formulate the basic notion and propose some kind of social
remedy. The following short essay was the result. Like
everything I wrote at that time, this was an "important
message" which I felt an urgent need to communicate
—that something very disastrous would occur unless
certain changes were made in our society, especially more
opportunities for people to "blow off steam" and to
"get pepped up." The "coolness and apathy of American youth" will sound strange to those who do not
remember how things were at that time—how deans
and professors had been complaining for years about
the "silent generation" and about seniors who, upon
being interviewed for jobs, were interested primarily
in the retirement plan! The young people have now
"come to life," found some Holy Causes, and developed
a youth movement which is so similar to what happened in Communist Russia (and to some extent in
Nazi Germany) that even the most pedestrian minds
are at last becoming agitated.

I was aware that the chance of getting any foundation
interested in supporting such a gymnasium as I proposed was very slim, but decided to try anyway. The
covering letters that I wrote, however, could hardly
have been less appropriate. Even when I drafted a
reasonable letter I could not resist throwing in misplaced
humor when typing the final version. At the time this
seemed highly appropriate, as it indicated that I was
the kind of "character" who would be needed to run a
gymnasium of this kind. My remark about becoming
very rich, for example, was intended as humor—tactless,
it is true—because actually I was preoccupied with my
"great" plans and ideas (another project, for example,
was to get all involuntary patients out of mental hospitals) and could hardly have been less interested, at

that time, in becoming rich (the idea now has great
appeal, but of course I would never say so in a letter to
a foundation—this is called "maturity of judgment").
A friend of mine paid me the dubious compliment that
I was writing "high camp" before the term had even
been invented.

My covering letter to the Rockefeller Brothers Fund
follows. I have omitted the names that I mentioned
from all my letters.

October 16, 1962

Dear Sirs:

It is my understanding that the Rockefeller
Brothers Fund often provides support for projects
which other foundations are unlikely to support, as
too risky or experimental, etc. The enclosed description of a gymnasium (two versions) suggests such a
project. This new type of gymnasium will have men
and women in it at the same time, but rules against
all kinds of illegal activities will be strictly enforced.

Among the people who have expressed interest
in this idea are ———, M.D., and ——— (letters en-
closed). Others, whom I talked with in person, are
Dr. ———, wrestling and gymnastics instructor at
———, Mr. ———, Superintendent of Recreation, City
of ———, who served at one time on the President's
Committee on Physical Fitness, Mr. ———, and Mr.
———, Director of the ——— Dancers Foundation.
All these men expressed enthusiasm for the idea, and
Dr. ——— agreed to teach classes in wrestling and
gymnastics.

Among the groups I am interested in working
with are old people, delinquents, and alcoholics.
These people are extremely difficult to help with the
usual "psychotherapeutic" methods.

I am very eager to set up this gymnasium on a paying basis, so that others can be set up, I can become
very rich, and our culture can be provided with a
desperately needed outlet for pent-up steam. As

there will be much shouting, jumping, crying, and laughing in my gymnasium, I am quite prepared to become known as the Aimee Semple McPherson of psychology. This possibility, coupled with my love of clarity and hatred of "politics" and my outspoken defense of individuals who believe they have the right to run their own private lives and not the private lives of others, may have something to do with my difficulties in trying to raise money for this project. As I appear on the surface, however, to be a sane and reasonable person, the more important difficulty is that the idea is unfortunately foreign to our culture.

The additional papers which are enclosed will reveal certain relationships to other ideas, which are by no means foreign to our culture but which are usually ignored or acknowledged only privately— or hidden in huge philosophical tomes or other scholarly works. These papers will also, I trust, make it abundantly clear that I will feel entirely free to attack any or all members of the "power elite" regardless of whether I receive any support from the Rockefeller brothers or not.

Please advise me as to further steps in applying for Rockefeller Brothers Fund support. I am more than willing to follow advice with regard to the business end of this project, as long as it does not involve entangling alliances with the medical profession or other forms of misrepresentation.

Very truly yours,

Enclosures:
   A Gymnasium for the Production of Dionysian Rites and Other Health-Giving Rituals
   A Gymnasium to Be Used for Primitive Dancing and Other Health-Giving Rituals
   The Neglected Psychology of Cowardice
   The Overemphasis on Sex in Western Civilization
   Limited Fighting and Friendship
   The Role of Deception in So-Called Mental Illness

Review of Lowen's *Physical Dynamics of Character Structure*
Review of Szasz's *Pain and Pleasure*
Differentiation and Dedifferentiation in Healthy Functioning
Letters from —— and ——
Vita
Brochure: Big Sur Hot Springs Seminars
Realism of Confidence Judgments
Laboratory Studies of Behavior Without Awareness
Training in Statistics for Nonmathematicians
Stamped, self-addressed envelope

As indicated, I enclosed two versions of the proposal, the first of which I called "a little 'far out' but essentially correct," and the second "more conservative, restrained, 'respectable.' " The last three papers and the two reviews listed were reprints from highly respectable journals. The reply was as follows:

November 12, 1962

Dear Mr. Adams:

Thank you for your letter of October 16 and its many enclosures. I have now had an opportunity to examine both the far-out and the respectable versions of your proposal and am sorry to have to say that the Rockefeller Brothers Fund cannot be of assistance. Much as we would like to live up to your expectations about tackling risky or experimental projects, we are just not in the business of building gymnasia.

While we hate to see such interesting and unusual material leave our files, I am sending back everything to you except your covering letter. I agree thoroughly with Dr. ——'s last sentence and hope that we will meet, should you come East again.

Sincerely yours,

After this response I changed the name to "workshop" and wrote a slightly revised version of the proposal, which I then sent to the Duke Endowment. My covering letter read in part as follows:

January 4, 1963

Dear Sir:

The enclosed paper, "A Workshop for the Production of Dionysian Rites and Other Health-Giving Rituals," describes a project for which I am eager to find financial support. As you will see from my vita and the biographical material contained in the two reviews, I have had a checkered career; however, the idea of using dancing as a health-giving device has been an ambition since my undergraduate days twenty years ago.

This proposed workshop is a much more important and far-reaching project than it may appear to be on the surface, as you will see from reading the enclosed material. U.S. culture, particularly northern culture, is in critical need of safety valves and more active participation rather than passive spectatorship. My ambition is ultimately to put this workshop on a paying basis, so that others can be built without being subsidized.

At first it may appear that this project is outside the scope of the Duke Endowment; one of the chief purposes, however, is to demonstrate the value of impulsivity, which from the days of the early settlers has been present in southern culture to a much greater extent than in northern culture, and which is now in danger of further submergence, with resulting undesirable explosions, as the attempt is made to standardize the population in accordance with the behavioral norms of the North. The ban on impulsivity and emotions is an extremely destructive feature of northern culture and will destroy us all if we do not destroy it. My project, therefore, if successful, would do more to benefit the South than a hundred mental health clinics operated according to the dominant philosophy of mental health in the U.S.A. today. I regard myself as an unintentional spy, having infiltrated northern territory over twenty years ago and having waked up only recently to the vast importance of the differences between the two cultures.

Palto Alto is an ideal location for this workshop, because it will be possible to work with people of different ethnic and racial backgrounds together, and yet there is a considerable influence of southern culture in the southern part of this state. In fact, the presence of two cultures has created considerable friction in the "mental health" programs in California, in which I am actively engaged.

. . . I have no interest whatsoever in devising ingenious methods of spending all the money granted, a practice which I have participated in at times but which I now find both repugnant and absurd.

Once these rituals are developed, it will be possible to engage in collaborative research on problems of biochemical, physiological, and psychological changes. I am painfully aware of the technical problems involved in such research, and as far as I am concerned it is only after one has obtained results which look very promising, on the basis of informal observations, that more careful measurements and observations are justified.

Among those who have expressed interest . . . Dr. ———, an endocrinologist at ———, has, among others, indicated willingness to engage in collaborative research.

Recently I submitted this proposal to the Rockefeller Brothers Fund, and am enclosing Mr. ———'s letter of reply. As a result of this letter, I have changed the wording from "gymnasium" to "workshop"; the latter is probably more appropriate in any case. One of the tragedies of our culture is the split between the cognitive, emotional, and physical aspects of man; this split is represented by such blanket policies as not supporting gymnasia. When I talked with Mr. ———, he indicated that specialists in recreation had been talking like this for years, i.e., talking about the important role of emotions in exercise—but of course they have no influence and no money (my comment, not his). On the other hand, the overgrown adolescents who donate large sums to build athletic facilities and hire big coaches to be devoted to a few stars are too often totally uninterested in the average individual and in the total development of the star athlete. The dance world tends to be dominated by anti-emotional and esoteric snobbishness, though neither Mr. —— nor Mr. —— fall within this category.

My letter to the Rockefeller Brothers Fund was even more informal than this one and perhaps gave a poor impression. Among other assertions was one that I am prepared to become known as the Aimee Semple McPherson of psychology, as there will be much shouting, jumping, crying, and laughing in my workshop. I was trying to indicate that I can withstand ridicule and can if necessary be a fanatical "character," which one may have to be to put this over. After working with so-called psychotics and having to spend a month in a mental hospital myself, I am not awed or cowed by "respectable" people.

Like most Texans. I assure you that I think big. If I can set up this workshop, I intend to bring in American Indians, among others, and to start an Ecumenical Dance Movement, eventually getting Kennedy, Khrushchev, and the Pope to do a war dance together instead of fighting each other. All kinds of people will come to my workshop (I know and like all kinds of people) and we will heal the splits between the athlete, the aesthete, and the scholar, the "bad" woman and the "good" woman, men and women, old people and middle-aged people, Christians and atheists, "respectable" people and "disreputable" people, etc. I claim to be the first fully qualified American paleface witch doctor, and will be glad to volunteer to dance with the African

witch doctors on a goodwill tour. I believe I know
how they help people—by stirring up their emotions,
as the revivalists did—first scare the hell out of them,
then make them feel safe in the arms of the Lord. I
was brought up as a Southern Baptist, by the
way. . . .

I have already followed Dr. ———'s suggestion to
work with groups in a preliminary way, but until I
have a building with suitable facilities and under
my own direction I do not expect to make any progress. Dr. ———, like the vast majority of other people, is entirely unaware of the enormous amounts of
hostility and other "diabolical" feelings that can be
released during dancing, and that folk dancing and
Arthur Murray studios leave completely untapped.

Please advise me as to further steps in applying
to the Duke Endowment for financial support. If
this project falls outside the scope of your organization, perhaps you can suggest some more appropriate
source of possible funds. I see that your address is
the same as that of the Rockefeller Brothers Fund;
if you care to see my previous letter or to show this
one to Mr. ——— I have no objection.

Sincerely yours,

Enclosures:
 [similar to previous list]

It did not take the Duke Endowment long to reject
this proposal. I received the following letter from the
executive:

January 7, 1963

Dear Mr. Adams:
 This is in reply to your letter of January 4.
 I regret to say that the nature of the Duke Endowment is such that it would be impossible for
the Trustees to consider a request for financial support for your proposed program regardless of its
merits.
 The Trustees of the Endowment are specifically

restricted to the support of institutions in the hospital, medical and educational field in North and South Carolina. For this reason, I am returning to you for your files the interesting enclosures which accompanied your letter of January 4.

Sincerely,

I next tried the Russell Sage Foundation.

March 12, 1963

Dear Sir:

I am trying to locate money for a program which potentially could do a great deal to improve social and living conditions in the U.S.A., but which is unlikely to find ready support from the usual sources. . . .

Honest economists admitted long ago that economic problems cannot be solved without some solution of the problem of finding satisfactions in living. I am passionately devoted to the maintenance and expansion of individual freedoms in this country, and we cannot maintain and expand our freedoms without teaching people how to enjoy living and how to be active participants more than passive spectators. . . . If and when most people go on a twenty-hour week, this kind of program will be invaluable in the constructive use of leisure time, rather than dissipating it in alcohol and other drugs, expensive travel and entertainment, passive staring at television, etc. (Television can be used in this program, with the emphasis on learning and participation, in the privacy and safety of one's own family room; we can produce cultural changes much faster than pessimists realize.) Any culture in which people do not dance, sing, fight, and love will die.

. . .

My workshop would have a library and I would give lectures as well as instruction in rituals; any

kind of silly or narrow cultism would be strongly
discouraged. Rivals or enemies of the program
would be invited to have their say. . . .

I am writing with the hope that the Russell Sage
Foundation itself may be interested in backing this
program, or, if not, that you can give me some advice in where to apply for support.

Very truly yours,

Enclosures:
[a shorter list]

The Russell Sage Foundation was prompt:

March 19, 1963

Dear Mr. Adams:

In reply to your letter of March 12 I must tell
you that your proposed workshop for the production
of Dionysian rites and other health-giving rituals
does not fall within the area of our current program
and consequently cannot be considered on its merits. The material enclosed with your letter to us is
being returned in the self-addressed envelope you
supplied.

Sincerely yours,

I next tried the McGregor Fund:

March 22, 1963

Dear Sir:

I am attempting to locate money for a program
which has a great potential for promoting the well-
being of mankind, but which is unlikely to find
ready support from the usual sources. . . .

As numerous observers have pointed out, there is
a tremendous need for the more active and constructive use of leisure time, instead of dissipation
in alcohol and . . .

The McGregor Fund declined my request with regret
on April 10.

*A Gymnasium for the Production of Dionysian Rites
and Other Health-Giving Rituals*

It can be argued in several ways that in order to maintain
the health of the individual it is necessary to provide suitable contexts in
which he can act highly impulsively, i.e., without deliberate conscious
control, and therefore "irrationally," if we define the latter term in accordance with views of "normal" behavior that are widely held in Western
cultures (as well as some others), particularly by the dominant culture of the United States, i.e., northern white middle-class urban culture.
These views of "normal" behavior are apparently now held even more
strongly by the dominant culture of the U.S.S.R.

Jung has repeatedly warned that certain kinds of experiences which
are expressions of the "deepest layers of the unconscious" must be
understood (to the extent possible) and provided for if Western civilization is to survive at all. If the "demonic" as well as the more benign aspects of the "collective unconscious" are not allowed expression in
constructive ways, they will emerge in an ever-increasing destructive
manner, as they have done in the past and are doing in the present (wars,
psychotic episodes, and other collective and individual horrors).

The southern Negroes are an example of an ethnic group that was
not only able to survive, in the face of tremendous physical and psychological hardships, but even able to enjoy life in a way that was often the
envy of the southern whites. The religious rituals of the Negroes, involving singing, dancing, chanting, shouting, and interpersonal dedifferentiation, played an important role in maintaining their physical, emotional,
and mental well-being. These rituals were in large part survivals of
African rituals, which were adapted to Christianity. It is usually assumed that a strong faith in God and in a hereafter were essential parts
of these rituals; there is considerable evidence that this assumption is
false. In order to enjoy the benefits of such rituals no highly speculative
beliefs at all are necessary.

There are many other examples of how large and small ethnic groups
have benefited from Dionysian rites. One of the most interesting groups

is the Shaker cult, because it illustrates clearly how such rites can to some extent take the place of sexual expression, without necessarily devastating results to others. Another example, a modern diabolical one which contains a warning that most Americans unfortunately do not understand, is the Nazi movement, whose rituals provided such enormous emotional gratification to the clean-cut German youth that they were willing to lose all individual integrity and all close interpersonal relations that were not officially condoned and regulated. The present-day coolness and apathy of American youth, their cynicism and acceptance of "relativistic" ideas, and their fear of close relationships that are individually regulated are extremely dangerous conditions. We are in the midst of a cultural revolution; there are many different trends which fortunately are not all in the same direction. There is still time to check the trends toward extinction of the individual, but these trends cannot be checked unless constructive opportunities are provided for intense emotional gratification and for the development of the courage, knowledge, and morale to act as individuals.

The mechanisms whereby Dionysian rites contribute to well-being are poorly understood. It seems highly plausible that once certain emotional states are produced, the resulting biochemical changes help to maintain health over a period of days, weeks, or months. The body can produce all the drugs necessary to the maintenance of health, if emotional gratification is made possible. The experimental evidence on this point, however, is almost nil, as the physiology and biochemistry of emotions is almost entirely a matter of speculation. Even anger is still an extremely obscure emotion, not only biochemically, but psychologically as well. For example, it seems likely that there are at least two kinds of anger, one which feels "good" and the other which feels "bad." This statement, however, cannot be supported on the basis of any well-controlled observations.

It also seems highly likely that some of the striking beneficial results of "depth" psychotherapy and of therapy with drugs such as LSD-25 are biochemical effects of emotions produced during therapy, and have little or nothing to do with "insights." These biochemical effects sometimes contribute to the individual's courage, both interpersonally and intrapsychically, and may therefore result in behavior changes that help to produce additional emotions and to maintain "health." This is not to say that cognitive processes are not highly important; on the contrary, unless the individual is helped to have some kind of rational understanding of his experiences, he may very easily form highly irrational convictions and become essentially a cultist, believing that his particular theology has now been verified.

It is proposed to construct a gymnasium specifically for the purpose of developing and using rituals in the maintenance of emotional well-being. The word "ritual" is not intended to preclude spontaneous acting-out within clearly defined limits. There is an enormous variety of rituals which could be developed, aimed at more or less specific feelings. Elation, for example, is a very beneficial feeling if proper safeguards are used to prevent a following depression. Elation can be produced, among other ways, by gradually accelerating primitive dancing, with appropriate music, costumes, etc. There are many adults who would be surprised at what can happen to them emotionally if they can drop their "dignity" long enough to engage in such an activity with others, or even alone. When dancing with others, an enormously satisfying dedifferentiation experience ("oneness") can occur, as in many "primitive" ceremonies. Many other spectacular effects can be produced, such as the phenomenon of "possession," but of course such phenomena are more hazardous. In addition to the "Dionysian" variety, there are many emotions of different quality which are also of great value, and work could also be done with these.

In the construction of the gymnasium, provision would be made for the production of constantly changing lighting effects, which even alone can have a considerable impact.

The gymnasium proposed would be set up independently of the medical profession, although collaboration with individual physicians would be welcome, as would collaboration with individuals from the fields of drama, dancing, recreation, physical education, religion, philosophy, the social sciences, etc. A preliminary estimate of the cost, including land, is approximately $200,000.

EPILOGUE: *The Failure of Grantsmanship*

> After my proposal was turned down by the McGregor
> Fund I put it aside and when I returned to it I decided
> to compose a "sensible," pedestrian-minded proposal

that would be less likely to arouse anxiety about either possibly wasting money or being accused of wasting money. These two great fears of foundations represent in part a very decent and responsible concern, but they result in wasting enormous amounts of money and in failure to support many worth-while ideas. All colorful language was eliminated; the reasons for such a workshop were soberly explained; and the activities were described in neatly outlined form. The emphasis was placed on recreation and education, with any therapeutic effects as a by-product (in this I had been influenced by Alan Watts, who liked the proposal but urged that the activities be engaged in for the satisfaction of doing them, not because they are "good for you"). I sent my new proposal off to the Rockefeller Brothers Fund with high hopes and the following covering letter:

November 27, 1963

Dear Mr. ——:

A year ago I applied to the Rockefeller Brothers Fund for support for a project with the somewhat appalling title, "A Gymnasium for the Production of Dionysian Rites and Other Health-Giving Rituals." In your letter of November 12, 1962, you stated, "Much as we would like to live up to your expectations about tackling risky or experimental projects, we are just not in the business of building gymnasia." I subsequently changed to the word "workshop," but, even so, my proposal was rejected by the Duke Endowment, . . . the Russell Sage Foundation, and the McGregor Fund. Since that time (April) I have not applied to further sources, but before beginning to make the rounds of California foundations, I thought I would try once more for Rockefeller Brothers Fund support.

The present proposal, "A Creative Workshop for the Arousal of Emotional Activity," makes clear that the scope extends far beyond that of a gymnasium.

Perhaps "school" would be an even better term. I should like to call to the attention of Governor Rockefeller and his brothers the seriousness of the situation in this country with respect to emotional health and the active, healthful use of leisure time. It is entirely possible that the majority of Americans could technically be classified as drug addicts. One of the basic reasons for this condition is the ban on emotional expression (and consequently on emotions)—a form of asceticism which has deep historical roots and is still very much alive.

A friend of mine who is Director of Research in a state hospital recently told me that $100,000 a year for ten years has suddenly become available for an experimental program within the hospital— this is Federal government money, which had not even been requested. He had to scratch his head for a quick plan to spend that much money. This is the kind of nonsense that goes on all the time within large organizations, while individuals with new ideas who want to work rather than play power politics can hardly get a cent. Yet many large organizations are so organized as to make the accomplishment of anything impossible. I may get to work with some patients at this hospital, but the usual consequence of a patient's showing any life or independence at this particular hospital is the electric shock table. I'm sure you know about these conditions already; I am suggesting that someone should set up a *foundation which would give grants only to individuals not connected with any large organization.* Perhaps H. L. Hunt will.

Thank you for your courtesy in replying to my previous request with information instead of a mere formal rejection.

Sincerely yours,

Enclosures:
[Similar to previous lists]

I received a cordial reply:

January 13, 1964

Dear Mr. Adams:

Now that the holiday rush in this office is over, it's a pleasure to renew our correspondence. I wish it were possible to send holiday greetings in the form of a favorable reaction to your revised proposal.

The Rockefeller Brothers Fund has an active interest in the constructive use of leisure time, as evidenced by contributions made to national parks, Colonial Williamsburg, etc. Support of efforts to improve the conditions at hospitals for the mentally ill has generally been channeled through the National Association for Mental Health. However, the type of experimental project you propose would not fit into our program—we would consider such a request only if it came from an established (not necessarily large) agency. Even then, our limited funds usually require that we restrict such support to agencies in the New York area. Therefore your plan to make the rounds of California foundations seems to be the best bet from your point of view.

I am returning the various enclosures in the envelope you thoughtfully supplied.

Sincerely yours,

I never made the rounds of California foundations and have done nothing since with this idea. Since this proposal was written, however, a number of developments have made such a gymnasium or workshop much more feasible. For example, the concepts of instant theater and of audience participation have been developed, as well as an amazing growth of free-style dancing and of interest in music. Whereas the staffing of such a gymnasium would have been difficult eight years ago, now there are large numbers of young people who would be both eager and able to work in such a place. Perhaps such gymnasia could even serve to lessen the generation gap.

 *3*

An Attempt to Reform
the United States Senate et al.

During the months following my first episode I had become keenly sensitive to the reactions of others to argument or disagreement—whether they regarded it as unfriendly, seemed to be afraid of it, or welcomed and enjoyed it. Although these reactions depend of course upon the way in which argument or disagreement is made, and by whom, still, the range of individual differences is enormous. Some people enjoy arguing with almost anybody and actually like people who argue with them, whereas others are offended by any disagreement whatsoever, no matter how courteously it is expressed or by whom. Most people fall somewhere in between these extremes.

My own background in this respect was much more unusual than I realized until the last few years. While I was growing up, my father, who was a lawyer, allowed me to argue with him about "abstract" matters concerning which he was far better informed than I. He enjoyed the arguments and was pleased when I could make a point. He did not allow me to speak to him in a way that he considered disrespectful, but he did allow statements that *his* father (who was also a lawyer) would have considered very disrespectful (he would occasionally say, "If I had talked to my father like that!"). It was probably largely because of this rearing that I tended to like and respect authority figures (e.g., professors) who were willing to tolerate some open disagreement and engage in open

35

argument, and neither liked nor respected those who were unwilling or unable to do so, but naturally I learned to discriminate and to get along more or less with most people.

For several months after my first episode, my discrimination between those who liked disagreement and argument and those who didn't broke down—I didn't care especially whether anyone liked my behavior or not, and in some situations I became, I am sorry to say, *offensive.* Strangely enough, however, those who did not challenge me to my face but who disliked both my behavior and what I was saying usually classified me as "defensive" (as I would learn later). The word "offensive" is not even in the vocabulary of some mental health experts—at least not with respect to people they see as "mentally ill." On occasions when I had been angry I was perceived (I learned later) as "anxious." Although I had experienced considerable anxiety during the sixty hours of autonomous experience, there was no anxiety whatsoever during the following months. It is very convenient to see behavior as "anxious and defensive" rather than "angry and offensive" as it enables one to fight someone behind his back with a clear conscience—after all, it would seem brutal to attack someone openly if he is already "anxious and defensive."

In 1960 there was a great deal of talk about which of the two major presidential candidates—Kennedy and Nixon—could stand up to Khrushchev, who was regarded as having a very forceful personality. One of my colleagues remarked that this concern was being emphasized out of all proportion to its true importance (he was partly right), and I emphatically insisted that, on the contrary, it was of the utmost importance; I had become so much more keenly aware than I had been of how decisions are so often made under the domination of "forceful personalities" rather than on any rational basis. I also became aware that people with forceful personalities are often fought behind their backs in ways that are less than honorable. I saw examples of this and realized that the same social processes go on at all levels of society and at all levels of government and international relations, with consequences that can be disastrous. This thought, like so many others during this period, was not new to me—I already "knew" it—but it became much more phenomenologically real, i.e., I could *see* certain qualities of human interaction much more clearly than before. Occasionally, for example, two people talking together would *look like* two animals that were fighting each other in a peculiar, disguised manner, instead of acknowledging their differences openly and trying to settle them more directly.

It is hardly possible to convey how deteriorated human interactions appeared to me during this period. Very few seemed open and straightforward; almost everyone seemed to work within a petty little clique, fighting other petty little cliques in roundabout, self-defeating, and self-deluding ways. Contributing to this perception were recollections of statements I had read during the 1950s that there had been an increasing tendency, in high places, for behind-the-scenes maneuvers rather than open discussions and encounters. It was not until 1961, however, that I wrote a short essay embodying these ideas. It was called "Limited Fighting and Friendship." Although I did not realize it at the time, one of the origins of this paper was probably an observation I had heard Gregory Bateson make informally several years before about Australia. Bateson said he had noticed a peculiar characteristic of the men of that country, at least those with whom he had any contact. They acted as though they wanted to fight; then, if and only if he indicated a willingness to fight, they wanted not to fight, but to be friends. This is the kind of observation for which Bateson is justly regarded by many (including the present author) as one of the cleverest men alive. It is worth far more than the usual results of an expensive research project. I believe Bateson picked up something which, whether generally true of Australian men or not, is true of many men in many societies, especially men of honor and integrity in their relationships with other men. It is a way of screening out men who are too afraid of you to challenge you openly (and who may therefore not be trustworthy), and at the same time avoiding dominance fights, and thus preserving a symmetry which is properly a part of friendship, and which is possibly nonexistent among other mammals.

Excerpts from this essay are as follows:

> In growing up, anger is recognized as a prelude to a fight, especially in an unprotected environment. Boys who are not afraid to fight tend to be more free in the expression of anger. Sooner or later, however, fist fighting becomes too dangerous, and even boys who have been quick to express anger tend to curb their tempers and to

treat other people less aggressively. Even bullies usually learn to curb the expression of anger within their own groups and with outsiders who are too powerful.

The free expression of anger, however, particularly when it is in the form of righteous indignation, makes one "feel good," feel "like a man," when one learns not to go too far, either physically or with words.

There are men who tend to like other men who "stand up" to them, by saying things to them in a somewhat "fighting" tone of voice, and by being willing to take the same tone of voice from them. This kind of interaction, if tolerated on both sides, may in some instances lead to heated arguments which both parties enjoy. Many people, especially women, have wondered at how some men can have heated arguments, even call each other names or say things that from their point of view are "insulting," yet remain the best of friends. The reason for this kind of friendship, however, which is unfortunately rare, is simply that men of this type respect other men of the same type, and usually do not respect men who have to be too formal all the time, who always remain "cold" when they argue, or who invariably prefer "discussions" to arguments.

Almost any two animals of the same species will establish dominance when placed together for the first time, and fighting is the most common way in which dominance is established, though the fight may be very brief and attenuated. Human beings are no exception; however, humans fight for dominance in many complex ways, and in many face-to-face interactions they are not aware that they are fighting. Many people react to any attempt to argue as though it is an attempt to establish permanent dominance instead of an attempt to establish a point. Once an argument is launched, one may feel embarrassed or humiliated at admitting that he is wrong, especially if the argument becomes heated. This is why among friends who like to have heated arguments one never "rubs it in" after the other has yielded, if one wants to show respect for one's friend; to do so is analogous to hitting a boy who has already yielded, as well as being recognized as pointless by those who see the argument as an attempt to establish the truth rather than a fight for dominance.

To be willing to engage in an argument, especially a heated one, is to put oneself "on the same level" with the other person. A person of a given size, status, or degree of power may be very choosy about whom he will permit to be on the same level with himself. The gentlemen of the Old South usually would not engage in heated arguments with people whom they considered beneath them; they expected others to yield immediately. Nevertheless, they tended to be more "democratic" in this form of interaction than gentlemen of the North, who would more often refuse to have heated arguments with anyone, even of their own class. The belief that emotion and rationality are opposed was much stronger in the North than in the South, although it was, and still is, present in both cultures and has been used in both cultures against women, whose emotional outbursts were variously regarded with amusement, embarrassment, or fear. These "female" emotional outbursts have often been irrational because the women were deprived of information, and they were deprived of information because they were "too emotional"; thus a vicious circle was established. The "proudest" people are those who expect others to yield to them with no argument whatsoever; many women are now in this category, but have been led to be by men who were too proud to argue with them. Men who are willing to have open arguments with women who are not their wives are rare, and this is one reason that women have tended to get the upper hand in some respects and why they are often excluded from certain all-male discussions, and why certain "secrets" still tend to be kept from them. The sad truth is that the majority of American men are now afraid of aggressive women.

The willingness to engage in heated arguments is always limited in certain ways, especially by men who are wise, because there are many dangers involved. People of different classes and different cultures have different standards of behavior, and this form of limited fighting can easily be perceived as an attempt to force someone to yield in a way that is felt as humiliating. Thus the interactions of people of different classes, different ethnic groups, different statuses, and of strangers within the same class or group tends to be surrounded with protocol, rules of "courtesy." In the settlement of disputes between classes, ethnic groups, labor and management, etc., protocol often prevents any frank expression of opinion, attitude, or feeling, and therefore prevents any kind of genuine relationship from developing, because each side wishes to refrain from "insulting" or "humiliating" the other, and yet both sides are too proud in that they are unwilling to yield in an argument, or even to become friends once an argument is launched. It happens occasionally that once there is a kind of limited free-for-all, in which people "put their cards on the table," those involved began to understand each other and to like and respect each other better. This happens only if they can overcome being too proud to admit that the other side may have a few points.

In international relations, protocol has been of extreme importance because of man's false pride, his insistence upon "saving face," which is part of what has been called the "sin of pride." Many wars have been fought because leaders have been "offended" and have been willing to send others to war (and sometimes even to fight themselves) to "save face," which in many instances has unfortunately meant insisting that the other side is totally wrong and their own is totally right, even when there are many obvious similarities in the two nations or cultures. Protocol and false pride have prevented leaders from getting to know and respect each other, and to work out a way of guaranteeing the rights of each. This is very obvious in the case of the Civil War, which might have been prevented if the leaders had engaged in more open debates, and had not been too proud to grant certain points on both sides, points which were actually admitted in private by moderates of both North and South, and by Negroes as well as whites. It is also highly probable that if Woodrow Wilson had been fought more openly by European diplomats, instead of by intrigue, the consequences would have been different and better. The same statement can be made for many human relationships; if there were more open fighting of a limited kind and less intrigue, people would begin to trust each other more, though many people would need to find new sources of interest and amusement.

Men, and women also, need to fight, but they do not need to kill, ruin, or humiliate each other. The fact that when people argue they too often act like two animals fighting to establish permanent dominance is recognized in the advice often given to someone about to marry: be sure to win the first argument. What is not recognized in this advice is that a person may "humble" himself by admitting he is wrong, then again challenge the other on a different point. Animals are generally unable to do this; once a fight has been won, dominance is rarely challenged. Humans can overcome this limitation if they become aware of the irrationality of acting as though arguments are fights for dominance, instead of attempts to establish the truth. *Men and women can become rational, can learn to respect differences in belief and attitude, if they are not too proud to do so.* Fighting and loving help people to stay young, whereas protocol drives people in the direction of self-contempt, intrigue, hatred, and impotence.

The old American boyhood tradition of "I'll fight or be friends—

it makes no difference which" has much to be said for it, in this day of gutless wonders, but it should be changed to "Let's fight a little, so we can respect each other and perhaps become friends." Such a principle would make people both strong and kind.

It was with a sense of urgency that I wrote this "message," dittoed several copies, and mailed them off with the idea of placing them where they might have an impact. My generalization about southern and northern gentlemen may be nothing more than a romantic idealization of the South; however, in my own experience the most high and mighty Americans have been northerners. At any rate, in scratching my head for someone in a high place who might possibly read what I had written, I thought of Senator Strom Thurmond (!), because of his southern chauvinism. In my covering letter to Thurmond I even mentioned an ancestor of mine born in Thurmond's home town—a childish tactic, but I was willing to try anything to "get through." I never received any reply or acknowledgment. It is very probable that he never even saw the letter or the paper, that both were screened out by the secretaries that must screen the thousands of letters received daily by United States senators. I read sometime later that Senator Thurmond got into some kind of physical scuffle on the floor (literally) of the Senate, but that was not quite what I had in mind.

October 10, 1961

Dear Senator Thurmond:

I have recently discovered a principle of human interaction which if properly used would be a great boon in both domestic and foreign affairs. When I say "discovered" I do not mean that others have not expressed similar ideas; in fact, this principle is in part nothing but "common sense"; in practice, however, it is unfortunately neglected, and the reasons for this neglect are complex and, when understood, lead to conclusions which are by no means "common sense" but are quite extraordinary.

Although I am in the process of trying to present these ideas in learned papers for our learned journals, I am enclosing a paper which is free of psychological jargon, in the hope that you will be interested in this principle and in perhaps encouraging others to try it. If I can be of any use in this respect, I would of course be very glad to come to Washington and engage in "limited fighting" with anyone you designate, to show how the principle works.

I am originally from East Texas, and my own cultural heritage has had considerable influence on what I have to say. My great grandfather, Elias Earle Adams, was born in Edgefield, S.C.

I am writing to you as an individual; other members of the Mental Research Institute do not necessarily share my enthusiasm for these ideas. In reply please use the following address: . . .

Respectfully yours,

I am aware that Dr. George Bach has been working along these lines for years; furthermore, more recently the entire encounter movement has developed. My main interest, however, has been in "limited fighting" about issues which are not primarily personal, but are often "abstract" (e.g., ideological) and sometimes far removed from the "here-now" and yet of great practical, as well as theoretical importance.[1] In this day of widespread violence and narrow-minded bigotry on all sides there is an urgent need for "limited fighting" of this kind, which could be shown on television. Young people desperately need models of mature men and women disagreeing passionately with each other without resorting to physical violence or insulting and irrelevant name calling. The academic world as well as the "power elite" should provide such models. The situation at present is remote from this ideal. I have heard members of leading departments of psychology say, "——[another member of the department] is a friend of mine, but we avoid talking about psychology." The theoretical differences are so bitterly held that they must be avoided! I am far from suggesting that academicians spend all their time in fruitless polemics, but some open arguments, which are bound to generate some heat, could be very salutary for both faculty and students.

For many years I was puzzled by the fact that certain people are satisfied only by 100 per cent agreement—99.9 per cent will not do. It had seemed that the patent unreasonableness and one-sidedness of such an attitude should be apparent even to the most authoritarian characters. Upon thinking about this problem in a different way, the "obvious" answer emerged. Once an animal has established dominance over another, it will fight even more fiercely to maintain dominance (on those rare occasions when dominance is challenged) than it will to establish

1. It was, nevertheless, gratifying to be told by a marriage counselor that he had found my essay to be of value in his own work.

it in the first place—as though it now has a "right" to it which it does not have on an initial encounter. Certain people act like animals: if you have failed to challenge them on a number of occasions (even for the very good reason that you happen to agree with what they are saying, or you know that they are better informed on certain points than you are) or, even worse, if you have argued and then admitted that you were wrong (because you were wrong), they will act as though they have already established dominance and will be outraged at any disagreement, no matter how minor the point happens to be, because it is taken as a challenge to their dominance. Dominance, like slavery, is unworthy of human beings, and full consciousness of the mechanisms involved can help to eliminate this subhuman quality in human relationships.

❧ 4

Deception and Intrigue in So-Called Mental Illness

PREFACE   After I had become much more open and spontaneous
with other people, I became aware (though not as
quickly as I should have) that my openness was not by
any means always reciprocated, and that *the more
effort I made to communicate with certain people, the
more guarded they became.* (As a matter of fact, my
attempt to communicate my "great discoveries" to one
Very Important Person in the vicinity, whom I had never
met before, led to my being enticed, cajoled, and pres-
sured into psychotherapy with a psychiatrist, whom I
saw almost every day for two months.) As soon as I
was labeled "mentally ill" or "emotionally disturbed,"
the guardedness and duplicity (largely unintentional)
with which I was dealt markedly increased and I realized, much more than ever before, how easy it is to
produce and to perpetuate "mental illness" by lies and
intrigues, *however benevolent in intent these may be.*
It was not until several months following my *second*

episode,[1] however, that I wrote the following essay, an
early version of which, entitled "The Role of Deception in So-Called 'Mental Illness,' " was presented at
the California State Psychological Association Convention in December 1961. Even though the basic idea
—that lies can and do sometimes produce delusions
and estrangement—could hardly be more obvious, the
psychological literature on this subject is extremely
limited, possibly because hypocrisy is so much an
integral part of our culture and in particular an
integral part of the traditional treatment of the
"mentally ill."

I continued to believe that I had stumbled upon
something of considerable importance and even went
so far as to send a copy of the early version to President
Kennedy in July of 1962. The paper was returned, via
airmail, by the office of the Director of the National
Institute of Mental Health, with a polite note saying
that the President had referred the paper to that office
and adding that they were "glad to have had the
opportunity to read your interesting paper." I realized
that I was in the position of being considered a "nut"
who mistakenly thought he had something important
to say. I must admit that I am still under the delusion
that the basic ideas of this essay, which could no doubt
be much better formulated and explained, should be
pondered and understood by the leaders of our society. It
was not published until 1964—hence the references to
two papers which were written later but published
at earlier dates.

---

1. During this second episode, one of the strange visions I had was of
an old print depicting a parade, with an Emperor and a Fool following behind him, with the following inscription: "Who rules the
universe—the Emperor or the Fool?" The print looked vaguely
Chinese, and was entitled "The Riddle of the Universe." I must have
seen a similar print during childhood, but have been unable to
locate it.

Deception and Intrigue in So-Called Mental Illness

Many of those who attempt to straighten out disturbed interpersonal relations have discovered that by insisting upon complete honesty in communication and by bringing facts out into the open, where they must be acknowledged by all concerned, rapid and extraordinary changes can be produced. On the other hand, everyone who uses this method has probably also become aware of certain hazards; the method might appropriately be labeled "dynamite," which can be constructive, destructive, or both, as destruction is often necessary to construction, in relationships as well as intrapsychically.

Deception and intrigue have a long history in Western civilization and have been institutionalized in various ways, as, for example, in professional roles. Judicial, religious, and curative roles are among those in which these processes obviously have been institutionalized, but they are also present in most other roles, such as those of man, woman, mother, father, child, spouse, unlike-sexed sibling, etc.

Those who are embedded in a social process and are carrying out a role prescribed by the culture, subculture, or immediate group are often blind to processes and effects which are obvious to outsiders, in case they are in a position to observe the process. Deputy sheriffs are sometimes in such a position, as, for example, when they arrive to escort a designated individual to a mental hospital after a commitment petition has been filed with the district attorney. Two deputy sheriffs have provided the following information on cases in which the designated individual had not been informed he was considered "mentally ill" prior to their arrival: [2]

1. A housewife called a social worker at a state hospital and complained that her husband was violent; the social worker then called the sheriff's office and passed on the information given by the wife. The

Reprinted in slightly revised form from the *Journal of Humanistic Psychology*, vol. 4, no. 1 (Spring 1964).

2. These cases were not selected to illustrate the maximum disregard for the rights of others, nor is any attempt made herein to describe the feelings and emotions of those involved.

wife then called the sheriff's office and said that her husband should be picked up immediately. When the deputies arrived, they found a seventy-six-year-old man attempting to dig a hole in his garden. He was stooped and feeble, walking with a shuffling gait, with difficulty. When confronted with the obvious impossibility of the kind of violence which had been described, his wife backed down and said that he played the radio too loudly. The old man explained that his wife wanted him to move out so that some of her relatives could move in.

2. A woman who was concerned about her thirty-three-year-old brother got in touch with the sheriff's office, and commitment papers were filed. She gave both business and home addresses of her brother, and when the deputies failed to find him at home, she called again and a second fruitless attempt was made. The deputies then went to his place of work, and found that his employer had wished to fire him but was afraid to do so. When told of their purpose, the patient became violent and had to be subdued. After he was released from the state hospital, new papers were filed. This time he went quietly.

3. A mother complained to the sheriff's office that she could not control her twenty-six-year-old son, and his father, who was living out of the home, backed her up in saying that the son should be committed. The mother wanted him to be picked up without his knowing that she had anything to do with it. This patient had already been in a state mental hospital.

4. The husband of a thirty-year-old woman complained about her to the sheriff's deputies and then said he could take her to the hospital, "because I can trick her." After going home, he called and said that he couldn't take her, after all. When the deputies arrived, the woman could not be found, so they left. Later, the husband took her to the hospital; at the desk she realized she was being admitted, ran out the front door, and had to be subdued.

5. An eighteen-year-old girl got married against her parents' wishes and lived in a motel without informing her parents where she was living. The parents had a petition filed and the papers were kept on stand-by. She was finally located and a matron and two men took her to the hospital.

One of the deputies also made an observation that is worth noting: In many instances the first reaction of the husband is simply to turn to his wife in surprise and say, "Why, honey—why didn't you tell me?" By the time he is carried out of the house, however, he is kicking and screaming, or at least trying to do so.[3]

The failure to tell the designated patient that he is considered "mentally ill" is the rule rather than the exception in the filing of commitment petitions through the district attorney's office, according to these sheriff's deputies. Of course, almost anyone who has worked with patients in mental hospitals is aware that such cases exist; what is not generally recognized, at least in the literature, is their high frequency and also the enormous impact that such a breach of trust and relationship can have upon the designated patient.

There are probably few patients who are deliberately "framed" in the sense of consciously malicious motivation on the part of others. Even in Case 1, above, the elderly man's wife had no doubt managed to rationalize her deliberate lies by telling herself that a mental hospital was probably the best place for her husband. Although many "experts" now realize that such tricks can alienate patients from other people, the manner in which the network of intrigue surrounding a designated patient can prevent effective rehabilitation while he is hospitalized and can prevent his re-establishment in the community is still very poorly understood. On the other hand, psychiatrically "untrained" deputies and policemen who are not afraid to deal directly and honestly with people sometimes see that the designated patient has been dealt with in a shamefully "dirty" manner—i.e., has not been given a fair chance of correcting his behavior before they arrive to remove him by force if necessary. They have also noted that certain facts are not brought out in the hearings, with the connivance of lawyers and physicians. Erving Goffman has provided one of the few professional attempts to describe these alienating processes, although neither in his *Asylums* nor in his *Presentation of*

---

3. I asked a psychiatrist what he would do if he found himself in such a situation; he answered that he would go along very quietly. I pointed out to the psychiatrist that most laymen do not have the knowledge and information that is available to him. Case 2, however, illustrates what is sometimes called "one-trial learning." By an interesting coincidence, the patient described in Case 2 was sent to the hospital in which this psychiatrist holds an important staff position. The most frequently used form of treatment, aside from tranquilizers, at this particular hospital is electric shock, which has been found to be effective in persuading patients to behave themselves properly. Some of the literature in experimental psychology on the use of electric shock is relevant; see, for example, Mowrer and Solomon (1954).

Self in Everyday Life does he indicate full awareness of the broader implications, i.e., the almost universal emptiness and alienation which "roles" produce. Literary descriptions have been in existence for many years, e.g., the poem "Patterns," written, understandably enough, by a rebellious Boston Brahmin, Amy Lowell.

Labeling has long been used as an excuse to deal with people indirectly, i.e., to deceive them and surround them with intrigue. All the labels used in the field of so-called mental illness, and their historical antecedents ("heretic," "witch," etc.) have been used in this manner, by professionals as well as laymen. The tradition in medicine of doing what is considered best for the patient has also included telling the patient what is considered best for him to hear, which has often not been the same as what the physician has privately considered to be the truth. T. S. Szasz, M.D., tells us that in seventeenth-century Europe it was considered a compliment to be told that one could lie "like a physician." [4] The old-fashioned family doctor in the United States often pampered women patients, concealing from them what he privately believed to be true (that they needed to get up and do some work, to go to bed with a man, etc.), in a way he would never have pampered a man, and in carrying out the professional role in this manner he was acting in accordance with the cultural norms in male-female relationships, norms embodying less honesty, at least in certain respects, than in man-to-man (a phrase which sounds alarmingly old-fashioned) relationships.

The following discussion is an attempt to present these ideas in a more systematic fashion, with some implications that are not obvious at first glance.

The word "deception" will be used to mean *any communication or other action which produces, strengthens, or affirms a false belief.* This usage is much broader than the popular usage, though not than such usages as "She was deceived by their spontaneously innocent expressions into believing that children cannot be cruel." Acts which are commonly called "lying" will be included under the term "intended deception," i.e., *an action (including deliberate withholding of information) which is*

4. T. S. Szasz (1961), p. 273. The prescribing of placebos or drugs which the physician believes are worthless in themselves is an example of deception "for the patient's own good," a form of faith healing. The physicians' belief that using the word "suggestion" among themselves distinguishes such prescriptions from those of "primitive" witch doctors is an interesting example of self-deception.

consciously intended to produce, strengthen, or affirm a belief which the actor himself believes to be false. The term "intentional deception" will be used to mean *an intended deception which is successful.* Deception may also be *unintentional;* in fact, any action, no matter how innocent or spontaneous, can produce, strengthen, or affirm one or more false beliefs and thus fall within the scope of the definition. Intended deception, as well as unintentional deception, may be accompanied by conscious intentions that are not malicious and may even be benevolent—the phrase "little white lie" denotes an intended deception that is without malicious intent. An intended deception may fail to produce the intended false belief, but may produce an unintended false belief, and thus be both an unsuccessful intended deception and an unintentional deception. A lie to the police can result in being seen as a liar in general and as guilty of a crime one did not commit. It is highly probable that habitual liars, like the boy who cried " Wolf!" always produce false beliefs that are unintended.

An especially important class of deceptions is comprised of *those which at the time of their occurrence are unintentional, but which can be seen by the actor, upon reflection, to have been deceptions, or at least highly probably deceptions, i.e., that they probably produced, strengthened, or affirmed false beliefs.* These will be called "spontaneous deceptions," and they are especially likely to occur when an individual waxes enthusiastic, when he gets "high" or becomes highly emotional, when he is in the presence of someone who dominates him, whom he feels very close to, or whom he fears to antagonize or is eager to please (or, in some cases, fears to please). Spontaneous deceptions, like intended deceptions, may be successful or unsuccessful; the actor may later believe that he probably deceived when in fact he did not. Performances of social roles are in many instances successful spontaneous deceptions.

It will be argued in the present paper that intended deception by others plays an enormously important role in the development of those states often called "mental illness" and that reduction of intended deception by others can lead to reduction in other types of deception and in marked improvement in feeling and in interpersonal relationships. Although this may seem to be an obvious thesis, the current emphasis by the dominant authorities in the mental health fields is on the reduction of "self-deception" and, to the extent that it is believed feasible, deception *of* others, especially of "experts." As stated earlier, it has been widely assumed by authorities, as well as by laymen, that "mentally ill" people should be told only very limited aspects of the truth as seen by others.

Two premises are of special importance for the argument. These premises are:

1. Intended deception of another person, Y, by a given person, X, increases X's distance from that person in important and identifiable respects. This premise means that intended deception leads to perceptions, feelings, and behavior on the part of X, the deceiver, that can be summed up by the common-sense meanings of "distance," "separateness," or "estrangement" from Y. An intended deception is by definition an attempt by X to produce a difference between X and Y, i.e., to induce Y to hold a belief which X does not himself hold, and perceived differences in beliefs are a common basis for distance from another person. Even more important, intended deception implies that X believes that he cannot trust Y with the truth in a certain respect; the distance produced becomes maximum when Y has explicitly asked or otherwise indicated that he believes himself to be entitled to know. This premise does not deny that intended deception may also be used to *decrease* distance in other respects, which X may consider more important. For example, in sexual seduction X may deliberately misrepresent himself or his perception of the other person to achieve intimacy which is not only physical but may have other aspects as well; nevertheless, the distance in certain identifiable respects remains, and can easily account for the limited satisfaction that occurs in seduction and the ultimate rejection of the seduced one.

2. Perceived intended deception by another person, X, increases Y's distance from X in important and identifiable respects. If Y sees that X is attempting to deceive him, Y's perceptions, feelings, and behavior become more distant from X, regardless of whether Y's perception is in fact correct, i.e., regardless of whether X is intending to deceive Y or not.

It is not hard to see how distance of X from Y can continue to increase, once there is an intended deception of Y by X, because if Y does not perceive the deception, then Y's communications to X are likely to elicit further intended deceptions from X (to preserve the original deception), which continue to increase the distance of X from Y, at least in certain respects. The interrelatedness of Y's beliefs is almost certain to produce additional false beliefs, which introduce further communication difficulties and further distance. If Y perceives the intended deception, but does not so inform X, then the distance from Y to X also increases, especially if Y "strings X along" and so adds increments to the distance from Y to X according to the first rule (in which Y is now the deceiver) as well as the second. Feelings during such sequences of mutual intended deceptions can vary along a tremendous range in both quality and intensity, e.g., from guilt, hatred, fear, contempt, or pity to cynical, playful, or enthusiastic acceptance of a "game." Among the more common features of such sequences, however, is guardedness, which may become manifest in muscular tensions, manner of speaking, etc., and which may give a certain "robot," "mechanical," or "phony" quality to the actor, as well as eliminate many kinds of feelings. On the other hand, some well-practiced sequences may be acted without any consciousness of deception at the time, and thus become spontaneous deceptions. In the Stanislavsky school of acting, actors are taught to run through well-practiced sequences not only with repression of any consciousness of acting, but with attempts to establish conscious connections with events in the actor's own past and thus to evoke emotions appropriate to the role ("emotion memory"). On the stage, "spontaneous" acting of this kind may indeed be a deception (members of the audience may form false beliefs about the actor himself), but it is hardly in the same category with spontaneous deception by an individual who is not on stage—or, at least, is not perceived as being on stage. The well-known quotation from Shakespeare, "All the world's a stage," may be an expression of the idea that even when people are most genuine they are still, being mere mortals, in some sense actors, but it can also be interpreted as expressing a perception of human behavior which can be very disturbing, namely, the perception of behavior as spontaneous deception, which may never be recognized by the individual as such, although it could be if he were to reflect upon it.

Many people derive satisfaction from "justifiable" intended deception, which is greatly enhanced if the intended deception is part of an intended intrigue, which may be defined as *a communication or communication network which is directly and consciously relevant to the future or some aspect of the future of one or more individuals deliberately excluded from the communication or communication network.* Intended deception is more likely to arouse strong guilt if it is part of an intended intrigue, and as a defense against guilt those engaging in intrigue may develop extreme cognitive distortions of the situation, without becoming aware that *the failure to confront the excluded individual directly per-petuates such distortions.* Intended intrigues, like intended deceptions, may be accompanied by the best of conscious intentions, as, for example, in reform movements, many of which start as intrigues, if for no other reason than that those who originate such movements are likely to be labeled as "fanatics" or "cranks." Intended intrigue tends to lead to feelings of alienation from the object of the intrigue; the person becomes an outsider. The word "intrigue" (more inclusive than "intended in-trigue") can be defined as *any communication or network which is about (or concerned with) one or more individuals excluded from the communication or network.* Some forms of intrigue are sometimes called "gossip," and many people recognize that this type of communication can alienate one from the individual concerned; the cognitive distortions in the perception of the excluded individual are recognized by those individuals who pay little attention to gossip and insist upon checking for themselves.

The process whereby intended deception and intended intrigue can bring about so-called mental illness can be illustrated by a type of se-quence which sometimes occurs prior to commitment of an older person to a mental hospital. Elderly people are often intentionally deceived, not maliciously but because they are thought to be incapable of understand-ing, likely to condemn or reject, or to be hurt or disturbed. Intentional deceptions are especially likely if the older person in question is unusually stubborn and proud, aggressive, sensitive, or vulnerable. Being deceived, the older person reacts in a way which from his point of view is appropri-ate, but which may begin to appear increasingly inappropriate to others, including those who have intentionally deceived him, because it is almost impossible to know what appropriate behavior is for an older person who is deceived, with his complex and interrelated conceptual systems and his identification with an older generation, with different standards. The older person looks "foolish," an almost always unintended result, which is accentuated to the extent that he is "open," i.e., talks freely. Old people who have time to think sometimes "put the world together" in ways that "make sense" to them at last, and it is sometimes the case that one ingredient of this "making sense" is to be open and honest, espe-cially if the older person has seen through the hypocrisies and absurdities of his own generation (each generation tends to have a different set).[5] This openness is sometimes accompanied by feelings of elation—the older person appears to be happy "for no reason." As what he is saying may be highly embarrassing and appears foolish, he may be labeled "mentally ill" or "senile" by his family, who may eventually enter into an intrigue, first with each other and then with the district attorney or the police. The older person may first learn that he is considered "mentally ill" when the police arrive to escort him to a mental hospital. His world may then undergo such a drastic and sudden transformation that he becomes extremely frightened and experiences an acute psychotic episode, in which he may see the police and his relatives as "robots." If he verbalizes this perception he is especially likely to be labeled "schizophrenic." This perception, fairly common during acute psychotic episodes, is probably valid, i.e., is probably the perception of people as playing roles without realizing that they are acting, a type of "behavior without awareness."[6] A "normal" person may have this kind of perception during an "experimental psychosis" induced by an hallucinogenic drug such as LSD-25.[7]

If, on the other hand, the older person senses, earlier in the sequence, that he is being deceived, he will naturally form hypotheses as to the reason for the deception, and these hypotheses, whether verbalized or not, can easily lead to his being perceived as behaving inappropriately and thus as being "mentally ill." He may, for example, be labeled "paranoid." Older people sometimes become reluctant to talk except in front of a lawyer or other reliable witness; these people are not necessarily unduly suspicious; they sense correctly that what they say is often not taken at face value and that they are talked about behind their backs —they are treated as though they do not know what they mean, and do not mean what they say, without even being accorded the decency of being so informed.

5. In some parts of the United States, e.g., small towns in the South, the term "privileged" is applied to someone who is allowed to say what he feels like saying in situations in which others have to be more cautious. This privilege often amounts to being allowed to tell the truth, i.e., what one believes to be the truth, in situations in which others would be required to lie.
6. This type of behavior without awareness cuts across several of the categories described in an article by the author (1957). It is, of course, a type that has been emphasized by many clinicians. See also Goffman (1959).
7. For an example of an ex-patient who is willing to live outside a mental hospital see O'Brien (1958).

A similar sequence occurs for many people in other age brackets and in settings other than families. After a person has been labeled "emotionally disturbed" or "mentally ill" by his relatives, friends, colleagues, or neighbors, a network of intended intrigue and intended deception is set into operation and the victim may never be able to behave in any way which is not interpreted as "inappropriate" by those who have constructed the network, except possibly by adopting a socially defined role which he finds highly inappropriate to himself.

The preceding statements should not be construed as asserting that victims of deception and intrigue are rational, healthy, sober, sweet, noble, honest, truthful, or well behaved, or that their faults spring spontaneously into being without a background in childhood. My point is that their condition is often aggravated and perpetuated by those with more socially acceptable and profitable pathology.

People who are perceived as being unable to understand or accept the truth, or, on the other hand, as being eager to bring the truth out into the open when others wish to conceal it, are among those most vulnerable to being made "mentally ill." These categories include unusually aggressive or unpleasant people, old people, women, people of different ethnic or class origins or identifications, people who will not listen to or try to understand anything with which they do not agree or which they insist is beyond their understanding, people of different status or of rival groups, uneducated people, and children, as well as people who are already labeled "mentally ill," "emotionally disturbed," as having a "psychiatric disorder," etc.

The statement commonly made today, "Everything is politics," means not the open fight, the open argument, but intrigue, seduction, and intended deception. That is one reason "mental illness" may increase if certain steps are not taken in time. In particular, the increasing isolation and aloneness of the individual, which Erich Fromm and others have described at length, can be accounted for in part by the processes of deception and intrigue previously described.

In 1958 an anonymous article appeared in the *Journal of Abnormal and Social Psychology,* presenting the theory that, roughly, the schizophrenic is a liar, i.e., that his peculiar behavior represents an elaborate method of concealment or deception, motivated by fear.[8] The author

8. "A New Theory of Schizophrenia."

failed to point out the almost universal nature of deception and concealment, especially through automatic role playing. Such hypocrisy was certain to develop in a culture with such strong pleasure-denying, body-rejecting traditions as ours.[9] Anyone who attempts to be perfectly honest is in great danger of being labeled "psychotic" and "too open for his own good." Furthermore, those who have experienced psychotic episodes have usually "seen" something which is not seen by "normals," but which is really there.[10]

Once a patient is admitted to a mental hospital, he is likely to be treated to an even greater extent as though his conscious processes, the ways in which he sees the world, have no validity. Mental hospitals, like our present society in general, tend to be cesspools of intended deception and intended intrigue, however well-meaning; the patient is often even less likely to hear the truth than before. There are great discrepancies between what is said behind the patients' backs and what is said to their faces, supported by the myth that it would be detrimental or pointless to tell them the truth directly. There are probably many noncommitted patients who would leave hospitals in disgust if they could hear tape recordings of what is said when they are not present, or could read the distortions, fantasies, and irrelevancies contained in the files; others might become greatly frightened or homicidal, while still others would be highly gratified to learn that they are not represented as totally evil. There are committed (or even merely admitted) patients who have seen that they are no more irrational than "normal" people, but are caught in a situation from which they see no escape; some of these decide they are the victims of conscious plots, perhaps by communists, whereas the truth is even more bizarre: they are in the grip of people who are supposed to be helping them but do not realize what a potent weapon against "mental illness" the truth can be, especially truths that "everybody knows anyway but nobody says." Patients, of course, also practice deception and intrigue, sometimes to an even greater extent than staff. Deception and intrigue on both sides alienate staff from patients and patients from staff; they preserve status differences at the price of fraternization and brotherly love, which patients often need more than anything else.

9. See pp. 70–72, 117–18.
10. See pp. 109–11.

The following statement by Norman Cameron is false, unless by "usual common-sense methods" he includes deception and intrigue:

> It goes without saying that by this time all of the usual common-sense methods for dealing with fear and suspicion have already been tried without success. Friends, relatives, and others have used reassurance, contradiction, reasoning, demonstration, and ridicule—often with skill and perseverance—but to no avail.[11]

Very seldom have those who have surrounded a prospective patient for a mental hospital failed to conceal highly relevant aspects of the truth, e.g., that they are afraid of him, that they believe he cannot understand certain matters, that he talks about matters that bore them or that they consider none of their business, that what he says is nonsense, that what he says is true enough but should not be said aloud, that he embarrasses them, that they consider his religious beliefs absurd, that they are tired of him, that the standards of his generation are different from the standards of their generation, that they consider him a highhanded or suspicious old fool, that they think he is "senile" or "mentally ill," etc.

Those engaging in deception and intrigue usually do so imperfectly, i.e., they emit incongruent messages, thus placing the receiver into a "double bind." [12] Deception is, of course, not the only way in which a "double bind" can arise.

As stated earlier, curative roles are among those in which deception and intrigue have been institutionalized in Western civilization. Such institutionalization is particularly obvious in some methods of psychotherapy, in which strict and "ethical" adherence to the "professional role" rules out certain communications, leading inevitably to deception of the patient, and in which supervision, "objective evaluation," and case conferences are forms of intrigue which work hand in hand with such deception.

An unknown but probably increasing number of psychotherapists have found that when they begin to talk as honestly as possible with patients, relying on their own convictions, regardless of whether these can be backed up with research data or authorities, changes in the patient not only occur, but occur with startling speed. Therapists who put their

11. Cameron (1959), pp. 334–35. An excellent critique of Cameron's position is given by Lemert (1962).
12. Bateson, et al. (1956).

cards on the table, as it were, as soon as possible, tend to minimize the likelihood of deception of the patient, and in so doing tend to protect both the patient and themselves, because they tend not to get into situations in which more is expected of them than they can deliver. When people begin to communicate honestly and openly with each other, they begin to trust each other, to feel more free to ask questions, to clear up misunderstandings, to see and accept each others' limitations, and they become less subject to spontaneous and unintentional deception. People who are consciously "on the level" with each other tend not to read into communications meanings that are not there, nor do they feel any need to "go into an act" (or assume a role) and thus practice spontaneous deception.

The idea that when people are deceived they act like "lunatics" who see things that are not there, and even fool themselves into disbelieving what is plainly before their eyes, is an ancient idea, expressed in the old myth of the emperor's new clothes (Andersen's story is only one version). Every culture deceives the individual early in life—only an "unspoiled" or "innocent" child or an "insane" person can see the truth which the culture, or its authorities (guided by sly advisers), has concealed. The power of the group to deceive the individual into disbelieving what is plainly before his eyes has been demonstrated in laboratory experiments of the type initiated by Solomon Asch.[13] The fact that a few of Asch's subjects became extremely disturbed when informed of the deception can be explained on the hypothesis that they saw some of the broader implications of the demonstration, which most subjects did not see.

Similarly, the idea that the truth can cure is very old—the biblical quotation "Ye shall know the truth and the truth shall make you free" is an early version, though not the earliest. It has been fought throughout the centuries by opposing ideas, such as that truth is unknowable (this doctrine has many forms, some very modern and sophisticated), promulgated by "practical" men, i.e., by cynics.

13. Asch (1952), pp. 450–501.

 5

The Overemphasis on Sex in Western Civilization

PREFACE   My second episode of madness occurred early in February 1961, a little more than a year after the first. For several months prior to this I had been delving into history, as I had become aware, partly through our research with LSD and the many strange notions and cults surrounding its use, that we were entering a cultural revolution, perhaps comparable to that of the sixteenth century, in which the notion of "mental illness" would play a leading and perhaps an ominous role. I was especially impressed by G. Rattray Taylor's *Sex in History,* which explores the important and largely unacknowledged role that sexual concepts and attitudes have played in historical developments.

Like many people I had assumed that the preoccupation with sex on the part of learned authorities had begun with Freud, but after reading Taylor's book I began to see this preoccupation as a recapitulation of history, leading perhaps to a comprehensive persecution comparable to the inquisitions, which dominated much of Western Europe for about five hundred

years. One sentence of Taylor's book struck me with
particular force: "It is hardly too much to say that
mediaeval Europe came to resemble a vast insane
asylum" (p. 19). The facts he presents provide ample
justification for this assertion. The world began to
look more and more irrational to me, and I realized
that my first episode of madness had enabled me to see
many things as they are. If this was true of my episode,
then why should it not also be true of many others? I
became haunted with the idea that the people who are
considered "psychotic" see many things about the
world more realistically than most "sane" people, and
that the process of declaring people "insane" is one way
in which the society protects itself against new insights
which would necessarily bring about some basic
changes. This idea and many more that were related to
it suddenly fitted together in a way that produced
extreme excitement. Even though I had had the experience of becoming psychotic through rage, it did not
occur to me that excitement might also produce
psychosis, nor would I have thought, in view of my
previous experience, that my *behavior* itself might get
completely out of rational control. This time, however,
I became a complete "lunatic," both internally and
externally. The following essay was written about a
year later, after I had read considerably more history.

The title is somewhat misleading, as it might give
the impression that I am arguing that sex is not really
so important. On the contrary, the point is that sex is
so important and basic a need that its widespread
frustration is and *has been* socially disastrous. Sex has
been overemphasized throughout the ages, in an almost
limitless variety of forms, because people have never
been freed to regulate their own sex lives and to pursue
sexual happiness. Prudishness and pornography are
opposite sides of the same coin (Wilhelm Reich

explained this long ago) and these are only two
varieties of overemphasis.

Although parts of this essay now strike me as dis-
jointed, rash, immature, and indiscreet, the main
theme is one that I will not only still defend, but can
now support with a considerably greater amount of
historical evidence. Recently I read H. C. Lea's *A
History of Auricular Confession and Indulgences
in the Latin Church,* which documents over and over
the absurd overemphasis on sexual sin. During the
early centuries of Christianity the three great sins (or
crimes, as there was little or no distinction between
these categories) were idolatry (which soon changed
to heresy), homicide, and unchastity (including
adultery, fornication, homosexuality, "perversions,"
bestiality, etc.). One of the origins of private confession
(public confession being the general rule during these
early centuries) was the practice of allowing adult-
eresses to confess in private, to protect them from being
stoned or otherwise harmed (Jesus' effort, valiant
though it was, in no way stopped this practice, which
had existed among the Jews since the time of Moses
and which continued centuries after Jesus). In the
same work Lea gives evidence for an attitude which I
knew must have existed but which I had not come
across in my previous reading. It had seemed incon-
ceivable to me that none of the clergy during the
Middle Ages and early modern period would have seen
the absurdity and cruelty of the overemphasis on sex
morality and have failed to resist that emphasis in
some way. Lea mentions the widespread popular
belief during these centuries that fornication was not a
sin, and tells of *priests who refused to enlighten their
flock in this respect, arguing that there was beauty in
their innocence.* To take this stand, in view of the official
emphasis upon the sin of unchastity, under some cir-

cumstances required considerable courage. Some of the
early missionaries, far from putting Mother Hubbards
on the "savages," scandalized the Church by allowing
their new converts to live in a way that was natural
and customary to them. The scandalous "laxness" on
the part of so many of the Catholic clergy in enforcing
the official sex rules, of which Lea speaks so disapprov-
ingly, was undoubtedly in many cases motivated not by
greed or hypocrisy but by kindness and good sense. I
should add that nowhere does Lea himself indicate that
in his opinion there is anything wrong with the official
rules against "sex immorality"; on the contrary, he
makes clear that he is in strong agreement with those
rules. My mention of Lea's "Protestant bias" (see
note 13 on p. 79) means merely his severe attitude
toward sex; he did his best to avoid bias in his writing,
sometimes confining himself entirely to Catholic
sources, as in his book on confession and indulgences.
Lea provided a very informative and spectacular example of the overemphasis on sex during the Civil War.
The Protestant Episcopal Bishop of Vermont had
published an article condemning the view that slavery
was a *moral* evil. By numerous quotations from the
Bible he had shown that slavery was accepted without
question in both the Old and New Testaments and so
must be considered as approved by God. To condemn
it on *moral* grounds (as distinguished from humani-
tarian grounds) was therefore blasphemy against the
Almighty. This article was reprinted and widely circulated as a Democratic campaign document in the
gubernatorial campaign of 1863 in Pennsylvania. Lea
wrote a parody of the Bishop's article using exactly the
same arguments, even to some extent the same words
and phrases, and quoting just as copiously from the
Bible, to demonstrate that it was likewise blasphemy
to condemn *polygamy* on moral grounds. Lea's parody

was printed as Union League pamphlet No. 62, November, 1863, and widely circulated (Lea signed it "Mizpah" but its authorship was widely known).[1] *This burlesque completely nullified the Bishop's article;* in other words, it was considered a *reductio ad absurdum.* The conclusion is inescapable that the institution of polygamy was regarded with more horror and disapproval than the institution of slavery, even in the North during the Civil War, and not only by the ignorant masses but by men as learned and cultured as H. C. Lea! This is even more extraordinary when one realizes that Lea was aware of certain terrible aspects of the history of slavery completely unknown to the average person, for example, that at many times and places of the Roman Empire, everyone was protected by law from torture *except slaves* and in some places the testimony of slaves was considered evidence *only* if obtained under torture! (Lea's *Superstition and Force,* which gives these gruesome facts, was not published until 1866, but he had done the necessary research years before.)

Crane Brinton is another historian who gives no indication in his *History of Western Morals* that he would be at all in sympathy with my argument—the last chapter in his book is modestly titled "In Which Nothing Is Concluded."[2] Yet he provides evidence for sexual confusion and misery throughout the ages, and highly recommends Zoé Oldenbourg's "admirable historical novel," *The World Is Not Enough,* which presents just as gloomy and messy a picture of marriage and adultery in the twelfth century as we have in the twentieth. Nor do Will and Ariel Durant, either in their monumental ten volumes of history or in their short *The Lessons of History* give me any reason to

1. "Bible View of Polygamy," in Lea (1942).
2. Brinton (1959).

think that they would agree in the least with my major
conclusion.[3] In view of the attitudes of these historians
(and no doubt many others with whose works I am
unfamiliar), compared with whom my own knowledge
of the past is of course piddling, my use of historical
material may seem highly presumptuous. Certainly if
my thesis is as "obvious" as I seem to claim that it is,
then the problem arises of why those who are apparently in a better position to see it than I are so oblivious
of it. I admit that I cannot answer this question any
more than I can explain why Wilhelm Reich was appar-
rently the first "mental health" expert to see that without a sexual revolution the problem of "mental illness"
is unsolvable. Recently I reread Reich's *The Sexual
Revolution,* having first read it many years ago, and
was amazed at how it is, if anything, *even more timely
today than when he wrote it,* perhaps because the current conflict over "sex education" and other contemporary events parallel events in Russia many years
ago of which Reich writes. The sexual revolution failed
dismally in Russia, and it will fail also in this country
unless many of us who are over thirty offer some moral
support and guidance.

Another sexual revolution that failed occurred in
Geneva more than four hundred years ago. In the
following essay as first I published asserted that most of
the old aristocratic families in Geneva were Libertines; this is probably an error, as they tended to
belong to another group which opposed Calvin, the
Patriots or Children of Geneva. They did, however,
provide leadership for the Libertines. Who can fail to

3. Because these modest authors repeatedly imply that their books are
   tedious, I should like them to know that there is at least one reader
   who started out to read only certain parts, and got so involved he
   couldn't stop until he had read the whole set, even though he reads
   very slowly (by preference as well as by capability). What a mag-
   nificent life's work! Eventually it will have a very important impact
   upon education in this country.

recognize the modern counterparts of this group, as described by Philip Schaff in *The Swiss Reformation?*

The Libertines or Spirituels, as they called themselves, were far worse than the Patriots. They formed the opposite extreme to the severe discipline of Calvin. He declares that they were the most pernicious of all the sects that appeared since the time of the ancient Gnostics and Manichaeans, and that they answer the prophetic description in the Second Epistle of Peter and the Epistle of Jude. . . . They revived the antinomian doctrines of the mediaeval sect of the "Brethren and Sisters of the Free Spirit," a branch of the Beghards, who had their headquarters at Cologne and the Lower Rhine, and emancipated themselves not only from the Church, but also from the laws of morality. . . .

The Libertines described by Calvin were antinomian pantheists. They confounded the boundaries of truth and error, of right and wrong. Under the pretext of the freedom of the spirit, they advocated the unbridled license of the flesh. Their spiritualism ended in carnal materialism. They taught that there is but one spirit, the spirit of God, who lives in all creatures, which are nothing without him. "What I or you do," said Quintin, "is done by God, and what God does, we do; for he is in us." Sin is a mere negation or privation, yea, an idle illusion which disappears as soon as it is known and disregarded. Salvation consists in the deliverance from the phantom of sin. There is no Satan, and no angels, good or bad. They denied the truth of the gospel history. The crucifixion and resurrection of Christ have only a symbolical meaning to show us that sin does not exist for us.

The Libertines taught the community of goods and of women, and elevated spiritual marriage above legal marriage, which is merely carnal and not binding. . . .

The Libertines rejected the Scriptures as a dead

letter, or they resorted to wild allegorical interpretations to suit their fancies. They gave to each of the
Apostles a ridiculous nickname. Some carried their
system to downright atheism and blasphemous
anti-Christianity.

They used a peculiar jargon, like the Gypsies,
and distorted common words into a mysterious
meaning. They were experts in the art of simula-
tion and justified pious fraud by the parables of
Christ. . . .

The sect made progress among the higher classes
of France, where they converted about four thousand
persons.[4]

Schaff, a distinguished scholar who was Professor of
Church History in the Union Theological Seminary,
tells of the terrible persecutions of the Anabaptists
(so-called by their enemies—they usually referred to
themselves as Christian Brethren) by both the Swiss
and German Reformers, and mentions the burning of
witches and of Servetus, the beheading of a child,
etc., but he shows the sex fanaticism of his generation
(late nineteenth century) by speaking with special
horror of the calumny spread by H. H. Bolsec, one of
Calvin's enemies, that Calvin had committed sodomy
in his youth, and the conclusion is inescapable that if
this had actually occurred it would have been, in
Schaff's opinion, much worse than the things which
Calvin actually did! He regards the conditional assent
which Luther, Bucer, and Melanchthon gave to the
"scandalous bigamy" of Philip of Hesse as "the darkest blot in the history of the German Reformation"!

Widespread sexual frustration builds up explosive
conditions that easily erupt into violence and virulent
hatred of the society itself. However obvious this may
be, our political leaders seem to be unaware that sex is

4. Schaff (1903), pp. 498–500.

of any great political and economic importance. This
obtuseness is remarkable in view of the fact that so
many of our young people have been attracted into
radical movements through being allowed sexual freedom (without having to slip around like criminals),
just as in Nazi Germany and early Communist Russia.
Every time a prominent person is involved in a sexual
scandal, there is an opportunity for that individual's
friends and associates, and even his political enemies,
to make a strong public statement that everyone
should have a right to run his own private life, and
that those not directly concerned should mind their
own business. It might be argued that such statements
would do no good, but as they are virtually never made,
there is no way of knowing whether they would
accomplish anything or not; my own conviction is that
a great many supposedly "narrow-minded middle-
class" people would respond very favorably to such a
stand. At the time of the scandal involving Mr. Profumo,
which is regarded by some political observers as having contributed considerably to the defeat of the Con-
servatives in the subsequent elections, the most sensible comment I saw was that of a London cab driver:
"Oh yes, those chaps do a bit of a run-around."

The Overemphasis on Sex in Western Civilization

INTRODUCTION

There are many aspects to what I, among many others,
believe to be an absurd, hypocritical, and destructive overemphasis on
sex in Western societies. In the following, some of these aspects will be
elaborated in detail and others will be merely touched upon. In general,
I have tried to concentrate more on material with which the majority of
psychologists are probably largely unfamiliar, to show relationships
which may not have been previously noted by the reader, and to provide

scholarly references for further study. The style of writing is intended to underscore absurdity, hypocrisy, and destructiveness, according to my point of view.

HISTORY

In sketching the historical roots of present-day attitudes toward sex, it is sufficient for the purposes of the present paper to begin with the Pauline epistles, in which there is an exaltation of virginity as a religious ideal, though one which Paul was well aware most men could not attain. In exalting virginity Paul was voicing an attitude which even at that time was not at all rare. For example, the practice of *syneisaktism* or spiritual marriage—cohabitation of the sexes under conditions of strict continence—was highly regarded by many, though eventually suspicions, often well-founded, tended to replace admiration, leading to a law which was passed in the year 420 under the Roman emperors Honorius (Rome) and Theodosius II (Constantinopole) forbidding all "so-called sisterly cohabitation." Meanwhile, the Council of Nicaea in 325 had strictly forbidden ecclesiastical concubinage, which had become very common and was frequently quite open. The first definite canon prohibiting sacerdotal marriage and prescribing and enforcing sacerdotal celibacy, even for those members of the clergy already married (of the grade of bishop, priest, or deacon), was confirmed in 385 by Pope Siricius. The Church then engaged in a long, intermittent, and often bloody struggle to enforce sacerdotal celibacy, with the emphasis gradually shifting to the prohibition of marriage, i.e., any strong and permanent relationship with the opposite sex, which might rival the tie to the Church, more than that of more casual sexual activities, especially if the latter were not too open and scandalous.

Religious fanaticism was common during the early centuries of Christianity, and it often took the form of sexual asceticism. Sexual asceticism may have originated largely as an avenue to mystical or transcendental experiences, but it soon became one of the most important ways of being "religious" or "moral." There were men of good sense within the Church

Reprinted in slightly revised form from the *Journal of Humanistic Psychology,* vol. 3, no. 1 (Spring 1963).

who realized the dangers of sexual asceticism and who warned that whenever practiced it should be coupled with humility, but these warnings, even when heard, were somewhat difficult to comprehend in view of the great stress on the virtue of chastity. Numerous sects of ascetics sprang up, and many of these were exceedingly self-righteous, fierce and warlike, and capable of great cruelty. There were also many hypocrites, enjoying the reputation of celibacy and concealing their sexual activities, not rarely going to the extreme of infanticide. As one would expect on the basis of general social-dynamic principles, there were also sects that advocated and practiced sexual libertinism as a religious observance; both these sects and those which advocated sexual asceticism for the laity tended to be considered heretical.

Toward the end of the third century asceticism received a great boost through the followers of the Persian Manes. Though Manes himself was flayed alive and his followers in Persia were slaughtered, his system had great influence in the West for more than a thousand years. It was known as the "Manichaean heresy." The Manichaean doctrine, that man's body is the work of the Evil Principle, engaged in an eternal war with the Soul as the substance of God, implied a rejection of all sexual intercourse and contributed greatly to the growth of asceticism within the Church itself.

Augustine (354–430) has been among the most influential of the Church Fathers, and his writings reveal an attitude toward sex which is extremely interesting in view of later developments. Augustine believed that, before the Fall, the genitalia were totally under voluntary control, and that Adam and Eve did not have sexual intercourse before their expulsion from the Garden of Eden, but that if they had done so coitus would have been without unregulated excitement, passion, or too much bestial motion. After the Fall, they were ashamed of the unruliness of their organs and sewed fig leaves together with which to conceal the telltale involuntary motion. Augustine believed that the sexual consequences of the original sin persisted in the inability of the will to govern the genitals (this practical thought reveals that he very probably had some of the same kinds of embarrassing trouble that most boys and men have had) and in the shame generally aroused by coitus. Augustine's own sexual experience consisted of a thirteen-year relationship with a concubine, who bore him a son. At the age of thirty he sent his mistress —without her son—to Africa and became engaged to another woman, meanwhile being unable to refrain from taking another mistress. Soon after, however, he ended his struggle with sexual lust by becoming converted to Christianity, vowing celibacy, and breaking his engagement.[5]

From 385 until the middle of the eleventh century the Church had little success in enforcing sacerdotal celibacy, in terms of abstinence either from concubinage or from marriage, despite dozens of councils and decretals devoted to the attempt. Many nunneries were essentially houses of prostitution; monasteries were notorious for sexual license, so that some were declared off-limits to all females, including animals, and many laymen were careful to see that their priests were provided with concubines, in an effort to protect their wives and daughters. In the eleventh century Hildebrand (Pope Gregory VII) gave a great impetus to the prohibition of sacerdotal marriage by authorizing the princes of Germany to prevent ecclesiastics guilty of concubinage from performing their priestly functions. The princes were most happy to oblige, as they were able to use the disturbance thus created to seize Church property and to free themselves from some of the control exerted by their emperor, Henry IV. The resulting persecution of priests, by mobs as well as by organized forces, was savage and cruel; some priests, for example, were mutilated and carried around to exhibit their shame and suffering. Many of their wives committed suicide, and the countryside was filled with wandering and homeless ex-priests and ex-wives. When Hildebrand's antagonist, Henry IV, who had attempted to protect the persecuted priests, also solemnly and formally prohibited marriage to the priesthood, an era began which virtually eliminated for several hundred years all formal opposition to the doctrine of sacerdotal celibacy, although concubinage, promiscuity, and secret marriage continued into modern times.

In the early thirteenth century Saint Francis and Saint Dominic, both renowned for their austerities, founded the Franciscan and Dominican orders respectively, and their sincere asceticism attracted men of similar types. These two orders, which soon hated and persecuted each other, provided most of the inquisitors during the next few centuries. The first inquisitions began after the Albigensian crusades had subdued Languedoc,

5. This brief account of Saint Augustine is taken from Bailey (1959).

the southern region of France. In this region the Cathari (also known as Patarines, Bulgari, Albigenses, Tesserants), who followed the Manichaean doctrines, were strong, and a considerable religious toleration of Cathari by Catholics—and vice versa—had developed. Neither the nobles, the clergy, nor the people had cooperated with the Papacy in putting an end to these conditions, and Pope Innocent III finally initiated the crusades, which after many years were successful. The inquisitions were then developed to root out heresy, but their scope became considerably greater than their stated purpose indicated. By their mode of operation, which included secrecy, placing the burden of proof of innocence upon the accused, withholding the names of accusers, and denying the right of counsel, the inquisitors were able to operate with standards of justice that were considerably below the secular courts of the day. As they were responsible only to the Papacy and not to the local prelates, they were able to exert great power in bending all to the will of the centralized authority.

In reading of the practices of the inquisitions it is very easy to form an erroneous impression of the inquisitors as men who were obviously full of hatred; such an impression makes it difficult to realize the full horror and significance of this period in history. They were for the most part conscientious men who were on the surface kindly and benevolent, and who were in the possession of (and possessed by) an ideology which enabled them to "abandon heretics to the secular arm" and witness their being burned alive with feelings of remorse that God's children had to be dealt with in such a manner, or, on the other hand, with feelings of self-righteousness in dealing a blow to the Devil. It is highly probable that many were largely unaware that some of their glorious feelings were feelings of power, status, and control, even though the instructions given by one of the most experienced inquisitors, Bernard Gui, indicates that such pleasures in their work were not unknown possibilities:

Like a just judge, let him so bear himself in passing sentence of corporal punishment that his face may show compassion, while his inward purpose remains unshaken, and thus will he avoid the appearance of wrath leading to the charge of cruelty. In imposing pecuniary penalities, let his face preserve the severity of justice as though he were compelled by necessity and not allured by cupidity. Let truth and mercy, which should never leave the heart of a judge, shine forth from his countenance, that his decisions may be free from all suspicion of covetousness or cruelty.[6]

The self-righteousness of sexual and other forms of asceticism was not confined to those of the clergy who kept their vows. The Cathari, especially those known as "perfects," were also self-righteous, and many went to their deaths as bravely and cheerfully as did some of the early Christian martyrs. It is not hard to understand how these rivals, who dared to be "good" in the way exalted by the Church and who yet refused to bow to its authority, could arouse the fury of the inquisitors.

Medieval theology was an ideal ideology for the carrying out of persecution with great self-righteousness. It was complex and thus could be mastered only by years of study; it was worded in a learned language (Latin) neither spoken nor understood by the vast majority of people; it had the appearance of objectivity, while at the same time subjectivity could enter in without being detected, even by the ideologist; and it enabled the ideologist to see that the "reality" underlying behavior was just the opposite of what it appeared to be on the surface. Not only could anyone be accused of heresy, but any departure from the "normal" manner of living, dressing, or "morality" could be used as a basis for the accusation of heresy. The "norms" were then, as today, largely in the fantasies of the ideologists. Medieval theology was the psychology of the time, by means of which behavior could be interpreted; and by suitable interpretations—coupled with citations from appropriate Church authorities, who varied among themselves in doctrine—it was relatively easy to label anyone a "heretic," especially as the burden of proof lay on the defendant himself. The secrecy in which the inquisitors worked added greatly to their power, as defendants were often informed neither of the names of their accusers nor of what they were accused of having done. Furthermore, it was dangerous to attempt to defend anyone accused of heresy, as the defender might himself be accused and placed in a similarly hopeless position. The inquisitions, therefore, can be regarded as a means of standardizing or "normalizing" behavior in accordance with the standards of the Church authorities, in particular the popes and the inquisi-

6. Quoted in Lea (1961), p. 167. It should be added that among those who eventually exposed the inquisitorial abuses and put an end to the horrors thereof were some of the inquisitors and other prelates.

tors. In the south of France the inquisitions provided the means of converting southerners into northerners; the devout Catholics in the south, as well as the Cathari, had to be "normalized," and the local prelates who tried to protect their people were rendered powerless. Even if it seemed inconvenient or impolitic to attack a person directly, he could be brought under control by proving that some dead ancestor had been a heretic, thereby rendering his inherited property subject to confiscation.

There was another respect in which medieval theology was an ideal ideology for the establishment of tyranny: it was sex-centered. With the increasing restrictions that the Church attempted to impose, and the increasing emphasis on the virtue of sexual "purity," it is not surprising that medieval theologians became obsessed with sex; many seemed to think of nothing else. All kinds of sexual practices and fantasies were discussed in great detail, and there was argument about how they should be arranged in order of sinfulness. There were numerous discussions of such matters as the sinfulness of different varieties of nocturnal emissions, homosexuality, the theological significance of semen, etc. One great advantage of such a sex-centered ideology was that it did not interfere with the indecent and tyrannical treatment of other people, as it provided a way of being "good" that had nothing directly to do with decent or fair treatment of others.

The liquidation of the Knights Templars, which occurred in the early fourteenth century and which is sometimes referred to as the "great crime of the Middle Ages," is especially significant in terms of the psycho-sociology of sex and power. The Templars, founded about 1118, were an extremely wealthy religious, fraternal, and military order composed largely of knights and nobles, whose power and privileges were feared and envied by ecclesiastics and rulers, and whose possessions were coveted by Philip the Fair, King of France. Jacques de Molay and other leaders of the Templars were trapped by means of intrigue, and the order was destroyed by the usual inquisitorial methods, not, however, without a valiant struggle which lasted over a period of years.

The charges against the Templars centered around their secret initiation ceremonies, and two of these charges are of special interest in the present discussion:

1. It was alleged that the initiate was stripped and then required to

kiss the preceptor on the buttocks, the navel, and the mouth, and sometimes on the penis.

2. It was alleged that the initiate was told that he must provide sexual relief to any brother who demanded it.

Homosexuality was extremely common during the Middle Ages, especially in monasteries, but like all forms of sex outside marriage—as well as many inside—it was officially strongly condemned by the Church, and in 1292 a scandal had led to the banishment of many professors and theologians of the University of Paris, presumably employed by old-fashioned administrators more concerned about their scholarly ability than their private lives.[7] For years it had been rumored that the initiation rites of the Templars included kissing posteriors; this rumor had been especially widely circulated by the Hospitallers, a rival and even more powerful order.

One might imagine that the extremely worldly, practical, realistic, and successful organization men of affairs who had risen to positions of power within the Church had quite a laugh over their ability to use these charges to destroy, with the most extreme cruelty and disregard of human dignity, an organization of aristocrats, knowing that homosexuality was so common and probably considering it privately a matter of relatively little importance. It is more probable, however, that they failed to see any absurdity in their proceedings, and that, like practical, realistic, and successful men of affairs today, they felt self-righteous in upholding "public morality," i.e., hypocrisy.[8]

As is well known, sacerdotal celibacy became an important issue in the Protestant Reformation. Several times the Catholic Church almost abolished the vow of celibacy, but those who sincerely insisted upon the ideal of celibacy and those who saw that any sexual relationship other than a casual one would interfere with the tie to the Church were able to perpetuate the official rule of sacerdotal celibacy, though not to prevent the

7. Lea (1961) tells us that about A.D. 1100 the Archbishop of Tours demanded that the vacant see of Orleans be given to a youth so generous with his favors that he was known as "Flora" and bawdy love songs addressed to him were openly sung in the streets. There was some opposition among the Orleans clergy, but the Archbishop, apparently too proud to be a secret hypocrite, beat down all opponents, some of whom then jested that the election took place on the Feast of the Innocents.

8. For modern examples of the upholding of public morality see Ploscowe (1951) and Adler (1953).

continued and widespread practice of concubinage and the use of confession for sexual seduction.[9]

The Protestant Reformation illustrates what can happen within a society when the discrepancy between official doctrine and actual practices —and private opinion—becomes too great. There were within the Church large numbers of exceedingly worldly men, many of whom must have seen the absurdity of the overemphasis on sex as having little or nothing to do with decent or kind treatment of other people and as an insult to any God other than a trivial-minded tyrant. Such men, however, were profiting from the most gigantic business in human flesh the world has ever known, and thus for the most part they went along with the hypocrisy of pretending to believe something they did not believe and of countenancing great sexual libertinism among the clergy, fearing only scandal, which arose repeatedly and was excoriated in the most scorching language by high ranking ecclesiastics themselves.[10] A fairly typical statement of the actual sexual practices throughout the Middle Ages is that made by Cardinal Hugo to the Lyonese in 1251, when Innocent IV and his retinue departed after a residence of eight years:

> "Friends, since our arrival here, we have done much for your city. When we came, we found here three or four brothels. We leave behind us but one. We must own, however, that it extends without interruption from the eastern to the western gate." [11]

The practices indicated by the preceding quotation were occurring at the same time during which the inquisitors placed great emphasis on "sexual immorality" when it suited their convenience to do so. The continual exaltation of sexual morality is indicated in the following:

> How the estimate placed on purity increased as virtue diminished is fairly illustrated in a characteristic legend which was very popular with ecclesiastical teachers in the thirteenth and fourteenth centuries. It relates how a pagan entering a heathen temple saw Satan seated in state on a throne. One of the princes of Hell entered,

9. The confessional box was invented in the sixteenth century in a futile attempt to stop the practice of seduction during confession. See Lea (1907b), vol. 2, chapter on "solicitation").

10. At first it may seem ridiculous to have feared scandal, as it repeatedly arose, until one considers that there was a new generation every twenty years or so, to be brought up with illusions.

11. Quoted in Lea (1907b), vol. 1, pp. 424–25.

worshipped his master, and proceeded to give an account of his work. For thirty days he had been engaged in provoking a war, wherein many battles had been fought with heavy slaughter. Satan sharply reproached him with accomplishing so little in the time, and ordered him to be severely punished. Another then approached the throne and reported that he had devoted twenty days to raising tempests at sea, whereby navies had been wrecked and multitudes drowned. He was likewise reproved and punished for wasting his time. A third had for ten days been engaged in troubling the wedding festivity of a city, causing strife and murder, and he was similarly treated. A fourth then entered and recounted how for forty years he had been occupied in tempting a hermit to yield to fleshly desire, and how he had that night succeeded. Then Satan arose and placed his crown on the head of the new-comer, seating him on the throne as one who had worthily achieved a signal triumph. The spectator, thus seeing the high estimate placed by the Evil One on ascetic chastity, was immediately converted, and forthwith became a monk.[12]

Of those within the Church who wanted reform, i.e., the elimination of the discrepancy between theory and practice, one would expect those officially on the side of severity to be in more powerful positions than those on the side of leniency. That is, men whose emotional gratification consists largely of feelings of power tend to achieve power; and, of those whose emotional gratification consisted largely of feelings of power, sincere ascetics of a nonmystic variety and cynics, whose sexual pleasures would be blunted by hypocrisy and lack of self-respect, would naturally predominate.

Luther and Calvin both hated the hypocrisy of the Church, but in eliminating the discrepancy between theory and practice they were as severe as it was at all realistically possible to be. Calvin, especially, was determined that everyone in Geneva should be "good," and he was not at all above sending spies out into the city, to be sure that no one had any illegal pleasure. The Reformation was in part class warfare, and it is worth noting that Calvin went to school with boys from old aristocratic

12. Lea (1907b), vol. 1, pp. 433–34. Thomas of Apulia showed that there was some sanity, nonetheless, during the fourteenth century, by advocating more love and less theology and Church ritual. The learned theologians at the University of Paris had his book burned and sentenced him to be burned also, but people in crowds had been listening to him, so they apparently thought it better to discredit him by allowing medical alienists to testify to his insanity and imprison him for life instead.

families, of which he was not, and that his schoolmates called him "the accusative case." Calvin later destroyed or drove away many of the old aristocratic families in Geneva, most of whom belonged to the political group known as "Patriots." [13]

In the witchcraft persecutions, launched in earnest in 1484 by a papal bull and continuing into the eighteenth century, sex played an important role. The witches were followers of a religion much older than Christianity, the Cult of the Horned God, which had continued to exist in rural areas and small towns, and included many of the landed gentry and the aristocracy who had clung to their old religion, as well as other "respectable" people and peasants. The inquisitorial treatment of the witches was even more cruel than that of the Cathari, Templars, Spiritual Franciscans (persecuted by the Conventual Franciscans because they insisted upon following the rules of Saint Francis), or Hussites had been. The old religion was not sexually ascetic, and it included sexual practices in some of its rituals; it was especially vulnerable, therefore, to the cold fear and hatred of sexuality and to the rules against sexuality built up by asceticism and hypocrisy. Most of the witches were women, and in torturing and killing these women it seems plausible that the inquisitors were torturing and killing the "seductive mother," the "dark sexual woman," the Eve who tempted Adam to his downfall. Women had long been blamed for sex and sin, by the early Church Fathers such as Tertullian, Jerome, Augustine, and Clement of Alexandria, and by numerous scholarly monks throughout the centuries; they had also been blamed as joy killers. Asceticism eventually took its displaced revenge, and the most ingenious methods of torture were devised, especially in Germany and other northern areas. In England, where the usual methods of torture were not allowed, a procedure euphemistically called "exploration" consisted of inserting a long needle all the way to the bone, on various parts of the body, including the genitalia. This procedure was also called "pricking." The fact that witches were widely accused of causing im-

---

13. The Protestants have tended in practice, though not in theory, to be more severe than the Catholics. Lea's Protestant bias is shown in his quoting with approval the treatment of a Protestant minister, Wendt, who was discovered to be "tampering with the virtue" of the children under his charge at an orphans' institution near Philadelphia in 1867. Whereas the Catholics tended to fiddle around in such matters, the legal authorities in the City of Brotherly Love sentenced the culprit to fifteen years of solitary confinement, "without a voice being raised in palliation of his crime" (Lea, 1907b, vol. 2, p. 360*n*.).

potence (a practice called "ligature"), especially among newly married couples, as well as being able to increase potency and fertility, provides added support for the thesis that the cruelty with which they were treated was an outgrowth of the overemphasis on sex and the resulting hatred of the "seductive mother" and the "prohibiting mother" also.

The hatred and fear of homosexuality also entered into the witchcraft persecutions, as the rituals included kissing the buttocks or anus of the "devil," i.e., the leader of the coven of witches, and there was some homosexuality in the sex "orgies" which occurred.[14]

At least as early as in the writings of Clement of Alexandria (died c. 215) there occurred the suggestion that avoidance of marriage might in some cases have its origin in cowardice instead of a love of continence, and if we follow this lead we can better understand the cruelty with which individuals and minority groups have been persecuted throughout the history of Western civilization.

Almost all boys wish to regard themselves as "masculine" and to be regarded as "masculine" by other boys, and this has probably been true continuously for at least several thousand years. Standards of masculinity vary considerably among different groups of boys, but among all (or almost all) groups these standards include the absence of cowardice or weakness, i.e., that which is perceived as cowardice or weakness; the differentiation of themselves from girls, as perceived by boys; and the emancipation of themselves from control by the mother, as the control is perceived by boys. Cruelty to outsiders can serve several of these functions at once, especially if it involves some risk, as nearly all mothers have attempted to keep their sons from being cruel (as cruelty is perceived by the mothers) and as girls have tended to be more gentle than boys, at least in Western civilization. Among some groups of boys the only activities which serve the function of creating a bond of "male solidarity" are those involving cruelty to or exploitation of outsiders. Kind or affectionate actions or feelings are regarded as effeminate—

---

14. These activities were often carried out only in symbolic form. Many people other than followers of the old religion were caught as "witches"; furthermore, the superstitions, terror, secrecy, and suspiciousness of this period, as well as the use of henbane and other drugs, precipitated much "diabolical possession," with appropriate hallucinations. It is not surprising, therefore, that there have been many controversies about the nature of the witchcraft persecutions.

"soft"—and thus become taboo, and homosexual activities are either tabooed entirely or are practiced only with outsiders, i.e., boys who are regarded as effeminate—"like girls"—or who are younger or smaller. In this type of homosexuality the outsider invariably plays the passive role and in some instances is forced to do so; the strong emotions generated in some men by the subject of rape may stem in part from this origin. Homosexuality may also be used within the group itself, to shame or degrade or in a somewhat less hostile way to establish or indicate dominance, as it is often used among other primates.[15]

Within most groups of boys success in relationships with girls is used for status, in terms of "masculinity," and in many groups this usage is exaggerated and degenerates into a crude exploitation by means of seduction. Some boys who cannot measure up to other standards of masculinity emphasize heterosexual prowess as the most important mark of a "real man"—an emphasis sometimes encouraged by women.[16] To "become a man" by having sexual intercourse has at least two advantages over other methods: it is usually pleasant and usually not too difficult, especially if the woman is willing to take some initiative, which many women are more than willing to do.

During the time that boys develop into men, and later as they mix on a more or less equal basis with men from other groups, it is very important to them that they be able to view their own behavior without the loss of self-respect, and this implies that they must not see their own behavior as cowardly. By shifting to different standards of behavior, the most cowardly actions can fail to be recognized as such by the individual. The medieval Church provided such standards under the headings of "morality" or "duty to the Church and to God," but it is important to realize that these standards were very similar to some which are today, and

15. The relationships between "bloods" and "tarts" in upper-class English boarding schools, described by Lewis (1955), are of a relatively nonhostile variety, with the bloods wooing the tarts, though considering themselves superior to them. A blood might have no objection to rooming with a tart, whose lover might be some other blood. According to Lewis, these schools were full of gossip about these activities— an indication of confusion and ambivalence. In some military academies in the United States there are only bloods, and the relationships are more Grecian, with little or no gossip.

16. Many women have helped men to develop some courage and strength by making them feel like "real men" during sexual intercourse. On the other hand, many women have helped men to fail to see their own cowardice; these women have often realized too late what a tragic mistake "help" of this kind can be.

probably were then, labeled "objectivity," "maturity," "self-interest," or "upholding public morality," and also to recognize that many men performed acts of great courage in adhering to these standards as they saw them. Nevertheless, such standards enable men to avoid any conflict in which they perceive even a very small probability of getting hurt, and in so doing to destroy other people who threaten them in any way. In this connection it is significant that the list of seven deadly sins, as standardized by Pope Gregory I (540–604), does not include cowardice, even though the latter is at least as destructive as most of the others listed: pride, covetousness, lust, envy, gluttony, anger, and sloth. To have included cowardice would have necessitated an elaborate explication of this concept, would have threatened or exposed many in power, and would have made it exceedingly difficult to bring people under ideological control.

During the Middle Ages the Church was the one social institution by means of which men could rise from humble origins to positions of high status, and it is not difficult to understand why men who rose to high positions tended to be filled with hatred and contempt, which often could not be recognized as such, but which could be manifested in extremely cruel treatment of others. Like all large organizations the medieval Church was rife with intrigue and deception ("politics"). Although lying was not listed as one of the seven deadly sins, it was forbidden in the Ten Commandments, and men who conscientiously strove to be "good," as well as men of honor who saw in lying a form of cowardice, would burn with resentment at having to "play the game of politics" to achieve positions of power. Nevertheless, by being ascetic, sexually and otherwise, a member of the clergy could still feel righteous and strong and contemptuous of those who were "weak." In torturing and condemning heretics and witches they could feel virtuous in serving God and Mother Church (run by men), at the same time venting their displaced hatred of their own mothers and fathers, of God and the Church, and of society in general, and emancipating themselves from their mothers by being extremely cruel under the heading of "objectivity," "masculinity," and "goodness." Lying was also a means of emancipation from the actual mothers, as most mothers try to get their sons to tell the truth and as the fathers then, as now, were probably more worldly and cynical (many of the fathers of priests were priests themselves). Hypocrites, on the other hand, would also have tended to be filled with hatred and contempt, as they were estranged from the heroic, strong, moral, or honest part of the self and as they were in fear of exposure. The necessity of "avoiding scandal" and of serving God and Mother Church provided a perfect rationale for operating in secrecy, using deception and entrapment, and in general "fighting" in such a manner as to give "heretics" and "witches" no fair chance to fight back, or in many cases no chance to fight openly at all. Thus, men who thought of themselves not only as "good" but as "strong" were able to operate with the utmost cowardice without perceiving it as such.

Clement of Alexandria's suggestion that the avoidance of marriage might in some cases have its origin in cowardice instead of a love of continence can be extended to attitudes toward homosexuality. Among some groups of boys homosexuality is not at all disapproved if carried on with sufficient precaution against discovery by adults. Boys can be very snobbish about such activities, and boys who are perceived as cowardly, weak, untrustworthy, or too "good" tend to be excluded, or to exclude themselves. Such boys might later take a revenge by severely condemning homosexuality as nasty, effeminate, and degenerate, thus attempting to prove to themselves and others that they are better than the "real boys" after all, or that they didn't miss out on anything worth-while. By labeling all strong affectionate and loyal relationships between men as "homosexual" and insisting that homosexuality is unmanly, friendship, which cowards have never experienced, can be destroyed much more thoroughly than overt homosexuality, and men can be more easily enslaved. The inquisitors were able to use charges of homosexuality—like other "departures from the norm"—as grounds for suspicion of heresy or witchcraft; men became afraid to be friends, and alienation was one of the common "syndromes" of these centuries. The witchcraft persecutions, like the persecutions of heresy, were not only disguised forms of matricide and sororicide, but patricide and fratricide as well.[17]

As would be expected, sex became an important issue in the shifts of power that occurred during the Nazi revolution. Hitler had a great deal

---

17. Erich Fromm's excellent account of the Reformation in *Escape from Freedom* is tainted by some of the same sentimentalism about the Middle Ages with which Arnold Toynbee has been afflicted. Even before the inquisitions, which began three hundred years before the Reformation, the majority of the population was far from being safely in the womb of the Church.

to say about sex and about how people should conduct their sex lives, especially the youth of the nation. Hitler himself was probably impotent, a not unusual condition with men who believe there are two kinds of women, "good" women and "bad" women. The bad (dark, sexual) women, the temptresses, were the Jewish and gypsy women, whereas the good (light, pure) women were the blonde Aryans. Hitler, like the inquisitors, took his revenge upon the "bad, seductive mother" by killing and burning Jews and gypsies, and he took his revenge upon the "good, pure mother" by being cruel and by telling the young blonde Brunhildes that it was their duty to yield sexually to young Nazi warriors who needed an evening of pleasure and relief, and to bear their fatherless children with pride. Hitler had been brought up as a Roman Catholic, and some of the practical, realistic, and successful cynics in power within the Church supported his program in the early phases of his rise to power. Another way in which Hitler took his revenge upon the "good mother" was eventually to render both the Church and the mothers powerless; the children were virtually taken away from both, who then had to countenance their being turned into robots, monsters, and "one-night stands."

The type of "masculinity" which Hitler fostered is that which is to be expected when the sensitive, gentle, and affectionate side of a man—which Jung has included under the "anima"—is not allowed expression, and when a man is seduced into becoming a moral coward, i.e., someone who will not stand up for what he privately reasons to be true or right despite the punishment that such action will bring from one's own reference group. Hitler turned the young men of Germany into robots who were able to feel "masculine" in performing such manly acts as beating women, children, and old men. This is the type of "masculinity" previously mentioned, the ability to act without any compassion whatsoever or without giving one's opponent any fair chance, while not feeling in the least cowardly in so acting. "There's nobody meaner than a coward" is an old saying which is probably true. Cowards are always full of hate because they are unable to do what they want to do, and they displace their hatred onto people who cannot fight back because they are too cowardly to fight those who are actually in the way; yet they cannot face and admit their own cowardice.

Hitler had for many years a close relationship with Captain Roehm, the homosexual leader of the SA (Roehm was the only man with whom

Hitler used the familiar pronoun *du*) and he may even have had one overt homosexual experience, but he expiated any guilt he may have experienced by liquidating Roehm and other homosexuals.[18]

It is important to realize how closely Hitler eventually met the standards of "respectability" which are widely held in the United States and many other countries today. He was neat and clean, and except for his mustache was clean-shaven. He used cologne and was probably careful never to "offend." He spoke with reverence of his country and of motherhood and said many things which people enjoyed hearing. He smiled and patted little children on the head; he probably had some genuine affection for children, i.e., Aryan children, because, unlike adults, they were "innocent." He removed people whom others did not want around, the Jews, and he cleared the landscape of the gypsies, who did not dress neatly, danced in an undisciplined manner, engaged in sex orgies and petty crime, were superstitious, did not look particularly clean, and did not always smell nice.[19] Hitler was thus, according to the moral standard prevailing in Western civilization for thousands of years, i.e., the standard of appearance or "respectability," a good man. Hitler did not have a "rare psychosis"; he had, on the contrary, the most common psychosis there is: putting power, status, and appearance or "respectability" ahead of human beings. The fact that he was extremely cruel does not in any way nullify the preceding statement, as extreme cruelty has for centuries

18. The sacrifice of others for one's own "sins" is a currently popular practice, engaged in by judges, politicians, psychiatrists, psychologists, professors, lawyers, business and military leaders, and other eminently respectable citizens. Ministers, having lost most of their power, are probably no longer among the prime practitioners, although they are often cooperative or neutral.

19. Among the many charges against the Jews in Nazi Germany was that they were "sex perverts." It is more likely that the average Jewish family was more prudish than the average Aryan family, especially with regard to homosexuality among boys, because of the Old Testament prohibition. An extreme attitude breeds its opposite; boys and girls brought up in prudish homes are more likely to feel alienated from their parents and their family tradition, in case they break the official rules, than those brought up in less prudish homes. Such alienation can easily lead to exclusive homosexuality and to promiscuity. By "prudish" I mean not merely disapproval of or friendly advice against sexual activities, but the kind of frightening patriarchal and binding matriarchal attitudes that can be effectively communicated with few or no words. To an anti-Semitic individual the exposure of a few Jewish "sex perverts" is sufficient to prove the wide prevalence of "sex perversion" among Jews, just as the exposure of a few "bigots" among southerners, DAR members, or American Legionnaires proves to many people that bigotry is more typical of these groups than of their own.

been one of the most respectable of all activities, as long as it is disguised as duty, objectivity, justice, masculinity, goodness, kindness, or service to an abstract ideal or ideology. Letters to the San Francisco newspapers stating that the "beatniks," with their sandals, beards, manner of dressing, and open disregard for the sex mores—instead of violating them discreetly—were "vermin" who should be "exterminated" express exactly the same kind of "psychosis" with which Hitler and some medieval and later Church authorities were afflicted.

OBSERVATIONS AND DISCUSSION

In the kinds of power shifts now underway in the United States and in Western civilization in general, it is extremely important for those eager for power to be, or to have available, ideologists who can justify the ruthless elimination or silencing of all individuals or groups who stand in the way. The advantages of medieval theology have already been enumerated; Calvin's theology was similar, except that he went a step further than the Catholics and described man as "depraved" rather than merely "deprived." Current ideologies that are presented as "science," however, go far beyond Calvin in downgrading human beings. Man is described as not only devoid of any moral sense (deprived, depraved), but as additionally a coward (similar to a rat, rabbit, or one of the more furtive primates), a weakling (woman is said to be stronger, but also human, therefore weak), and an irrational fool who is inferior to machines and, according to at least one computer expert, will be superseded by machines as the next evolutionary step upward.[20]

Sex continues to play an important role in power upheavals. In supporting ideologies that present a cynical view of the basic nature of man, it becomes extremely important to silence or discredit any powerful individuals or groups who have been able to afford close friendships and to maintain certain standards of respect for individuals, and who thus are

20. Clarke (1961). The contempt toward human beings expressed in Clarke's article, although very probably unrecognized as such by the author, goes far beyond that expressed by John Calvin and possibly even Adolf Hitler. Both Calvin and Hitler are sometimes mistakenly called "idealists" because they believed that men can—and should—strictly obey large sets of rules. Those who are cynical about the basic nature of man are usually in favor of extensive rules of conduct (though not necessarily their strict or equitable enforcement): if man is basically a dangerous and ruthless beast, then obviously he must be "kept in a cage."

not likely to share cynical views. Such a group is the old aristocracy, the families and groups which have held power for generations. This group, therefore, is discredited on the basis of its sexual practices. In times like these it is "discovered" that the old aristocratic families and power groups do not lead "good" sex lives, according to official standards. Although they are behaving in about the same way aristocrats have always behaved, or misbehaved, they are presented as not only promiscuous but as seductive and destructive. In this way, any attempts which they make to uphold any standards of decency or honor, or any old and unwanted religions, can be discredited.[21] The destruction of the Knights Templars, preceded by the "scandal" at the University of Paris, is a historical example. Sexual practices can also be used to discredit heroes of the past who may stand for some ideal that might prove an obstacle to the Brave New Era. George Washington, for example, who with considerable justification represents the ideal of telling the truth, is described as an "adulterer" and as "homosexual" (because of his close friendship with a handsome and brilliant younger man, Alexander Hamilton), as though it has now been discovered that he had feet of clay and was not quite up to our standards of what a hero should be.[22] Washington was a southern aristocrat and behaved about like other southern aristocrats, except that his standards of courage, integrity, loyalty, honor, and friendship were unusually high even for that group.

Concepts such as courage, especially moral courage, honor, friendship, loyalty, and integrity tend to drop out of existence or to be regarded as anachronisms in times like the present. The word "cowardice" has never appeared in the subject index of *Psychological Abstracts,* which has been published continually since 1927 and covers most books and journals, domestic and foreign, in the fields of psychology, sociology, education, philosophy, anthropology, psychiatry, physiology, and neurology and parts of religion, political science, history, economics, and zoology. There are exactly ten references under "courage"; of these, five are in foreign languages and five are authored by members of one psychological school, Adlerian. The latest reference was in 1948. It is remarkable that a man

21. This is not to say that "aristocrats" usually make such attempts, or have usually done so in the past. They have more often accumulated fatty tissue, especially under their scalps.
22. Now that heroes can be selected in advance, their sex lives can also be checked, to be sure that we do not have another George Washington.

in John F. Kennedy's generation could write a book like *Profiles in Courage* and could even be elected President! This book is frequently regarded as "sophomoric" by young people and sophisticates and must be a constant source of embarrassment, in view of the book's heroes' predilection to stand up for what they believed to be the truth, to the "practical" and "realistic" cynics who tend to surround rulers and to give the usual advice: the public cannot believe or even understand the truth. Hitler was by no means the first to state that the people will not believe the truth but will believe Big Lies; this principle has been known to most if not to all the tyrants of Western civilization, and particularly to their smart advisers.

The current doctrine that any strong affection between men is "pathological" has always been present among certain classes and certain groups, and this doctrine is now especially pleasing to worthless scions of great wealth and to men who have climbed the ladder of "success" and were unable or unwilling to afford friends on the way up. One "scientific" form of this doctrine is that given by Weston La Barre in *The Human Animal,* a widely used text in anthropology: "A boy must become a man by similarly admiring manliness—in a rival he may hate or envy—through the mysterious love of male *logos,* not of physical males." [23]

In other words, one should not love his father, his brothers, or his friends; in fact, to Dr. La Barre physical males are so unlovable that it is even puzzling that women can love us.[24] In Dr. La Barre's defense, however, it should be added that he uses the word "love" to mean a possessive and jealous attachment, as he asserts that homosexual love robs the loved person of his or her love of the other sex. The "romantic" love which involves possessing and being possessed by another person ("belonging to each other," marrying Mommy or Daddy) probably always involves a large component of hatred (of slavery, unrecognized as such), which must be repressed. Dr. La Barre apparently sees such hatred only in homosexual "love."

Extreme doctrines tend to give rise to doctrines equally extreme in the opposite direction; thus, one also hears that exclusive homosexuality is "normal" for some people, in other words, that strong affectionate or erotic feelings toward the opposite sex are, for these individuals, "patho-

23. La Barre (1954), p. 218.
24. La Barre (1954), pp. 215–16.

logical" or impossible. In fact, some men decide that they are "in reality" women, and some women that they are "in reality" men. These doctrines, however absurd, are not nearly as vicious and destructive as the doctrine that affectionate and erotic feelings and physical intimacy between men and between women are to be condemned and eliminated, because to eliminate them is to lead men and women to hate and fear their own sex and eventually the opposite sex as well, covering up their hatred and fear with superficial "friendliness," possessiveness, or an exacting and jealous "camaraderie" such as that found among the Nazis. In societies in which people are allowed to be bisexual, sincerely affectionate ties with both sexes tend to arise quite naturally. Freud, a gentleman of the old school, should be credited with courage and integrity in surmising, in Victorian Vienna, that we are all by nature bisexual, although this surmise was an obvious truth not only to the ancient Greeks, whose bisexuality was tainted by the failure to grant women equal status with men, but to many others throughout the history of Western civilization, as well as to many American Indians, Orientals, South Sea Islanders, and Africans.[25]

Although Freud is often credited with—and blamed for—the overemphasis on sex in Western civilization, it should be obvious from the foregoing that the currently dominant sex-centered psychodynamic theories are current forms of sex-centered ideologies that have been dominant for about two thousand years, and in some ways are even more absurd than medieval theology. Like the latter, they offer excellent vehicles for rising to power and hoodwinking and controlling human beings: They are complex and therefore can be mastered only by years of study; they are worded in a language unfamiliar to the vast majority of people; they have the appearance of objectivity while at the same time allowing plenty of leeway for subjectivity to enter in, so that they can easily be used in the service of the ideologists themselves; and they enable a given kind of behavior to be interpreted so that it is "in reality" just the opposite of what it appears to be on the surface. Furthermore, *any*

25. Ford and Beach (1951). If Freud had lived in certain parts of the United States, he would have had a much better chance of checking his hypothesis while growing up.

Spain is a country in which close affectionate relations exist between men; men are expected to be emotional and graceful, as well as strong; and homosexuality is not severely condemned as long as it is not pursued in an offensive manner. Spaniards are not noted for their cowardice, lack of honor, exclusive homosexuality, or hatred of women.

departure from the "norms" can be used as a basis for suspecting or inferring a departure in some other respect (this is one of the functions of complexity).[26] This is not to say, however, that these ideologies are entirely false or unscientific; like medieval theology there is much truth in them (some of which is useless and trivial, to be sure), especially when they are believed to be true and the self-fulfilling prophecy can operate.

Meanwhile, the overemphasis on sex continues to exist within religion, although there, as within the mental health professions, there are healthy counter-trends. Following a world tour a "leading" evangelist commented that Russia was the most "moral" nation he and his wife had visited, as they saw no one kissing anyone in public.[27] England, on the other hand, seemed dreadfully immoral, as they observed a couple having intercourse in a public park.

In films such as *La Dolce Vita* and *The Roman Spring of Mrs. Stone* the American public is being led to believe that the Holy City has recently become a city of vice, led by old aristocratic families, whereas the truth is that for more than two thousand years, since Greek culture came into Rome and was elaborated and corrupted, the Holy City has been notorious for vice of all sizes, shapes, and manners. As Lea points out, during the fifth century, according to Salvianus, Bishop of Marseilles, Rome was "the sewer of the nations, the centre of abomination of the world, where vice openly assumed its most repulsive form, and wickedness reigned unchecked and supreme." [28] It has continued in like manner down to the present. As previously, great emphasis is put upon appearance ("respectability") as the predominant moral standard; according to a recent court ruling it is unlawful in Rome to kiss anyone in public even if the kiss occurs in a closed car with frosted windows. As for the aristocracy, they are perhaps the people least likely to trick others into bed, to steal the money one has provided for postage stamps (as some hotel clerks do), and in general to treat others with unnecessary

26. Cf. pp. 119 and 123. The inference would be true, if for no other reason, simply because every individual, whether regarded from a genetic, biochemical, psychodynamic, environmental, developmental, or learning-theory point of view, is different from every other individual in more than one important respect.
27. This was before the Russian astronauts landed and Khrushchev and another official smacked them right on the mouth in front of news cameras.
28. Lea (1907b), vol. 1, p. 85.

indecency and cruelty; thus, it is especially important to discredit them because of their refusal to obey conventional standards of "sex morality" and to silence them with threats of blackmail, etc. The same is true, in a less spectacular way, of the old southern families in the United States, who have some remnants of decency, kindness, loyalty to family and friends, and respect for the privacy and rights of others, as contrasted with the newly rich "respectable" people who find it convenient to main-tain a system of morality (sex morality, going to church, saying words, wearing the proper clothing) which does not interfere with their ruthless or deceptive activities in climbing the ladder of success.

The hatred of women, especially old women, is another characteristic sign of the times. Old women are portrayed as tyrants trying to run ev-eryone's private life. It is almost fashionable to hate one's mother, if the hatred is covered up with the proper words and gestures. The taboo against hating and killing one's mother is a wise taboo, and one that no civilization can repeatedly violate—as Western civilization has done in disguised form—and survive. Only a coward who cannot sever the sym-biotic tie hates his mother. Someone has said, "Every coward is a Nero in disguise"—every coward not only fiddles while Rome burns, but also wants to kill his mother, and will, if he can do so without being aware of what he is doing.

Women have historically been kept in ignorance of the facts of life with regard to the world of men, at least until they are old and helpless. A recent incident illustrates that such withholding of the truth is still occurring and further that women often show great practical wisdom about human relationships when given the facts. A grand jury, made up of thirteen women and eight men, recommended that prostitution be legalized in Philadelphia. Despite the historical precedent for this recom-mendation, one made by Saint Augustine, Saint Thomas Aquinas, and the historian W. H. Lecky, among others, the "liberal" mayor, Richardson Dilworth, said that the suggestion was "not worthy of comment," and other leading citizens, both men and women, expressed "shock" at the proposal.[29] Women, when the facts are made available to them, often prefer clarity and honesty in interpersonal relations whereas historically the majority of men have preferred to live in a cesspool of hypocrisy rather than attack the so-called moral standard of their day—"You

29. *New York Times.* March 4, 1961, p. 45; March 5, 1961, p. 81.

can't fight City Hall!" It is probably for the latter reason that women have been excluded from high positions of authority in many organizations, and why they are feared and fought largely behind their backs in politics, to an even greater extent than are men. Jesus was a notable exception, and one highly probable reason for his crucifixion was his admonition to a group of "respectable" men not to throw rocks at an adulteress unless they were "innocent" themselves, thus interfering with their fun (i.e., their cruelty) and their financially profitable hypocrisy, and at the same time implying they were no better than she was.[30] Here was a man who was obviously not a coward running around advocating love and kindness, so there was nothing to do but to kill him.

Current attacks upon fraternities are another sign of the times. All fraternal organizations, religious and otherwise, are vulnerable to the charge of homosexuality, not necessarily overt, but "latent," an even more dangerous syndrome! It is true that these attacks are usually made on other bases, such as racial and religious discrimination, absurd snobbishness, etc., but the hypocrisy in such attacks leads one to suspect that they are over-determined.

Another form of the overemphasis on sex is the prevalence of destructive pornography, i.e., "dirty" jokes and the portrayals of erotic activities as dirty, perverted, or sinful which appear almost daily in news items and motion picture advertisements and in widely read magazines and books. The censors leave most of the destructive pornography alone (it works hand in hand with prudishness), concentrating their fire upon efforts such as those made by D. H. Lawrence to stand up for the right of the individual to regulate his own sex life or to purify "dirty" words.

CONCLUSIONS

Societies of Western civilization have tended to set up rules (laws, economic and other social sanctions) which are too restrictive and infringe upon the rights of the individual to live in accordance with his basic nature; such rules lead to a vulture-like society in which a large percentage of people watch each other carefully, though furtively, to see who is breaking the rules, crucifying those who get caught (in

30. In the article as originally printed I had "a prostitute" instead of "an adulteress." (See preface, p. 63.)

some instances, glorifying them) and privately cursing the stupidity of the official restrictions and the dullness of their existence. Certain individuals are highly paid to act out forbidden impulses: Marilyn Monroe was such an individual, and her suicide was possibly in part the result of seeing that she had been made into a totem animal, one which is glorified, laden with the collective guilt of the tribe, and then destroyed. Her widely quoted statement, "They take pieces out of you," would support such a view.

With true sexual freedom, i.e., responsible individual sexual self-regulation and respect for the rights and privacy of others, would come a de-emphasis on sex, which would become much more satisfying and much more frequently an expression of affection and intimacy and would no longer be the preoccupation of a whole civilization. Individuals so freed could develop an enjoyment of many aspects of living (talking, thinking, singing, dancing, listening, explicit games, walking and other participant sports) which are at present ineffective as sources of satisfaction partly because of sex starvation and the resulting varieties of preoccupation, compulsivity, displacement, etc. It should also be emphasized that, as honest economists admitted long ago, economic problems cannot be solved independently of some solution to the problems of satisfaction in living. When basic avenues of satisfaction are closed, a large percentage of men and women live for power and status, rendering the solution of economic problems impossible. Power corrupts because it is so unsatisfactory as a primary or exclusive satisfaction in living—thus more and more is needed. The old-style southern Negroes are a rare example of an ethnic group able to find considerable satisfaction in living without formal power and status, and such satisfaction can be understood in terms of certain healthy features of African cultures which were retained. Many of these Negroes are by no means "inferior," racially or culturally. We should emulate them as much as we should try to "improve" them.

The forces against freedom are very strong indeed; when the legal code was revised in the state of Illinois in 1961, so that fornication, homosexuality, and adultery, engaged in by adults in private with mutual consent, are no longer against the law, the story was killed in most newspapers and other large communication media, not only outside the state but within it as well. The fight against letting the "masses" know the truth continues, in some respects stronger than ever. Many men, both of the "power elite" and of the respectable and practical "middle class," act wittingly or unwittingly as though they are determined that people shall not be free, and thus they hasten their own destruction, as these classes have done in the past.[31]

SUMMARY

Several aspects of what this author considers an absurd and destructive overemphasis on sex in Western civilization have been described and discussed, concentrating on material, especially of a historical nature, with which most psychologists are probably largely unfamiliar. The style of writing has been intended to underscore absurdity and destructiveness, as well as to reveal the author's bias. References for further study have been provided to supplement the necessarily sketchy presentation.

31. Many arguments, some quite complex, have been advanced against telling the public what one believes to be the truth; the author regards all those that he has heard as self-deceiving rationalizations of cowardice. As was said by many good Americans of earlier times, lying is cowardly.

This article should not be construed as anti-Christian. Although the majority of people called "Christians" are largely ignorant of the history of Christianity (so called), some Christian priests and ministers would like Christianity to become genuinely kind and truthful. In a showdown between the old religion of Christianity and the new religions in disguise, the author might be on the side of Christianity. Jesus was, after all, relatively sane.

~ 6

The Still Neglected Psychology of Cowardice

During the fall of 1945, while on a weekend pass from Camp Lee, Virginia, I visited the state mental hospital at Williamsburg, and because I was in uniform and was at that time working in the neuro-psychiatric clinic at Camp Lee, I was conducted through several of the wards, including that which housed the most disturbed patients. On the latter ward, the aides paused outside one of the small rooms and told me that inside was a "criminally insane" patient who fought them every time they opened the door. I looked through the small horizontal slit in the door and saw a large, powerfully built, and hirsute man.

One of the aides suddenly called the patient's name and said, "There's a friend of yours here to see you."

The patient came to the door and looked at me.

"Don't you recognize him?" the aide asked.

The man continued to study me for a few seconds and then slowly shook his head. I was both embarrassed and appalled by this cruel teasing and told him that he had never seen me before.

On the day of my second episode this scene flashed vividly back into my mind, especially the man's eyes looking out the slit in the door. His predicament of being in a situation in which he was confused by false information and in which anything he might do could easily be interpreted as "insane" struck me with an uncanny horror. Then I realized that I had not thought about this incident at the time I went into training in clinical psychology in 1956, nor had I thought about it at any time during that training, even while I was working on the "maximum security" ward. It occurred to me that if I had recalled this incident, then perhaps I would have been *afraid* to enter such training. From this I jumped to the conclusion that by going into clinical training I was attempting to prove that I was willing to walk into a room with a "dangerous, criminally insane" patient and thus to prove that I was not a coward. This insight released a flood of ideas, on a wide variety of topics, which fitted together in a way that was completely new to me, and which produced the mounting excitement described in the preface to Chapter 5. Later, during the episode, I fantasied that the "criminally insane" patient had once been a southern gentleman, and that I was destined to live out the same sequence, ending in a small room with a slit in the door. When three uniformed men came to take me away I protested, "*I'm* no southern gentleman! I don't want to go back to Virginia!" Within an hour I was alone in a small room with a slit in the door. . . .

Months later I found that the dimension courage-cowardice had been neglected in learned books and journals to an even greater extent than I had suspected during my excitement, and this general neglect seemed to be part of an extremely unsavory trend within our society. Although I mentioned this in "The Overemphasis on Sex," I thought it worth expanding into an additional paper, "The Neglected Psychology of Cowardice," which I wrote in 1962 but which was not published until 1965. Although the *Journal of Humanistic Psychology* is among those covered by the *Psychological Abstracts,* for some unknown reason this article, along with those on differentiation and dedifferentiation and the overemphasis on sex, were not abstracted; thus, as of 1970, the word "cowardice" has not yet appeared in the index and the psychology of cowardice is still neglected. In this it seems to me that the experts are taking a grave risk. What if it should be "discovered" that cowardice is a form of "mental illness"? How could the experts claim to be authorities on this form of "mental illness" if they have no literature on it? As I have apparently written the only paper on the subject (a dubious distinction!), perhaps I should be acknowledged as the leading expert and asked to examine some authorities for signs of this "mental illness," among which signs might be deceptiveness and an avoidance of public debates. I hasten to add that I do not think of myself as very courageous, and there is certainly no reason that I should. The most courageous men in my generation are probably dead—they died in World War II. As I did not risk my life—I never even went overseas, and I was by no means a conscientious objector, as so many young men are today—the least I can do is to stand up openly for what I believe to be true and right.

Until a few years ago I was puzzled by the fact that many men who did risk their lives and who were decorated for bravery still do not feel especially courageous and are uncomfortable about the whole subject. An ex-combat veteran explained this to me. Even though a man has risked his life in combat more than once, he can usually think of a situation in which he failed to risk it, or at least failed to take the *maximum* risk. There is always another hill to be taken, another machine-gun nest to be infiltrated. Standards of courage can be so high that they can never be satisfied except by suicidal attacks. It would be one of the cruelest and most unjust ironies of all, if it were to come to light that in addition to all the other horrors of war, even men who are heroic are made to feel like cowards.

Although "The Neglected Psychology of Cowardice" is not reprinted in this book, because most of the material covered is included elsewhere, I should like to correct two errors in that paper: I had assumed that Freud did not write about courage because the word was not listed in the index of his collected works which I consulted; but when I looked up "courage" in the *Syntopicon of the Great Books,* I found that he had made a few remarks on the subject, which were unfortunately cynical. Also, I unjustly accused my favorite historical villain, John Calvin, of having been afraid to fight openly with Servetus. Upon reading Philip Schaff's fine volume on the Swiss Reformation I learned that Calvin was willing to accept Servetus' challenge to open debate but the Council would not allow it. Many years before, Calvin had accepted a challenge to a private argument in Paris, and, at considerable risk to his own life, had waited at the appointed place only to find that Servetus failed to appear. Calvin's admirers would also maintain that he was above any personal resentment toward Servetus (implied in my paper), especially as at the time almost all members of the clergy approved of the execution and as Calvin recommended the sword rather than the stake for the execution (to no avail). This is more debatable.

7

Psychosis: "Experimental" and Real

PREFACE Early research on LSD was dominated by the notion
that the drug produced a "model psychosis," which was
typically a very frightening, disagreeable, and unpro-
ductive experience. A number of researchers, however,
most of whom were outside the sphere of psychiatry,
discovered a principle known to many "primitives"
for centuries, namely, that the preparation and expectations of the subject and the conditions under which
the drug were administered could modify the drug
experience in many different directions, and that the
resulting experiences could be very beautiful, gratifying, and constructive.[1] Unfortunately, those who
knew how to produce these "transcendental" experiences usually took the position that such experiences
had nothing whatsoever to do with psychosis.[2] This
position paralleled a much older one among religious

1. Much later, Timothy Leary and Richard Alpert designated this
   principle, which had continued to be ignored in the most wooden-
   headed manner possible by "official" medicine, by the convenient
   expression, "the influence of set and setting."
2. A third position, popular among psychiatrists, was that the "model
   psychosis" was a toxic condition very dissimilar to functional psychoses.

99

people, defending mystical experiences against the charge that they are pathological and even psychotic.

Humphrey Osmond was possibly the first to attempt to reconcile these two attitudes concerning the use of psychedelics. He was interested in a biochemical theory of schizophrenia and believed that research with drugs such as LSD would prove very fruitful in understanding psychosis, but at the same time he was aware of the constructive aspects of drug experiences and he suggested the term "psychedelic" ("mind-manifesting") to indicate these aspects.[3]

In the fall of 1958, when our work with LSD began at the Mental Research Institute, I was initiated into the "transcendental experience" method by "laymen" who had experimented informally for several years and knew a great deal about how to administer this drug, and throughout our research we were very much aware of the enormous variety of experiences that can be produced with LSD and similar drugs. I felt very strongly, however, as I still do, that "psychotic" experiences are sometimes among the most valuable, and that perhaps the most important contribution that research with LSD has made to our knowledge is that what Western societies have been calling "psychosis" is very often, if not usually, in part an awakening, a growth or individuation process, or an attempt by the organism to function more naturally, completely, or healthily. Carl Jung took this position many years ago, but his viewpoint in this respect is still that of a very small minority within the mental health professions. Psychiatric residents, for example, are usually taught that they must stop the patient's psychotic process by almost any means at their disposal. It is often claimed that if the psychotic process is allowed to continue, the person will never again be the same; I believe this

3. Osmond (1957). Osmond's suggested term was largely ignored until popularized by Leary and Alpert.

claim to be quite correct. Among living psychiatrists, John Perry and R. D. Laing are perhaps the most outspoken in their defense of the value of psychotic experience.

The following essay was written in 1963; it presents a cognitive theory of psychosis which attempts to reconcile the many apparently conflicting phenomena and attitudes surrounding this dreaded subject. Naturally I drew heavily from my own experiences in developing this theory. It should in no way be considered a denial of my own pathology—on the contrary, I was two or three times as pathological as the usual psychotic. I am, after all, a native Texan, and I even had one "typically Texan" delusion—that I had fallen into the hands of communists. That is all beside the point. It may be very noble to assume full responsibility for one's psychosis and to see all the pathology as within oneself, but it is an enormous and cruel injustice to see "mental illness" as entirely within someone else, called a "patient." Even when one is experiencing absurd hallucinations and delusions, there can occur perceptions of reality that are startling in their clarity and validity. The hallucinations and delusions are relatively easy to get over—as soon as the acute episode passed I saw that the communist menace was not around, and I have long been able to laugh at the idea that I thought I was a reincarnation of John Calvin. The hardest experiences to get over are the perceptions of reality that are valid, especially those aspects of the world which are right before people's eyes but which they do not see because those aspects run counter to the prevailing ideology of the society. There could hardly be a more hackneyed idea than this (to highly educated people), or one that is less well understood. The advantages that I have had over the vast majority of those who have become psychotic are too many to list, but I can mention a few. I was in a small, well-staffed

private sanitarium, under the care of a psychiatrist
whom I had known, liked, and respected, and who,
while I was in training, had performed the unprecedented experiment (at that hospital) of living on his
own ward with the patients for a week, including
dressing like a patient. My wife refused to give per-
mission for electric shock, despite considerable pressure on her to do so—for this I will always be grateful.
After the acute episode subsided, I was allowed, on my
own request, to discontinue tranquilizers, as they were
making clear thinking impossible. I was under no
financial pressure. After the acute phase I knew how
to be a model patient, to get along fine with the aides
(with whom I had had early altercations—in many
places I would have been beaten), nurses, and other
patients. My slight knowledge of Jungian psychology
was of tremendous aid in surviving the hallucinations
and in avoiding deluded interpretations of them (such
as that I had actually encountered three gods, one a
ferocious tiger-like figure, one with an ancient, rubbery
face, and one with a long beak, like a huge bird of
prey). With regard to the valid and disturbing perceptions of the world, even then I knew enough history to
know that I was seeing things that some people have
seen throughout history and have tried their best to tell
others about. (As one reads about the sixteenth century he may wonder why more people did not, like
Luther, see the world as covered with excrement.)
Those of us who have plenty of "book learning" may
not realize what an asset such knowledge can be until
it becomes of vital use; the plight of the person who
"sees something" that overwhelms him and who has no
conceptual framework within which he can make any
sense of it and no knowledge of anyone who has ever
experienced anything like it is an unbelievably lonely
and pathetic situation. It is possible that almost everybody who becomes psychotic must at some point have

sufficient confidence in his own perceptions and reasoning power to say, at least to himself, "This is so," *even
if no one else agrees with him.* To many patients such
a stand would be completely out of the question; in
fact, even to oppose the authorities or the majority of
people who surround them would be unthinkable. The
best cure for the delusion that authorities and majori-
ties cannot be wrong is the study of history.

The bitterness in this book stems, it is true, not only
from sympathy for those whose lives are wasted in
mental hospitals, but also from my own frustrations in
trying to do something to help them. For example, a
few months after being discharged from the sanitarium
I applied for a job in a large mental hospital, at a low
salary, and even though I was told by the head of psychology that he would "give his right arm" to have
me on his staff (a statement I later learned was grossly
hypocritical), my application was refused. Later, I
proposed a research project which would study the
effects of courses in "mental illness" upon patients.
The director of research was sufficiently enthusiastic
that he wanted to be co-director of the project. After
initial encouragement and after a mutually satisfactory
proposal had been drawn up, he told me we might as
well drop it—the older and supposedly wiser heads
at the hospital were too suspicious and afraid. I was
planning to teach the patients the ideas of Szasz and
Goffman, as well as Jung, Reich, Sullivan, and others.
(True, this might have upset things a bit.) Mental hospitals should be operated more like schools, where
patients can learn things that will protect them from
the destructive game of "mental illness." They should
also be able to learn new vocations and professions;
some of the best psychologists and sociologists would
be produced by such schools! They should also operate
more like retreats ("asylums" in the good sense), with
a frank and open acknowledgement that the outside

world is irrational and has been irrational for thousands of years. (Many patients know this already, but would be greatly gratified if the authorities would finally acknowledge it.)

Then I proposed a study of the legal aspects of actual cases of commitment to a professor of law, who was highly enthusiastic and assured me that we could secure a sponsor, then suddenly wrote that it was unfortunately not possible.

On the other hand, by working on a committee of the county mental health association and on a committee of the American Civil Liberties Union, I was able (together with others, some of whom worked much harder than I did) to be of some help—but it was like swimming through molasses, and the biggest obstacles to all such efforts, especially those involving the legal rights of "patients," are psychiatrists (though some are helpful) and especially psychiatric organizations. At one point I seriously considered studying law, so that I could somehow be instrumental in having kidnapping charges brought against psychiatrists and others. If a few prominent psychiatrists could be kidnapped and clapped into mental hospitals, we would soon see some truly startling progress in the field.

For years I have done nothing for the "mentally ill." If I could write something in this book to make some experts angry enough to go to bat for their "patients" I would certainly do so, even if their anger were directed partly at me. Many experts know that one of the biggest obstacles to progress in the field is the existence of absurd superstitions, but they will not oppose the ignorant bullies who too often exercise power in our communities. The belief that mental patients are likely to be child molesters, for example, is on a par with the belief of the Romans that the early

Christians cooked and ate babies, a belief held many centuries later by the "Christians" about the "witches." Yet this superstition has resulted in great restrictions of liberty for hospitalized patients, which in some cases are tantamount to condemning patients to spend the rest of their lives in prison. People quite understandably and justifiably want to protect their children, but they should be told, in as blunt language as possible, that well-dressed business and professional men are more likely to molest children than hospitalized patients. And the fact that some people will allow their relatives or others to be locked up indefinitely to avoid scandal should be publicized and exposed for the hideous atrocity that it is. Superstitious and ignorant men and women in the community should be invited to come to mental hospitals and work as volunteers, and if they refuse, they should be told to be silent about something of which they insist on remaining uninformed.

Psychosis: "Experimental" and Real

> *Now is there something wrong with this entire circus.*
> —CARL GIESE

> *Consistency, thou art a jewel.*
> —ORIGIN UNKNOWN

I shall attempt to present a theory of psychosis centered around the topics of cognitive structure, emotion, role, cultural norms, and communication, and to relate my theory to the cultural revolution through which we are now passing, with comparative references to past revolutions. The contribution of the psychedelic drugs in understanding both "psychotic" and "normal" behavior will be described according to this author's convictions, which have much in common with those focused on "transcendental" experiences, but also with those which have placed drug experiences and behavior in the "model psychosis" context. The presentation is necessarily sketchy, because psychosis involves many problems interlocked in such a way that they must be solved simultaneously rather than piecemeal in any reasonably adequate theory. Many readers, however, have doubtless been thinking along similar lines and will have little difficulty in filling in most of the gaps.

It is assumed that the reader is familiar with the idea that the processes of socialization result in the individual's perception of some objects and events as they in fact are, and of some objects and events as they are not.[4] No animal can survive without some validity in his perceptions, but no animal has only valid perceptions; man is no exception to either of these assertions, but, unlike other animals, his culture (e.g., that of the northern United States), subculture (e.g., proper Presbyterian, midwestern large city), and immediate groups of reference (e.g., his nuclear family, family of origin, clubs, professional affiliations) determine to a considerable extent not only what cognitions will occur, but also the degree of validity of a given class of cognitions. As we move from basic cognitive processes such as figure-ground formation and color perception to more complex organization of the cognitive

Reprinted in slightly revised form from *Psychedelic Review*, vol. 1, no. 2 (Fall 1963). Also published in *The Psychedelic Reader* (New Hyde Park, N.Y.: University Books, 1965).

The ideas expressed herein are in large part the result of the observations and experiences of the author during the two years of his tenure as U.S. Public Health Service Fellow, 1958–1960, and as a staff member of National Institute of Mental Health Project MY-2621, located at the Mental Research Institute, Palo Alto Medical Research Foundation, Don D. Jackson, Principal Investigator, James Terrill, Staff Psychologist, Charles Savage and Jerome Oremland, Research Associates. Grateful acknowledgment is made to Thomas Gonda, Department of Psychiatry, Stanford University, who sponsored my fellowship application, and to Leo Hollister, Richard Hamister, and John Sears, who cooperated in the biweekly administration of LSD-25 to two hospitalized patients over a period of many months at the Veterans Administration Hospital, Palo Alto. The views expressed herein are emphatically the sole responsibility of the author, who experienced a psychotic reaction lasting several months following a 200 mcg. LSD-25 session, without hospitalization, and one year later managed to experience a spectacular psychotic episode without benefit of drugs, resulting in one month's hospitalization. The statements herein are by no means free of the biases or values of the author; for example, I do not like to see people kept deceived or locked up for years in order to help preserve respectability, the sex mores, or status systems. I have no complaints whatsoever concerning my own treatment, and I consider myself extremly fortunate indeed.

4. The epistemological position of the author is similar to and perhaps identical with that taken by the founders of Gestalt psychology long ago (see, for example, Koffka, 1935, and Köhler, 1938) and recently discovered by many others.

field and to perception of objects as members of a class and as thus possessing certain properties attributed by the perceiver to members of that class, cultural determinents usually play a greater and greater role, and differences between groups become concomitantly greater. Within groups the situation is more complex, as group norms tend to minimize some differences and to maximize others, depending upon the specific group. The generalization can be made, however, that *within every group each individual is deceived into living in a world that is only partly real, when, of all animals, he has the greatest potentiality of living in the real world, and of modifying the real world in ways that are to his advantage.*

The thesis that the individual perceives only part of the reality available to him is hardly an original creation of the present author. It has been expressed throughout the centuries in various forms, some much more adequate than the brief statement above. For example, the ancient and recurring statements that people are "asleep" or "blind," or that they are "actors" without realizing that they are acting, are expressions of more or less the same thesis, as are numerous more recent expositions by philosophers, ethnologists, psychologists, sociologists, general semanticists, novelists, psychiatrists, etc. Alan Watts prefers to say that the individual is "hypnotized" by the culture; Erich Fromm has also used the analogy with hypnosis in describing the individual's empty role-taking and alienation from parts of himself and from others.[5]

Alfred Korzybski, Eric Hoffer, and Ernest Schachtel have written about similar processes, though with different words and emphases.[6]

In thus grouping together such a wide variety of formulations, I do not mean to deny important differences between them, or to argue that the general thesis is correct simply because many learned people have held it, but to emphasize that it is continually rediscovered and expressed in ways that sometimes obscure the underlying similarities. It is probably our false pride and our status striving, as well as the impossibility of reading everything, which often prevent our seeing and ac-

5. Watts (1961), Fromm (1941). A beautiful and moving literary expression of the idea that people are only half awake is found in Thornton Wilder's play *Our Town*. Al Hubbard, one of the pioneer workers with LSD-25, expressed this idea very well by the informal remark, "Most people are walking in their sleep; turn them around, start them in the opposite direction, and they wouldn't even know the difference."
6. Korzybski (1948), Hoffer (1951), Schachtel (1947).

knowledging that others have been trying to express that which we believe (sometimes correctly) we can formulate more clearly and succinctly. My own preference for a formulation in terms of deception stems from the fact that in child-rearing practices, as in adult interactions, many concrete examples of intentional deception and of withholding of information which results in unintentional deception can be cited and corrected by telling the individuals concerned, in language they can understand, what one believes to be the truth. Comparisons with hypnosis and sleep, while valid, are both harder to exemplify and also less clear in terms of their implications; this is not to say that they are less important theoretically, or that they are not needed in a more complete account of socialization processes and remedies thereof.

It is largely by means of language and definition of role that groups cast a veil of illusions over the individual. Language, especially, is a convenient vehicle for achieving some uniformity in illusions, as well as in valid perceptions, from one individual to another, in an especially deceptive and insidious manner.[7] Definition of role is, however, at least a close second. Roles not only prescribe the "moves" which an individual is entitled to make in relationships with others; they penetrate the interior of the individual and prescribe his perceptions, thoughts, and feelings.[8] Role behavior is an expression of cognitive structure and vice versa.

If one examines any given processes of communication prescribed by roles and limited by language, one may become aware of something that is "not supposed" to be seen within the culture, namely, that the *processes under examination perpetuate the delusions and illusions of the members of the culture.* For example, the restrictions on communication in judicial processes tend to prevent the participants, including the defendant, from seeing that what is called "justice" is sometimes a hypocritical and tragic farce. On the other hand, a lawyer or a judge may, during the course of his career, gradually "wake up," and may continue to "play the game" and/or work toward judicial and legal reforms.[9]

Restrictions on communication very often serve the function of pre-

7. Schachtel (1947), Adams (1953).
8. Goffman (1959), Sarbin (1954).
9. Bazelon (1960), Ploscowe (1951).

serving false beliefs, and this function is frequently not recognized even by those who impose the restrictions. The "excommunication" of an individual, for example, whether from a religious community, a professional group, or society in general, can permit false beliefs about the individual to be perpetuated. When comments about an individual are made in his absence, for example, he has no chance to correct whatever false beliefs are expressed, or to contribute information that is lacking. *These false beliefs and incomplete information about excommunicated individuals play an extremely important part in the social life of the community.* This principle is partly recognized by those who refuse to form their beliefs about an individual on the basis of gossip and insist upon informing themselves firsthand, but the more general conservative function of exclusion is rarely perceived.[10]

It has been recognized for many years that "psychotic episodes" can be precipitated by insights into oneself. It was for this reason, in fact, that Freudians tended to avoid taking "pre-psychotics" into treatment, whereas Jung took the unpopular and "mystical" position that such episodes, preferably confined to the interviewing room, are the most effective, though admittedly hazardous, road to individuation.

The precipitation of pyschotic episodes by insights into the outside world has been less well recognized, at least within the mental health professions. To acknowledge such a possibility is to acknowledge that the culture permits, teaches, or trains the individual to be blind or deluded; thus it locates pathology outside as well as inside the individual (and in his relation to the outside) and in particular it locates pathology in the most powerful institutions and authorities of the culture. Whereas the location of pathology within the individual is in accordance with the Western cultural tradition that the individual is "ignorant," "bad," "sinful," "deprived," or "depraved," except for the saving grace of outside forces, the location of pathology in the dominant institutions of the culture is hardly in accordance with the tradition of any culture. On the other hand, Western civilization, unlike some "primitive" societies, has contained and nourished also a tradition of critical examination of the world as well as of oneself, a tradition inevitably in conflict with institutions or cultural patterns which blind the individual. This duality is particularly obvious in northern United States culture,

10. Lemert (1962).

which from the days of the first Puritan settlers contained a strong trend toward critical self-examination—with surprising psychological sophistication—as well as strong conservative forces, without which no culture can survive.[11]

It is not difficult to see how insights, whether into oneself or the outside world, can precipitate psychotic episodes, and why from that point onward the individual is likely to find it difficult to articulate with the culture. There are at least two ways in which an "insight" can trigger a neurological "jam session": (1) by arousing an intense emotion and thus altering the chemical composition of the blood and consequently the functioning of the brain, and (2) by a sudden collapse of boundaries between two or more cognitive structures previously kept separated from each other, within that particular individual's total set of cognitive structures. Cognitive structures are presumably related in some manner to the structure of neurological processes.[12] A sudden change in the former is therefore presumably accompanied by a sudden change in the latter.

These two mechanisms are not mutually exclusive, and perhaps in most episodes they work hand in hand. The most important insights are probably those in which two or more cognitive systems, each available to consciousness, are brought into relation. The defense mechanism that breaks down is *compartmentalization,* which has been relatively neglected in the literature, possibly because it is a defense par excellence of most people called "experts," "scholars," "intellectuals," "technicians," or "scientists." Theorists are usually very particular, for example, about what is relevant to their discipline or specialty, what they are or are not supposed or required to know or to do in their roles, exactly how an idea should be worded and the great superiority of one wording over another, etc. From the fields of logic and mathematics many clear examples can be drawn of valid isolation of cognitive systems and of apparently slight changes in wording which do in fact produce enormous differences in implications or in efficiency, and also some examples of invalid compartmentalization and of quibbling over symbols which obscures the similarity of underlying conceptual structures.

The evidence for the breakdown of compartmentalization in psy-

11. Smith (1954).
12. Köhler (1938); Hebb (1949); Miller, Galanter, and Pribram (1960).

chotic episodes is both phenomenological and behavioral. Phenomenologically, things seem to run together in ways that may be alternately bewildering, amazing, inspiring, amusing, bizarre, uncanny, or terrifying. Speech during such episodes is what would be expected when decompartmentalization occurs. What the individual says does not make sense in a conventional way; he does not stick to the point and instead drags in matters that appear to observers to be completely irrelevant. In other words, a massive dedifferentiation of cognitive systems and linguistic habits occurs, which may be as bewildering to the individual as to those with whom he may attempt to communicate.

For any given individual the massive cognitive dedifferentiations called "psychotic episodes" result in more valid perceptions and beliefs in certain respects—the individual has now seen through some of his delusions and illusions, idiosyncratic and/or culturally taught—but they usually result in new delusions and illusions and in even less accurate perceptions and beliefs in some respects than before. Cognitive processes such as memory, attention span, control over impulsivity, and especially judgment are often impaired for much longer periods than the acute episodes themselves, and euphoric or dysphoric emotions may continue, often appearing "inappropriate" to others and sometimes to the person himself. The way in which the individual is classified according to the official psychiatric nomenclature depends on the stage and circumstances during which he is examined, as well as on who examines him.

As each individual has lived in a somewhat different phenomenal world and has belonged to a different set of reference groups from every other individual, and is subjected to a different environment and sequence of external events during his episodes, the *individual differences and communication difficulties among those who have experienced psychotic episodes tend to be much greater than among those who have not,* especially as the insights and ideas developed are often among those which cannot be expressed within the vocabulary of the individual or, even worse, among those which the language of the culture tends to militate against or rule out of existence or awareness. The kindness a long-term patient may show toward a new patient in a mental hospital is perhaps usually accompanied not by an understanding of that individual but simply by the realization that his phenomenal world, whatever it was, has collapsed, as did the long-term patient's world at some time in the past.

A general principle of social psychology is that members of groups are usually less open in their communications to outsiders than to other members of their own groups: they tend to give less full and accurate information, and to voice their convictions or doubts less freely.[13] The importance of this principle for the field of so-called mental illness can hardly be overemphasized, because the labeling of an individual as "mentally ill," "emotionally disturbed," "psychotic," "schizophrenic," "paranoid," etc. immediately moves the individual either entirely outside the group, or at least toward the periphery. Whereas the designated patient often needs fuller and more accurate information than before, the information he receives is usually both less complete and less accurate. At the time when he is suffering most from feelings of alienation, he is likely to be treated in such a way as to increase his alienation, especially as he may behave in a way that is especially unattractive or repellent to others. Any demand for additional information is easily construed as "paranoid" by those who see no reason for his lack of trust, and who are thus blind without realizing it.[14] When people lie or withhold relevant information they usually, if not always, do so imperfectly; in other words, they emit incongruent messages. These incongruent messages often place the receiver into a "double blind." [15] *Lying and withholding of relevant information are perhaps the major causes of "mental illness," as well as the major ways in which such "illnesses" are perpetuated.*

Jung emphasized long ago that the road to individuation is narrow as a razor's edge, fraught with peril, and that only a few fail to lose their way. As an individual begins to see things as they are, in a way he has not done before—to see clearly not only his own blind and seamy past

13. This statement assumes that group membership is *defined* in other ways; in other words, the statement is intended as an empirical assertion, not as a tautology. Important exceptions sometimes occur when anonymity is guaranteed, when the recipient of information is sworn to secrecy, etc. The free exchange of "confidential" information about designated "patients" between "experts," whose group membership is defined in terms of being "expert," accounts for the feeling of alienation which some experts have toward their patients, to whom these experts never say anything they believe would not be "good" for the patient. Such experts are very similar to many other politicians.
14. Goffman (1961).
15. Bateson, et al. (1956).

but also the stupidity, irrationality, cruelty, and blindness of his own culture and groups of reference—he must have not only great tolerance for pain, including feelings of alienation and uncanny emotions; unless he has advantages such as knowledge, power, status (albeit this is a two-edged sword), devoted friends and relatives, and financial independence, the burden is likely to be beyond the endurance of any human being. The restriction of the "sacred" mushrooms to high-caste individuals, found in some societies, makes considerable sense in this respect.

The solution found in Zen Buddhism and formulated clearly by Alan Watts of becoming a "joker," i.e., one who has seen through the arbitrariness or absurdity of social "games" but is able to "play" them anyway, is helpful but not sufficient, because, as Watts would presumably agree, *some social "games" must not be played but broken up* if we are to avoid a complete Hell on Earth. For example, the game of Blame the Jews, "played" in Nazi Germany and in many previous and subsequent times and places, e.g., in Western Europe during the fourteenth century, when the Black Death was blamed on the Jews, must be broken up, although to be a "joker" might under some conditions be necessary as a device enabling one to operate underground in a different way, i.e., decently.

Some patients who refuse to leave mental hospitals are no longer interested in the games that people on the outside insist on playing— among these games are "blame it on the ex-patients," "be kind to ex-patients but be careful about trusting them or telling them the truth," "one step forward, one step back," "your private life is my business," "last things first, first things last," "if you don't believe it, pretend you do anyway," "don't let your right hand know what your left hand is doing," "be both prudish and pornographic," "be both mechanistic and mystical," "sentence first, trial afterward," [16] "be both a coward and a gentleman," etc. Some patients also have a partly justifiable punitive attitude toward society: "Since you say I'm crazy, you can pay my room and board, indefinitely."

All the psychedelic or "mind-manifesting" drugs attack the defense of compartmentalization and thus make it possible for an individual to

16. " 'No, no!' said the Queen. 'Sentence first—verdict afterwards.'
" 'Stuff and nonsense!' said Alice loudly. 'The idea of having the sentence first.'
" 'Hold your tongue!' said the Queen, turning purple. . . ." (Quoted by Jourdain, 1918, p. 96, from *Alice's Adventures in Wonderland*.)

see through some of the absurdities, including status systems, of his own behavior, and of his own culture and groups of reference.[17] This, I believe, is the most important basis for attempts to ban or restrict the uses of these drugs, even more than the fact that, unlike alcohol, they make possible great pleasure without subsequent punishment, contrary to the long-standing "moral" dicta of Western civilization. The distinction, however, between "transcendental experiences" and "experimental psychoses" is, in my opinion, extremely unfortunate, and has resulted in a failure to recognize the great contribution that can be made by these drugs to an understanding of what we have been calling "psychosis." Several years ago the author heard Harold Abramson remark that *every time someone takes a large dose of LSD-25 he undergoes an experimental psychosis.* At that time I thought Dr. Abramson, who had worked extensively with this drug for several years, old-fashioned, and privately congratulated myself on being more informed and up-to-date, or even ahead of my time. Now I am in complete agreement with his statement, granted that the term "experimental psychosis" can give a misleading impression about drug experiences and that an "experimental psychosis" and a "real psychosis" are usually very different in some very important respects.[18]

The fact that an experience is extravagantly satisfying, in terms of emotions, sensations, and fantasy, complete with technicolor and sound track, creatively and productively loaded with valid insights, does not justify our not labeling it "psychotic," unless we are to drop the word altogether. To avoid using the word "psychotic," reserving the latter only for the frightened, suspicious, obviously deluded, depressed, constricted, or empty experiences, is to overlook what mental health experts —with the exception of Jung and a few other voices crying in the wilderness—have traditionally minimized, i.e., the *constructive* aspects of psychosis. That "psychotic" experiences can be emotionally gratifying

17. Unfortunately these drugs have sometimes resulted in new status systems which compete in absurdity with any others in existence, including those in psychoanalytic circles.
18. It is especially important that the subject understand that the drug is responsible for his craziness or his loftiness and that his craziness or his loftiness will be only temporary. When drugs are given without the subject's knowledge, as, for example, certain criminals are reported to have done in India with a mixture of marijuana and datura, the "experimental psychosis" can become very real indeed. See Osmond and Hoffer (1958).

is grudgingly recognized in many descriptions of patients, but seldom does one find even a grudging recognition of the possible beneficial effects of these emotional orgies. The views of religious mysticism that have been held by most psychologists and psychiatrists make this one-sidedness particularly obvious. There is virtually no recognition of the possible value of *dysphoric* emotions. When it comes to cognition, there is again very little recognition of the constructive or creative aspects of psychosis, despite the repeated lesson from history that people who put forth truly new ideas—or old ideas that are unpopular or unfashionable —have often if not usually been said to be "insane," and that there has often been some truth in such accusations.[19] In fact, labeling the inno-vator as "insane" has been a standard method of fighting genuinely new ideas, as opposed to old ideas whose deceptive rewordings are eagerly accepted as the latest fashion. It was the irrationality of this kind of opposition to new ideas which led William James to remark that one of the least important objections that can be made to any theory is that the man who invented it was insane. James's remark can be generalized: *one of the least important objections that can be made to any statement whatsoever is that the man who made it is "psychotic" or "mentally ill" or "emotionally disturbed."* By "least important objection" we understand that we are concerned with the *validity of the statement* and not with the question of giving the individual power over others, set-ting him up as a model for others to attempt to emulate, or encour-aging the wholesale acceptance of everything he has said, or will say in the future.

Hell is at least as instructive as Heaven, and out of the Hell called "experimental psychosis" can come changes in the individual that are just as valuable, or even more so, as those arising from "transcendental experiences." The tendency to give the patient or subject as gratifying and "wonderful" an experience as possible, to protect him from later trouble, and to assert that those who have "bad experiences" or later conflict have not taken the drug in a "proper" context or with the "proper" preparation is a form of conservatism; the preceding word is

19. Sir Isaac Newton is an example of someone who became "psychotic" after putting forth a new idea, experimentally demonstrable, and seeing how his learned col-leagues in the Royal Academy reacted. He did not publish again for about twenty years, meanwhile writing "metaphysics" (which is kept locked up, a source of embarrassment to physicists).

not intended, however, to assign this attitude to the lowest regions of Hell. It is kind to help people to grow, change, or regress (in the service of the ego, of course) gradually and relatively painlessly, but *it should not be assumed that gradual and painless change is always possible, or even necessarily desirable.* In a world as irrational as ours, to be fully human one must be capable of taking great and sudden pain.

Although raptures about "transcendental experiences" often focus primarily on the visual splendors and lofty insights into the meaning of existence and the universe and the increase in aesthetic sensitivity, the real source of enthusiasm is much more likely to be the strong feelings and bodily sensations aroused, often for the first time in many years or since the individual was very young. The ban on emotional expression, especially in Anglo-Saxon cultures and especially among men, makes the enthusiasm and wonder arising from drug-induced states readily understandable, because without emotional expression the emotions themselves wither away.[20] To attribute one's enthusiasm to feelings and sensations is less congruent with these cultures than to praise the "higher level" processes. The same has been true in religious mysticism although it has been pointed out many times that the bodily sensations in religious mysticism have become painfully obvious on occasion, e.g., when saints have "gone wild" and shouted that they desired the body of Jesus.[21] In revivalism also, emotional gratification is apparently the most important source of enthusiasm, although to the individual who has been "saved" the cognitive "insights" are believed to be the primary source.[22] Some individuals who have been "saved" have frequently felt good for months and have been able to live comfortably without searching for feeling through "sin," only to "fall from grace" eventually. Similarly, following gratifying emotional orgies during drug sessions, many subjects have been able to live for a time in their usual routine manner without boredom, eventually to crave another gratifying orgy,

20. Smith (1954) tells of the history of what the early Puritans called the heresy of Antinomianism, of giving way to subjective conviction, emotion, and impulsivity. Southerners were considered generally tainted with this terrible heresy. It survives as a form of "mental illness" or a "sign" of mental illness, especially according to northern experts.
21. It has usually not been noted that such a desire may be very rational in a world in which men consider some parts of their bodies "dirty" and look upon virginity as the "highest" state of womanhood.
22. Sargant (1957).

which may be conceptualized primarily as an opportunity to rise to a "higher" level of existence or knowledge. The same can be said of many individuals who have experienced intense emotions during "depth" psychotherapy. The search for "meaning" in life is usually in large part a search for feeling; unless the individual becomes aware of the nature of his search, he may spend his life in a never-ending pursuit of cognitive "insights" or "understandings," like those scholars and scientists who keep searching for a "discovery" when their greatest needs would be met by standing up openly for what they already know or believe, thus exposing themselves to the danger and excitement of external conflict.[23]

All paths to individuation, whether through "psychosis," drug states, psychotherapy, Zen Buddhism, general semantics, philosophy, solitary confinement, Catholicism, Calvinism, thinking and reading on one's own, etc., are effective only if the individual can accept the chaff with the wheat, only if he can look squarely at the horrors of the world as well as its joys and beauty, can tolerate a variety of emotions (and thus supply his body with a variety of drugs), and can summon up the courage to act in accordance with his moral principles as well as his more obvious needs, and thus have some self-respect. In a society as hypocritical as ours is today, *the most socially unacceptable and dangerous acts are those which are most in accordance with the private moral convictions of the individual.* This is true not only for "intellectuals" and "worldly" people, but for "peasants" and "small-minded" people as well, because there are powerful individuals and groups on most sides of most fences, and because there is widespread cynicism about "fighting City Hall" and about standing up openly for one's private knowledge and convictions.

Western civilization has gone through a number of cycles or spirals which can be described as (1) the setting up of rules or "games"; (2)

---

23. Much of what is called "epistemology" and "methodology" is a complex and deceptive rationalization of cowardice. This has been particularly obvious in the field of philosophy, in which the convenient though double-edged idea developed very early that one cannot know or communicate anything: "Nothing is; or, if anything is, it cannot be known; or, if anything is and can be known, it cannot be communicated" (Gorgias, c. 450 B.C.). The principle is also readily discernible in psychology, history, and the social sciences. One form of this principle was called the "good-taste psychosis" by Harry Elmer Barnes, who added that the good-taste psychosis among respectable historians was the greatest enemy of truth in his field.

the development of hypocrisy, i.e., a discrepancy between the way things are—and are privately known to be, especially by those having access to large amounts of accurate information—and the way they are publicly acknowledged to be; and (3) the reduction of some forms of hypocrisy and the setting up of "new" rules. All three phases are present at any one time, with one or another phase dominant with respect to a given set of rules. Hypocrisy develops when official rules make satisfaction in living difficult or impossible, as, for example, excessive official restrictions on emotional expression, sexual conduct, open conflict, excessive definition of role, etc.

In eliminating or reducing hypocrisy a *standardization* or *normalization* of the population has in past times occurred, and such normalizations have been extremely cruel and unjust, as certain individuals and groups have served as totem animals, taking on the projected collective guilt of the tribe, arising from hypocrisy, among other sources.[24] The "new" rules have tended to be the old rules in disguised form, or modified versions that have been even worse; some forms of hypocrisy are retained and new forms are created. To a limited degree one must agree with the prophets of doom (Spengler, Toynbee, Sorokin) that Western civilization has been rolling downhill.[25] The normalization may occur under various headings: in southern France (Languedoc) in the thirteenth and fourteenth centuries and in many other areas during the same and succeeding centuries under the heading of eliminating "heresy"; in Calvin's Geneva during the sixteenth century, under the heading of turning the citizens into sincere and honest "Christians"; throughout Western Europe during the sixteenth and seventeenth centuries, under the heading of eliminating "witchcraft"; and in twentieth-century Russia and Germany, under the heading of developing good Communists and Nazis, respectively. *Each of these headings concealed certain normalizations which would have been impossible or more difficult to carry out if seen clearly for what they were.*

24. Among these have been especially the following: women, children, old people, followers of old religions, the old aristocracy, people in the "provinces," uneducated people, especially of the "lower classes," Jews, gypsies, and people who are "odd." Most of these totem animals cannot easily fight back; that explains their selection as totem animals. Remnants of the old aristocracy who have managed to retain some power are discredited on the basis of their "bad" sex lives, or allegations thereof.
25. Geyl (1958).

Secrecy has been of obvious advantage in normalizations. A second weapon is a principle made explicit by the inquisitors, by Calvin, and by the Communists and Nazis, which has been stated as follows: *a person who is off the norm in one respect is likely to be off in another respect.* For example, a person who dressed oddly was suspect as a heretic. One of the most cruel of the inquisitors, Robert le Bugre, a reformed Patarin (Cathar), claimed to be able to detect a heretic by the manner in which he moved.[26] Although ordinary citizens could help in routing out heresy by informing anonymously on anyone who seemed "off the norm," *only an ideologist (inquisitor) could determine whether the individual was actually a heretic.* Since statistical studies were even worse than they are today, the "norms" themselves could be located conveniently in the fantasies of the ideologists, and could also be decreed by them to a considerable extent, as they gained power. Thus, the ideologists were able, in all these times and places, to "normalize" the population along whatever lines they desired or thought necessary. Languedoc had a culture distinctly different from that of Northern Europe, and was in general more advanced. Under the heading of eliminating "heresy" it was transformed in the direction of northern France— the southerners, including devout Catholics, had to be "normalized." [27] The elimination of "witchcraft," from the latter part of the fifteenth to the early part of the eighteenth century, was, among other things, the virtual liquidation of the remnants of a religion many centuries older than Christianity.[28] Calvin transformed the image of man a step downward from that of the Catholic theologians, from "deprived" to "de-

26. The English word "bugger" and similar vernacular expressions in French and Italian stem from the word "Bugre," a term by which the Cathari were designated because of their Bulgarian origin. The full significance of this derivation is not known to me, but Robert's cruelty illustrates how dangerous it can be to reform someone. He was finally locked up himself.

27. Current attempts to describe southern United States character structure in pathological terms can be partly understood in terms of the general phenomenon of acculturating conquered territory. This is not to say that these attempts are invalid, but that northern character structure is also pathological, though in a different way. The northern treatment of Negroes, for example, is at least as irrational as the southern treatment, though in a way which differs behaviorally and psychodynamically. There has never been a culture that has not created pathological character structures, i.e., all "national character structures" are pathological in some ways and to some extent.

28. Christianity as actually practiced was by no means always clearly distinct from the Cult of the Horned God, just as in comtemporary Latin America Christianity is not always distinct from the indigenous Indian religions.

praved," and liquidated or drove away the old aristocratic families of Geneva. (It is worth noting that although Calvin never set foot in the New World, he has been probably as important to the development of the United States as any other man of modern times.) [29] The early communist ideologists planned freedom in personal life and the "withering away of the state," but as class warfare progressed it was discovered that sex "immorality" was incompatible with being a good communist, and that the State was helpful in keeping the masses in their proper places.[30] During the Nazi revolution the Prussian military leaders, the old aristocracy, had to become even more cold and cruel than they had been before and to revise their standards of honor in the direction of those of a middle-class individual much more cynically contemptuous of average human beings than they were.

During and immediately following a normalization, no one is allowed to be himself, as no one fits the "ideal" which is officially held and enforced; thus, alienation from parts of oneself is produced, with resulting fear and hatred which are then displaced toward those who are discernibly "different," i.e., outsiders, who are made into scapegoats. The great cruelty during normalization can be at least partly explained on the basis of this kind of process.

The drastic ideological changes and shifts of power that occur during normalization increase the frequency of psychotic episodes and other disturbances. *Mental illness is thus mixed in with religious, class, ideological, racial, and ethnic warfare.* The thesis that many of the "witches" were "mentally ill" is not incompatible with the thesis that many were followers of the Old Religion, or that many were members of the old landed gentry, who sometimes cling to old religions, especially out in the provinces, or that many were poor and ignorant. When one considers the existence of practices such as forcing children to watch as their grandmothers or mothers were burned alive—by Protestants and Catholics alike—it would seem strange if "mental illness" were not prev-

29. One of the author's grandiose delusions during his real psychosis was that he was a reincarnation of John Calvin, among other historical figures. My conviction that it would be salutary to lock everyone in solitary confinement at least once during his lifetime shows that this delusion, like most, has at least a grain of truth. I was also tortured by the delusion that I was an actual descendant of that mean hypocrite, John Knox, the founder of Scottish Presbyterianism.

30. Reich (1946b).

alent during that period.[31] These children probably saw, without being able to formulate their perception clearly, that they were in the hands of destructive giant robots unaware of their irrational cruelty. Many of the children being labeled "schizophrenic" today may have had similar perceptions.

Both hypocrisy and the reduction of hypocrisy tend to increase the incidence of mental and emotional disturbances. During both phases behavior tends to be formal, secretive, and robot-like; people feel alienated and distrustful. Information "leaks out" or is deliberately provided, and *the people who are most likely to be precipitated into psychotic episodes (by sudden insights) are those from whom certain facts have been carefully concealed, in other words, women, especially old women.* When normalization starts, many people are "scared stiff" and thus are even more robot-like, suspicious, and cautious. The "schizophrenic" perception of individuals as mechanical puppets is probably a valid perception; the "schizophrenic" sees the robotization that Fromm and others have described.[32] This perception can also be attained by means of the psychedelic drugs.

The greatly increased exposure to facts and ideas, through mass communication media, travel in foreign countries, etc., can greatly increase the frequency of psychotic episodes, according to the present theory. It is interesting, for example, that an "uneducated" person in a small town can purchase a paperback in a five-and-ten which can reveal to him that some of the peculiar ideas which for years he has taken as a sign of his secret insanity or depravity have been written about by Plato, Whitehead, Russell, Freud, Fromm, Carnap, and others.[33]

Hypocrisy is an unstable social condition, as everyone has to operate in a fog, but the reduction of hypocrisy can in theory be brought about by openly allowing people to be different and human, without a normalization. If our country avoids a normalization, it will be the first accomplishment of this kind in the history of Western civilization; nevertheless, there is reason for hope. Normalization requires the consolidation of power, and it is much more difficult to consolidate power in the United

31. Lea (1939).
32. Fromm (1941).
33. Many philosophers, among them Nietzsche, Schopenhauer, Wittgenstein, have gone "insane." It seems probable that they saw through the absurdities of their own cultures, i.e., they ate of the forbidden fruit of the tree of knowledge (cf. May, 1961).

States than in any of the previous times and places, for the following reasons: There are two major cultures (with many influential subcultures), two major political parties, several large communication media, many powerful individuals and groups, and there are many checks and balances on an overconcentration of power within government. Furthermore, women, who find it more difficult to be deliberately cruel than do men, have much more power. Nevertheless, there is danger, as indicated by the following signs of the times: the tendency for activities to go "underground," so that it is difficult to obtain information which one believes that he has a right to know;[34] the ridicule of old women (most of whom have done the best they could with what they have known); the emphasis on the public importance of one's private life; the attacks on fraternal organizations; the attacks on the old religion of Christianity; and the formation of new secret societies.[35]

There are those who wish to normalize this country under the heading of having only "good Americans"; others wish to normalize under the heading of eliminating or preventing "mental illness."[36] An example of the first is an item that appeared in *The New York Times* (Western Edition) on November 1, 1962, headed "Ideological Split Fills Amarillo with Bitterness and Suspicion." Among its other activities, the John Birch Society had attempted to purge schools and libraries of "communist" reading matter. Several books, however, were removed for alleged "obscenities"; among these were four Pulitzer Prize novels and George Orwell's *Nineteen Eighty-Four,* a satire on collectivist society. Thus, under the self-deceptive heading of "eliminating communism" comes a "clean-up," even though the Russians are apparently much "cleaner" than Americans and have objected to the "immoral" behavior of Americans visiting their country. All the previous normalizations have included "clean-ups"—that is why Europe is so clean. "Sex perversion," for example, was "cleaned up" in Germany by the inquisitors and later by the Nazis; these "clean-ups" account for the current absence of "sex perversion" in that country, just as the "clean-

34. Several writers, for example, Hanson Baldwin, have recently written of the prevalence of the mentality that values secrecy even when it is clearly unnecessary.
35. The secret patriotic societies of the 1840s and 1850s, members of which were called "Know-Nothings" by outsiders, are interesting antecedents of such societies at the present time.
36. Szasz (1961), Gross (1962).

up" of prostitution in San Francisco in the 1930s accounts for the current absence of prostitution in that fair city. What has been virtually eliminated in "clean-ups" has not been "unclean" acts, which have if anything increased as exclusive pursuits, but love and friendship, which cowards envy and take satisfaction in destroying, reducing everyone else to their own empty and lonely condition. Any "lower" animal which could be taught to revile or be alienated from parts of its own body and the bodies of other members of its own species could easily be seen to be "mean and crazy." There are few data on this point; an experiment by Birch is relevant.[37] In this experiment, hoods were placed around the necks of pregnant rats so that they were prevented from the usual self-licking of the ano-genital region which is increased during pregnancy. When their young were born, these mother rats, with hoods removed, ate most of their pups and failed to nourish the rest adequately; none survived. The most "mean and crazy" humans, however, have not been female.

The possibility that normalization could occur under the heading of "eliminating mental illness" is illustrated by the fact that the words used earlier, "A person who is off the norm in one respect is likely to be off in another respect," are quoted from an address by a leading psychoanalyst, Dr. Bernard Diamond, before the Santa Clara County (California) mental health association. Dr. Diamond himself is a relatively outspoken defender of the rights of individuals to live their private lives in the manner they choose rather than the manner he would choose for them; his statement, however, could easily be used in the service of tyranny by experts or others more power-hungry. Szasz has made a brief comparison between institutional psychiatrists and inquisitors,[38] but even better analogies can be drawn between some psychotherapists in clinics and in private practice, and inquisitors. Members of the public, teachers and physicians, for example, are encouraged to watch for "subtle signs of mental illness" (signs of heresy, signs of witchcraft) and to refer or report such individuals to the proper authorities for help, and outpatient treatment is now offered on an involuntary, as well as a voluntary basis. Psychiatrists may be able to achieve much more power than they have at present, but if they do not align themselves on the side

37. Birch (1956).
38. Szasz (1961).

of the rights of individuals, they will become even more hated and feared than were the inquisitors. This remark should not be construed as an endorsement of "rights" such as walking down the street shouting insults or making scary faces, physical assault, vandalism, urinating on a busy street in broad daylight, etc. If we are to preserve our freedoms, however, *involuntary* confinement resulting from such acts should be for a stated maximum length of time, not an indefinite stretch the termination of which is to be decided by an ideologist.

During cultural revolutions the dominant ideologists provide the rationalization for normalization. Psychology, broadly defined, is now, as before, a focal point of ideological controversy. Modern psychodynamic theories (and some learning theories and theories of interpersonal relations) share with medieval theology (the psychology of that era) the following characteristics: (1) complexity; (2) formulation in learned language unknown to the vast majority of people; (3) the appearance of objectivity, at the same time allowing sufficient concealed and self-deceptive subjectivity to be used in the service of the ideologists; (4) the principle of reversal, so that someone or something can be shown by the ideologist to be "in reality" just the opposite from what he or it appears to be to the unlearned observer; and (5) an emphasis on sex and other puzzling and troublesome aspects of human or extra-human relationships such as status, power, or control. These are highly desirable characteristics for an ideology which can be used to divide, conquer, and establish tyranny.

Concepts that would interfere with normalization and with those forms of hypocrisy that are retained or created tend to become extinct or to be considered inadequate, irrational, or old-fashioned. Among these concepts are courage, honor, decency, integrity, loyalty, truth, friendship, honesty, love, kindness, fun, and fair play.[39] These concepts have been largely ignored in the psychology of our time.

Ideologies preserve certain attitudes and ideas within the culture and

39. A reputable psychologist has been unable to find a publisher for a manuscript on love behavior containing empirical data of a non-obscene variety. One publisher informed him that the topic was not of sufficient interest. When a professor of psychology at one of our leading universities announced that a graduate student was planning a dissertation on the subject of friendship, another member of the department exclaimed in surprise, "Friendship! What kind of damned topic is that?" The Association for Humanistic Psychology has been formed to attempt to encourage interest and research in these and related concepts.

eliminate others. Old ideas and attitudes are reworded and claimed to be new discoveries by the ideologists, especially those who are ignorant of history and of the sociology of knowledge. The dominant ideology of the United States has been Calvinism, and some psychological theories and methodologies (as well as some varieties of "common sense") are more or less disguised forms of Calvinism.[40] Calvinism had several facets, including a mean and crazy aspect exemplified by the beheading of a child in Calvin's Geneva for striking her parents, thus upholding "parental authority." This mean and crazy aspect of Calvinism was carried to the United States in many ways, e.g., in the old Connecticut blue laws which gave fathers the legal right to kill disobedient sons.[41] Calvin outlawed most types of pleasure, even in the privacy of one's own home, and this aspect of Calvinism was also imported.[42]

Individuals who oppose powerful social institutions are sometimes labeled "insane." An instructive example is Thomas of Apulia, who in the fourteenth century, when Western Europe resembled an old-fashioned asylum, preached that what was needed was more love and less theology and Church ritual, that the reign of the Holy Ghost had supplanted that of the Father and Son, and that he was the envoy of the Holy Ghost sent to reform the world. The learned theologians of the University of Paris burned his book, and he was pronounced insane by medical alienists and committed to life imprisonment, probably as a means of discrediting his work (crowds had been listening to him) more than as a "humane" alternative to the stake. Yet men like Thomas have been relatively sane, whereas *homo normalis,* as Wilhelm Reich called him, has often been mean and crazy, and this has been especially true of his cynical leaders.[43]

One method of reducing hypocrisy and at the same time preventing

40. Fromm (1941).
41. Dollard and Miller (1950).
42. Smith (1954). For example, whereas the State of California has outlawed drunkenness only in public places, the City of San Jose has an ordinance against being drunk anywhere within the city limits, including one's own home. It is true that no attempt is made to enforce this ordinance, but neither is it repealed as absurd. The state statute is used discriminately: "respectable" citizens found drunk in public places are either left alone or escorted discreetly to their homes, whereas "lower-class" people are often thrown into the "drunk" tank or taken involuntarily to a mental hospital. This is an example, though not one of the worst, of hypocrisy as defined earlier.
43. Reich (1949).

normalization is to defend the right to be "crazy" in the sense of (1) seeking and loving the truth; [44] (2) loving people instead of hating them; [45] (3) openly respecting the rights of others to be different from oneself and one's own friends or colleagues; (4) living primarily in accordance with values other than status, power, security, or material possessions; (5) openly challenging powerful authorities and institutions; and (6) being a socially unacceptable truth-teller instead of a socially acceptable liar.

SUMMARY

A theory of psychosis as a sudden and drastic change in cognitive structure has been presented. The ways in which socialization, including deception, creates cognitive structures that change rapidly on exposure to new information have been described. The psychedelic drugs attack compartmentalization and thus produce insights into some of the absurdities within the individual and also within the social struc-

44. Translated into what is sometimes considered "scientific" psychodynamic theory, this means that someone has repressed his desire to sleep with the null class. The idea that the concept of truth is dispensable is an old idea, "discovered" by various scientists and philosophers of this century. La Barre (1954) gives one form of this idea, stating that truth in mathematics is relative to what is called "mathematics" within the culture. This is similar to the view of mathematics presented to psychologists by S. S. Stevens (1951), with a different formulation. It is correct for parts of mathematics but not for other parts, especially the oldest parts such as the theory of numbers (Myhill, 1952, 1960).

One of the most deflating papers ever written is that by Ness (1938). In this paper Ness demonstrated that people, selected more or less haphazardly, expressed all the concepts of truth to be found among the writings of philosophers. One can imagine how this discovery endeared him to his learned colleagues.

On loving psychology, see Bugental (1962a).

45. Although I do not love everybody, I try not to hate anyone. Sometimes, however, I apparently do not try hard enough; I would be delighted to read in the newspaper that certain "experts" had been eaten by crows, and that some of the oversized cowards in high public and private office had fallen overboard on one of their many voyages, been caught in nets, sliced up and boiled down for whale oil. In baboon societies the larger and stronger males remain on the outskirts, as the colony moves along the ground, and thus are the first to encounter danger. This demonstrates that large baboons tend to have more courage and *noblesse oblige* than many large men. There are, nevertheless, some large men of the right type—ones who are not afraid of someone who shows that he is not afraid of them. Mr. Crawford Greenewalt is an example of a man in a high position who could do a great deal more for this country than criticize the psychological testing industry (Gross, 1962). Like Gross, he fails to see, or at least to say, that this horrendous industry is carrying out the directives of more powerful agents and of impersonal social forces.

ture in which he is embedded. The constructive aspects of psychosis, "experimental" or real, have been greatly neglected in the literature. Psychology is a focal point in ideological conflict, as it has been in past cultural revolutions. Normalization, i.e., the reduction or elimination of certain individual differences and human qualities, has accompanied the reduction of hypocrisy in previous cultural revolutions, but there are reasons to believe that hypocrisy can be reduced in the United States without such normalization. Suggestions are made for the accomplishment of this objective.

8

Cynicism and Matricide

PREFACE   During the LSD session in late December 1959 which
precipitated my depression, I lay on the couch and lis-
tened to some record albums, among which was Yma
Sumac's *Legend of the Jivaro*. In the timeless phenomenal space produced by the drug, she seemed to be
the Earth Mother, wailing for her sons, who were being
repeatedly taken away by strutting warlocks. The experience was overwhelmingly poignant. Not only warlocks but all men seemed guilty of some terrible conspiracy and crime against women. During my ensuing
depression, so abruptly terminated by rage a few days
later, I was concerned only with my own guilt and
worthlessness, not that of other men at all, but in the
following months and years, as I probed into the history of the witchcraft persecutions, I found that there
had indeed been a conspiracy and crime against
women, much more extensive and terrible than anything I would have thought possible. This thesis was
mentioned in "The Overemphasis on Sex," but it obviously warranted a much more thorough treatment. I
was determined, however, not only to present a

cogent argument, but to *move* the reader, as I had become convinced that only by arousing emotions would my writing have any effect. The title was chosen in 1962, but I was unable to write the paper itself because I realized that my previous style of writing did not allow any build-up of the horror, sympathy, rightous indignation, and determination to act which I wished to evoke.

In the summer of 1966 I finally succeeded in putting my thoughts on paper and also in the delusion that I was composing a savage and beautiful essay. Upon rereading the manuscript I was reaffirmed in my previous conviction that I am not Hemingway, so I ask the charity of the reader in judging my style.

The manuscript was rejected by *Playboy,* to which I submitted it with the hope of reaching an action-oriented audience most of whom would be surprised by the contents and yet might be in sympathy with the main conclusions. *Playboy* is somewhat cynical but many of its readers are not. I then considered submitting it to one of the women's magazines, but decided against doing so—it seemed traitorous to my own sex.

A few minor additions and changes were made in 1970, after considerably more study.

Cynicism and Matricide

THE CYNIC

The cynic is usually a genial man. This statement may surprise those who apply the word "cynic" to men who, like the Cynics of ancient Greece, rave, rant, and ridicule, men like H. L. Mencken, for example. But in the way I am using the term, Mencken was far from being a cynic, because he never ceased fighting, in his own inimitable fashion, for what he believed to be the truth; he never ceased trying to point out, or to blast through dense and resistant skulls, that which he saw as destructive or absurd. The true cynic, on the other hand, prides himself inwardly upon having accepted what he sees as Reality or Nature, unpleasant though it might be, and he lives comfortably within this Reality. He is ordinarily a master of the friendly manner; in fact, if he is a highly successful cynic, he has just the right degree of friendliness for each occasion. He wears many masks and plays many roles; he "plays the game" like a good fellow; he has learned that rocking the boat is hardly the way to win friends and influence people, and he is careful never to be seen as a boat rocker—unless, of course, it is some hated outsider's boat. He knows that he will be judged by his appearance and his behavior, not by what is in his head or in his heart, and he acts accordingly. When it comes to letting others know what he is actually thinking, he is a snob, but he knows that snobs are not popular, and therefore he is very careful never to be perceived as one. He is an expert of the candid manner, if not of manners in general.

The cynic does not usually rave and rant, but that does not mean that he does not fight. He fights, but in his own way. He fights carefully and judiciously, as a practical and realistic man ought. He fights to win, but in such a way as to minimize the danger to himself. He fights so that it is difficult for anyone to fight back. He fights anonymously, when that is convenient, because it is very difficult to fight someone whom one cannot see, and one of his many masks is the mask of anonymity or invisibility. As he is a good fellow and can be counted on to keep secrets from outsiders and to lie convincingly whenever necessary, he is in on many intrigues, and thus is often in a position to act anonymously, for example, as a member of a committee that does not reveal how individual members voted, or as an adviser to someone in power who takes full responsibility for his "decisions." But there are other useful methods of fighting in a way that makes it difficult for anyone to fight back; for example, one may convince others that his actions, whatever they are, are simply parts of the role that he is supposed, in fact, duty bound, to play. One may fight to win, in a way that falls considerably short of Marquis of Queensberry rules, as a good party man, convincing others, and perhaps even oneself, that one's fighting is good not only for the party but also, by a happy coincidence, for the country as well. Or, if one is a learned authority, a professor at some renowned university, one may utilize the services of graduate students without giving too much thought or time to the question of whether such utilization is good for the students, all in good conscience; for does not the university pride itself on the productiveness of its faculty?

What does the cynic fight for, in his genial and reasonable manner that appears to be devoid of fight? He fights for power or status, as the realistic and practical man that he is, but he also fights, at least on occasion, either to preserve or to change the society in which he lives, depending upon what appears to be to his advantage, or to the advantage of those whom he feels to be an extension of himself. If he feels himself to be an integral part of some whole, then he fights for what appears to be to the advantage of the whole, because there is then no distinction between what is best for the whole and what is best for him. But in any case the method of fighting is secondary, and to his way of thinking only an unrealistic fool or an innocent child would think otherwise.

The cynic believes that he sees things the way they are, that, in this sense, he is an impeccable realist, and that he accepts Reality as a man should. He has a theory of basic human nature—that people are animals with the high-minded motto "Me First"—and he accepts basic human nature as unchangeable. By this kind of understanding acceptance he avoids hating those of his fellows who are also realistic enough to live and thrive by the same motto. He can in all sincerity accept his fellow travelers in a spirit of true and comfortable camaraderie—comfortable because when and if his comrade falls by the wayside he need not help him if it is very inconvenient or embarrassing to do so, according to the code to which they both adhere. He does not have friends by whom he sticks no matter what; he has heard that such relationships exist, but he is suspicious of them as due to some lack of understanding of Reality, or to some other unrealistic, infantile, or sinister factor.

The cynic accepts things the way they are, and if there is a big discrepancy between the way things are and the way they are officially supposed to be he accepts that discrepancy too, as being part of Reality, for who, except those relative few who are successful cynics like himself, can possibly see things the way they actually are? None other than Mr. Walter Lippmann, who fails to qualify as a cynic, unwittingly expressed the credo of the cynic on nationwide television in 1960, after an American plane was shot down in the Soviet Union and President Eisenhower first denied, then admitted, that he knew about the flight, angering Mr. Khrushchev to such an extent that the latter committed an unusual breach of diplomatic etiquette by banging on the conference table with his shoe. Mr. Lippmann was shocked by President Eisenhower's behavior.

"Everybody knows," said Mr. Lippmann in an exasperated tone, "that every large nation spies on every other large nation, and everybody knows that when a spy is caught the Head of State pretends that he knows absolutely nothing about the spy's activities, and everybody knows that he is [here Mr. Lippmann hesitated] not telling the truth, but the reason for the denial is to allow the other country to save face and not to declare war." I have quoted Mr. Lippmann from memory and therefore not exactly, but the substance is correct. The remarkable and important aspect of Mr. Lippmann's commentary is that it was given, with obvious sincerity, with no indication that this learned spokesman saw anything amiss in this game that heads of states play, and should keep playing, according to Mr. Lippmann.

I have said that Mr. Lippmann formulated the cynic's credo. It is true that he was talking about spying, but he provided the perfect paradigm for many other hard cold facts of life. Something goes on which is not officially admitted and "everybody" knows it. By "everybody" is meant, of course, everybody who counts, everybody who is anybody, everybody who is in the know. When this something is brought to light, through some carelessness or indiscretion—or vigilance on the part of outsiders—then everybody who is anybody pretends that he knew absolutely nothing about it. And everybody who is anybody knows that everybody who is anybody is just pretending. But the reason for this game of pretend is—? Here I do not know what Mr. Lippmann would say, but I do know what the cynic wants to avoid at all costs: *putting up an open fight for what he privately knows or believes to be the truth.*

There is no moral principle that the cynic hates more than the principle that one ought not to lie, for he is a liar par excellence and proud of being one. He is convinced that lying, especially in his genial way, is not only a necessity but is much kinder than telling the truth, and is therefore more moral than truth-telling. Has he not seen how the truth hurts people, whereas lies or evasions make them happy? The cynic believes that people, like cud-chewing moo cows, should be as happy as possible. Besides, who can understand the truth except a man like himself? The cynic may or may not be learned—many of the most successful cynics are not—and he may never have heard of Erasmus, but he can wholeheartedly endorse that great thinker's recommendation concerning telling the truth. "Piety requires that we should sometimes conceal truth, that we should take care not to show it always, as if it did not matter when, where, or to whom we show it. . . . Perhaps we must admit with Plato that lies are useful to the people." [1]

The cynic finds it difficult, nevertheless, to keep his genial manner when pushed a bit on the subject of truth-telling versus lying, because deeply embedded in his psyche is a shadowy figure which haunts him, a figure he feels dependent upon in a way that at times feels like slavery, a figure he needs but fears, and at times even hates if he dares, a figure he wishes would stay in its place. The identity of this figure was given in a simple response of a young man to whom I put the simple question, "When you were growing up, who urged you to tell the truth?" The answer came in a monosyllable, given as though he were hypnotized. The answer was, "Mom."

THE MORALITY OF LIES AND CONCEALMENT

Philosophers have traditionally been interested in universal principles, not mere matters of convenience or usefulness, and one of the traditional questions that has been raised in many a course in ethics is, "Are there any universal ethical principles, and, if so, what are they?" In such courses there will often be someone naive enough to bring up the possibility that telling the truth is one such principle. The professor, especially if he is a cynic, has been lying in wait for this opportunity. A sly and self-satisfied look appears on his face, like that of a hunter who is sure of his prey. To show that a principle is not universal it is necessary merely to produce one counter-example. His counter-example is a powerful one indeed, one which always wins, for anyone who dared to deny its force would show himself to be a monster, arguing not for good but for evil in its most blatant form. In the manner of a man perfectly sure of himself, the learned professor begins his counter-example.

1. Durant (1957), p. 288.

"Suppose your mother were on her deathbed; that is, assume that you had every reason to believe that she had only ten minutes to live. Suppose that she asked you a question, and suppose further that you knew that a truthful answer would make her last minutes unhappy, whereas a lie would make her last minutes happy, or at least peaceful. Would it be ethical to tell the truth in this situation?" The example varies, the grandmother sometimes being substituted, as older and more appropriate for college students, and the time may be one hour or one minute, the latter being more sure to win the argument. The medical evidence that death is imminent may be detailed, to make the example more realistic. Sometimes other examples demonstrating the harm of truth-telling will be given, such as situations in which it is necessary to lie in order to save the life of a friend. Truth-telling does not necessarily fare well as an ethical principle in philosophy courses.

It is interesting that the father is apparently almost never, if ever, used to demonstrate the immorality of telling the truth, and that there appears to be much more enthusiasm for showing the dire consequences of truth-telling than the dire consequences (in other situations) of lying or withholding the truth. Both these points indicate that professors of philosophy who appear to be highly abstract dreamers are not so different from practical and realistic men of affairs as they might seem to be. Women have been used by men throughout history for almost everything under the sun, and one of the most widespread uses at the present time is that of an excuse for not telling the truth, on the grounds that they would be hurt, or they would not understand, or they would not put up with something that men know to be necessary. The situation with respect to woman's oldest profession is a case in point. From time to time a spectacular newspaper story appears telling of the arrest of a madam and some of her employees. The names and photographs of these terrible women appear, together with more or less juicy details of their method of operation. There is usually also mention of the distinguished nature of their clientele—prominent socialites, business and professional leaders from all over the country, even government officials. Occasionally the finding of a little black book with the actual names of the distinguished clientele is reported. Their names, however, are never printed, and even if a few customers are present when the roundup is made, they are kindly and discreetly allowed to return to their respectable niches, untainted by a public scandal. And why? The cynic has a ready and plausible answer. In the first place they are not evil men; they had no intention of hurting anybody; they are simply Big Boys, and Big Boys will be Big Boys, having what they want when they want it. In the second place, it would do no good to reveal their names, and it would do incalculable harm. It would harm their wives and their children, and it would harm others who look to them for leadership, and it would harm the organizations and the communities to which they belong. Whereas it is right and necessary to arrest and expose the Bad Women, their customers are not bad, being simply men, and it would be positively evil to expose them, as it would hurt the Good Women. Think how many Good Women would have been harmed if Miss Polly Adler had written with less taste and discretion about the considerate fathers who provided their Ivy League school sons with introductions and generous allowances, so that they could go to Polly's rather than pick up riffraff off the sidewalks.[2] The cynic knows that prostitution is here to stay, unless everyone were constantly watched or monitored, and it cannot be legalized because the Good Woman would not stand for it. If the Good Woman were not so good, then perhaps there would be no need for prostitution, but there is a need for Good Women and a need for Bad Women, and that's the way of the world. To put the situation into a blunt paradigm: Big Boy has the fun; Bad Woman takes the rap; Good Woman takes the blame.

Actually, laws against prostitution were passed long before women had a vote. Further, the Good Woman is not always resistant to the notion of legalizing prostitution when she is given some facts.[3]

In allowing the Bad Woman to take the rap and in blaming the Good Woman for the necessity of unrealistic and corrupting laws, the cynic plays a very old game that men have played for many centuries, the game of "Blame it on a woman." During the early Middle Ages it was firmly established by the theologians that it was primarily Eve's fault, not Adam's, that man fell. For hundreds of years various monks, studying and writing in their dungeon-like cells, elaborated the theme of woman's guilt. It was pointed out over and over again that were it not for women, men could live in brotherly love. Is it surprising that those

2. Adler (1953).
3. Cf. p. 91 above.

who were seen as guilty of destroying the bliss of Eden and of preventing brotherly love should become objects of hatred? [4] These monks were supposed to have no direct knowledge of women, in the biblical sense of "know," and some of them did in fact not, though many of them did, as Lea tells us in painstaking detail in the most fantastic book on sex ever written, *The History of Sacerdotal Celibacy in the Christian Church*.[5] Celibates and hypocrites, therefore, were the men who built up that formidable, complex, and mystifying indictment against woman that was to come to its full and awful fruition in the fifteenth, sixteenth, and seventeenth centuries, and to deal a crushing blow from which Western civilization has yet to recover.

THE TABOO ON MATRICIDE

There is possibly only one taboo which is universal to all cultures, and that is the taboo against matricide, the killing of one's own mother. Patricide, though extremely rare, was part of the cultural pattern of certain Eskimos, who found it difficult or impossible to provide enough food to feed old men who could no longer contribute their share of prey. As the Eskimo father aged he dutifully followed the role prescribed by his society by taking long lonely walks through the snow, without looking back, for he knew that the day drew nearer when his son would follow him, stealthily, would slip up quietly behind him, and swiftly, without warning, would crush his skull. The best that an Eskimo father could hope for, at the hands of his own son, was a quick and merciful death.

Even the Eskimos, however, did not kill their aged mothers, "useless" though the latter might become. I asked an anthropologist who had described the patricide of the Eskimos what happened to the mother, and this young man, who could hardly be described as maudlin, said, after a moment's hesitation, "Well, she dies of a broken heart." The same fate awaits mothers, not all but too many, of our own society and perhaps of most societies. They die, not necessarily suddenly, of broken hearts, and, further, their hearts are broken all too often by the very men they have loved and nourished.

4. See the short summary by Durant (1950), p. 825.
5. Lea (1907b).

It is human to want to destroy that which we hate. The man who hates his mother thus has a problem, because mothers are protected from their sons by the universal taboo against matricide. Man is an extremely clever and ingenious animal, however, and the problem is not insurmountable. The most famous case of matricide, nevertheless, shows that even a powerful tyrant, "deified" after his mother's death, does not dare to be completely honest and direct about killing his mother. After having his mother, Agrippina, murdered, after viewing the corpse and remarking, "I did not know I had so beautiful a mother," Nero, with Seneca's reluctant help, explained in a letter to the Senate how Agrippina had plotted against him and had killed herself, when her traitorous intention was detected. The senators showed themselves to be practical and realistic men by not only accepting the explanation, but also coming as a body to welcome the young Prince (he was only twenty-two) back to Rome and to thank the gods for having kept him safe.

Nero certainly did not consider himself a woman hater. It was, after all, his unconsummated lust for Poppaea, the wife of Salvius Otho, that led him to kill his mother, who had given her support to Nero's wife, Octavia. He loved Poppaea so passionately that he presented her with Octavia's head, whereupon the Senate again thanked the gods for having preserved the Emperor. Even his famous homosexuality was of an active variety; after Poppaea's death (from, it was said, a kick in the stomach during advanced pregnancy) he found a young man who bore a close resemblance to his beloved wife, had him castrated, married him in a formal ceremony, and "used him in every way like a woman." Nero, like many mother haters of today, considered himself very fond of women; in fact, he could not resist them. We are given some hint, however, of his degree of love and respect for women and, in particular, of mothers, by the information that he "voided his bladder upon an image of the goddess whom he most respected, Cybele." The goddess Cybele was the Magna Mater, the Great Mother. Agrippina's last words as she bared her body to Nero's henchmen were appropriate: "Plunge your sword into my womb." [6]

If it is necessary for an Emperor-Deity to lie and conceal in order to murder his mother, then think how devious and deceitful must be similar actions by lesser men. But man is indeed ingenious, and the

6. This account of Nero is taken from Durant (1944), pp. 274–85.

medieval theologians found a way, without, it must be emphasized, realizing the horror of their actions. It is very doubtful that even Nero could have done with full consciousness what they did, and certainly they could not have acted with full consciousness, for consciously they were for the most part men who were guided by duty, not by lust or hatred, in the construction of their hideous and deadly ideological weapons.

MAN THE KILLER

It is not difficult to make a strong case for the thesis that man is the worst and least rational of all animals, for nowhere else in the animal kingdom do we find any rival to the insane and unnecessary cruelty with which man has treated other members of his own species. Nero's actions, the cynical acceptance of lies by the majority of the Roman senators, the scapegoating of the Christians, accused of starting the great fire in Rome, can be multiplied backward and forward many times in the pages of history. Backward to the time of Pharaohs to whom human slaves were not as important as the stones which they labored to pile together for the enormous tombs in honor of the Great. Forward to the "year of our Lord" 1966, when thousands suffer hideous death and other horrors of which I shall say more later. Robert Ardrey, author of the excellent and stimulating *African Genesis,* insists that even if we escape the horrors of recorded history by going back to man's origin, we gain small comfort, for we are direct descendants not of peaceful vegetarians, like other present-day primates, but of killer apes, whose most distinguishing characteristic, according to Mr. Ardrey, was their ingenious use of antelope bones as death-dealing weapons. The author goes on to argue that deeply and inextricably ingrained in man's nature is the making of weapons, and that his preoccupation with this endeavor is as natural as the mating patterns of howler monkeys, which he discusses with considerable charm. Ardrey aims a stunning attack upon the "Illusion of Original Goodness," Rousseau's doctrine that man is basically good, becoming corrupted by civilization, a doctrine carried on with sophistication by Thomas Jefferson, by the eminent anthropologist Sir Grafton Elliot Smith, and even, according to Ardrey, by Karl Marx. Ardrey makes the cogent point that found throughout the animal kingdom are the instincts for dominance and territory, including eternal and unremitting hostility against all neighboring social groups of the same species (as, for example, among colonies of that irresistible but rude comedian, the howler monkey), and in his enthusiasm for the courageous acceptance of man's predatory origin and basic instinctual urges he defends, or rather glorifies, the switchblade delinquents of *West Side Story* as "normal adolescent human creatures," living in a world "consummately free." [7]

The medieval theologians did not have the advantage of knowing that man is descended from the killer ape, but they did not need it. There was even at that time ample evidence that there was no good in human nature itself. They did not even need to examine history; there was plenty of bloody evidence all around them. Ralph Glaber, monk of Cluny, tells of the horrors of the eleventh century: "Wayfarers were seized by their stronger fellows, and torn limb from limb, and cooked and devoured. . . . Many also enticed children with an apple or an egg, and led them far away to kill and devour them. The bodies of the dead were torn from their graves in very many places, as a defence against famine. . . . as though the eating of human flesh had now become customary, one man at Troyes brought it cooked for sale in the market, as though it were the flesh of cattle. When men seized him, he did not deny the nefarious crime; so they bound him and burned him in the fire. Another, who disinterred this man by night and devoured him, was burned also in like fashion." [8]

Man had gone far beyond his unknown predecessor, the killer ape, and his bestial nature was such that the monks reasoned that any good that appeared to be in him was obviously from outside himself, from God, who was perfectly good, and who was, of course, masculine. Cybele, the Magna Mater, was a fraud; she did not exist. The feminine had no good to contribute and it was woman who ruined the Garden of Eden. The glorification of God and the denigration of man and woman grew and grew and was endlessly elaborated by men who could always remind themselves that they were fortunate enough to reside in the womb of the one institution dedicated to the true God, with a developing monopoly on the Keys to the Kingdom—Mother Church (run by bachelors).

7. Ardrey (1961).
8. Coulton (1938), pp. 4, 5.

THE VALUE OF CYNICAL PHILOSOPHIES

A cynical philosophy of the basic nature of man is necessary if one is to liquidate human beings as though they were insects, and the medieval theologians had no trouble in constructing a suitably cynical philosophy. But their task was much greater, for in the centuries to come human beings were to be liquidated not like insects but as creatures much worse than insects, not to be killed quickly, with or without pain as a matter of indifference, but slowly, with ample time to pay an excruciating penalty for their sins. This more difficult task was accomplished by making use of the fallen angel, the dark figure completely beyond redemption, the Devil. It was the Devil, even more than Eve, who was responsible for man's fall from grace and man's cruel torments ever after. Just as God was the perfect good, so the Devil was the perfect evil, a foe which one must fight relentlessly and eternally, with any means at one's disposal, a foe deserving no quarter, no honor, no fair play, no mercy.

The Devil was actively at work everywhere, tempting, seducing, destroying, leading souls off the precipice into the eternal fire. Was it not good to fight such a monster by any means? And fight the learned theologians did, by the construction of that elaborate psychology known as demonology, which exhibited in painstaking detail the role of the Devil in human affairs. And in no other aspect of human affairs did the Dark One exercise his awful powers as in that realm in which he could be inextricably linked with woman—the realm of sex.

There is a widespread impression, even among college graduates, that the verbal obsession with sex with which learned authorities are afflicted began with Sigmund Freud, and that psychoanalytic theory is the first complex sex-centered psychology, unintelligible to outsiders. This is an unfortunate impression, for there is an important lesson to be learned from that sex-centered psychology of the late Middle Ages and the uses to which it was put.[9] Although Paul had indicated a lack of enthusiasm for sex as a joyful human enterprise, and although the most important Church Fathers of the early centuries of Christianity, e.g., Tertullian and Jerome, had reinforced Paul's attitude, it was not until

9. See pp. 74–76.

centuries later that some of the learned theologians, the psychologists of their time, were writing of almost nothing but sex. That this obsession with sex occurred should surprise no one; in fact, it would be remarkable if that particular obsession had not developed, for when men are deprived of any basic bodily need, they are very likely to think, in one way or another, about the satisfaction of that need. During World War II certain conscientious objectors were utilized as subjects for experiments on severe food deprivation; these men not only spent enormous amounts of time fantasying and talking about food, but would even purchase pots, pans, and other cooking utensils which were completely useless under the circumstances. An obsession with food is usually easily observed in societies where food is scarce.

The medieval theologians, however, were not officially permitted the satisfaction of fantasies in which their sex needs were gratified. To fantasy in such manner was a sin, just as deadly, according to some authorities, as the forbidden acts themselves. One might sin even while asleep. One of the burning questions of the Middle Ages was under what conditions a nocturnal emission was a sin. After much argument it was settled that it was a sin if accompanied by lustful thoughts or feelings. The sin of sex was made greater and greater until it overshadowed all other sins, including murder.[10]

Sex was the Devil's realm par excellence, for had he not, in the form of a serpent, tempted Eve and thus brought about the act which led both Adam and his seductive companion to cover their genitalia with well-justified shame? Sex was the Devil's realm and woman was the instrument through which he exercised his sovereignty. "If it were not for women, men could live together peacefully, in brotherly love." How many learned authorities on the nature of man muttered this malediction to themselves in the Middle Ages? Not that homosexuality was to be permitted either—this form of gratification was also severely condemned by Mother Church (with the nuns having no vote).

One has only to read Lea's *History of Sacerdotal Celibacy* to learn what limited success, over a period of about fifteen hundred years, the Church has had in its attempts to force chastity upon its priesthood. Some popes and cardinals were famous for their mistresses and their numerous offspring, and at least one monastery and nunnery had a

10. See the quotation from Lea on pp. 77–78.

connecting underground tunnel as a convenience for lovers. At some times and places priests were so notorious that leading citizens would take pains to provide any new parish priest with concubines, in an effort to protect their wives and daughters. Seduction during confession ("solicitation") led finally to the sixteenth-century invention of the confessional box. Nevertheless, some learned authorities on the nature of God and man did keep their vows of celibacy. It is important to keep in mind that the clergy of the Middle Ages included almost every conceivable type of man, from the most sincere to the most hypocritical, from the kindest to the most cruel, from the most ruthlessly ambitious (the Church was the one and only means whereby a man could climb from the lowest strata of society to the highest) to the most self-effacing, from the most learned to the most ignorant, from the bravest to the most cowardly, from the most industrious to the laziest, from the most gentle to the most warlike (a complaint was made at one time that the bishops of the region were indistinguishable from the barons), from the most honest and forthright to the most cynically sly, and from men devoted to truth to the biggest liars and forgers in history.[11] There was no unitary trend, except the gradual accumulation of power by that organization misleadingly known as Mother Church, having within its fold not only the humble servants of God but the weavers of that web of illusions and half-truths, that potent black magic known as demonology.

The destruction of the goddess Cybele, the Magna Mater (or, more precisely, the destruction of belief in her, for that is the only means of destroying a god or goddess), was perhaps the first great act of matricide committed by the Christian ideologists, installing Jehovah (more accurately, Yahweh) the God of the Jews, as the sole sovereign of heaven. But gods and goddesses do not die quickly and gracefully. It is said that it took many blows to kill Agrippina, but it took many more, over many centuries, to kill the Great Mother, and even then she arose, within the relative safety of the Church, in the figure of Mary, who reigns today in many areas, especially the more "primitive" ones, as the figure to whom prayers are most often directed. Cybele, like nearly all the gods, was not noted for her kindness. In 205 B.C., after importing the black stone believed to be the incarnation of the Magna Mater, the

11. The repeated mendacity and forgery is given in detail by Lea (1896).

Roman Senate was shocked to learn that the fertility goddess had to be served by self-emasculated priests—in her reincarnation as Mary she has improved considerably in kindness. The fight against Mariolatry within the Church parallels, in a very attenuated form, the fight against Jehovah's great female rivals (Cybele, Demeter, Venus, Diana) in the early centuries of Christianity, leaving aside for the moment the savagery of the fifteenth, sixteenth, and seventeenth centuries. Jehovah's masculine rival, the Horned God, much more ancient than the God of the Jews, who was much more permissive than Jehovah with respect to man's sexuality and other "bestial" traits, had to be disposed of also. The Christians were left with only Jehovah,[12] who had to be both mother and father, without being allowed to be androgynous. Jehovah was said to be a loving God, but in practice to serve Him fully demanded the utmost "austerities," i.e., all possible denial of bodily needs and pleasures. Asceticism led a fortunate few to true mysticism, that fantastic breakthrough whereby the human being lives in a world very different from the world perceived by others, a state in which there is indeed much bodily pleasure in terms of sensations and emotions, including that rarest jewel of emotion, joy—but the mystics were not organization men. The theologians, dedicated to reason but prevented by dogma from exercising their reason fully, ran Mother Church, or, more precisely, provided those verbal formulations which those with power found appealing and convenient. Prevented by their rules from fully human feeling and by their dogmas from fully human rationality, it is not surprising that their psychology was strange and horrible, even to the point of being bizarre. A very significant example of their reasoning powers is the conclusion at which the learned fathers arrived as to the joys of Heaven. As angels were good, and as goodness and pleasure were opposed (remember that we are speaking of the theologians, not the mystics), there was a problem. One of the agreed-upon joys, however, permissible even in Heaven, was the view of the eternal torment of the souls in Hell. This happy thought is perhaps suggested by the Book of Revelation; it was explicitly introduced near the close of the second century by Tertullian, who, after a blistering denunciation of Roman spectacles, describes his own anticipated delight in viewing the roasting

12. And his incorporated Son, who in turn quickly absorbed elements of Dionysus, Adonis, etc.

of kings, magistrates, sages, philosophers, actors, and charioteers.[13] The idea caught on and lasted for many centuries without being detected as a thinly disguised form of sadism. Even as late as the eighteenth century that great American Presbyterian revivalist, Jonathan Edwards, asserted, "The view of the misery of the damned will double the ardour of the love and gratitude of the saints in heaven."[14]

Cybele demanded self-emasculated priests; Yahweh demanded a sex-denying priesthood, after giving His Son, presented as the perfect man (though sexless), born of a mother said to be untainted by sex after, as well as before, her Holy Son's birth.

There are some warm-blooded animals that become mean and irrational when mistreated, and in some cases it is sufficient to deny them the right to live in a way natural to their species. Man is such an animal, and those who constructed demonology, the psychology of the late Middle Ages, were indeed mean and irrational. It is as though their desire for revenge asserted itself in a disguised form, a form in which it could do its deadly work undetected as revenge, which was forbidden. Hate is much more palatable if it is disguised as love, just as lying is more acceptable if it can somehow be seen as supporting truth. One can easily feel pious in doing wrong, if one is persuaded that what one is doing is right. It is extremely dangerous to emphasize any kind of morality that has nothing directly to do with honesty, fair play, or kindness, because such an emphasis can easily lead to self-righteous cruelty. Demonology was the perfect psychology for the blinding of the ideologists to what they were in fact doing; under its guidance the darkest chapters in man's history would be carried out in the name of a loving God and His gentle Son.

OLD WOLVES IN NEW SHEEPS' CLOTHING

"We are living in one of the most exciting eras in history," said John Kennedy when he was president. There are other characteristics too, which Kennedy probably had reasons for not discussing too openly. This is a time of rapid cultural change, of widening gaps between generations, of many different trends in many directions, some diametrically opposed. There are all kinds of goings on and all kinds of

13. Durant (1944), pp. 612–13.
14. Sargant (1957), p. 149.

possibilities for the future. Almost anyone can find some trends and possibilities that he is glad to see, that offer great hope for the future, but if he looks carefully he will also see those that threaten to destroy whatever he values most. Every large organization has within itself conflicting trends. People have within themselves, individually, conflicting values and beliefs, and many of us are frequently confused about what our values and beliefs are. This is a time of ideological change and of radically new doctrines, or at least of doctrines which *appear* to be radically new.

Consider, for example, the following two statements:

1. Cultivated mind is the guardian genius of democracy.

2. We must consider carefully the public image which we project in our roles as mental health experts.

Which is old and which is new? The first *sounds* old, like something we heard—as some of us in fact did—back in the distant past when we were naive, before we grew up and began to see things as they really are. The second, on the other hand, sounds strictly twentieth century, right out of the slickest offices of Madison Avenue. The second sounds like the kind of statement a mature, practical, realistic man of affairs should take seriously, if he does not want to fall by the wayside or be ridiculed as a fool, whereas the first sounds like something a high school commencement speaker might say if he believed it would sound good and if he were willing to be sufficiently phony to say it.

In terms of words and sounds the second is new and the first is about a century older. Prior to the twentieth century no one spoke of "public images," much less of "projecting" them, nor of "mental health," nor of "role" in the sociological sense. But let us reformulate this slick up-to-date advice:

"Most people consider us to be authorities on human nature and look to us for guidance, so we'd better watch our reputations, boys."

This reformulation may be a bit crude and may miss the nuances of the more refined version, but it catches the essential message and lays bare the awful truth: this is the same old threadbare advice that smart, practical, and realistic men have followed for thousands of years. It is cynical advice. Be very careful about telling just anybody the truth. Be very careful about allowing outsiders to see us as we really are. Reputation first, reality last, says the practical, realistic cynic. This twentieth-century advice was carefully followed by the psychologists of the Middle Ages, the learned theologians, who, like all practical realistic men, were deathly afraid of scandal. Even though scandal broke out repeatedly, there was always more that could have been exposed, through carelessness, and there was a new generation every twenty years or so, which could be brought up with the correct illusions.

Mirabeau B. Lamar's statement, on the other hand, archaic and "nice" though it may sound, has a *meaning* that is just as daring, radical, and unpopular today as it was over a hundred years ago. It is taken from a message in 1838, while Lamar was President of the Republic of Texas, and it was adopted as part of the motto of the University of Texas. It is Jeffersonian in philosophy, Jefferson having probably been the first man in history to believe that the "common" man had the potentiality of understanding anything of any real importance in the art and science of living. Jefferson, the great democratic aristocrat, actually believed that the "common" man could be let in on the "secrets," and that he could eventually have some of the honor, integrity, and idealism that was previously believed to be the exclusive domain of a chosen few, at most.

We do not have education in Jefferson's sense of that word, nor have we or any other country ever had it. To illustrate how far we deviate from his ideal, I need only to relay some information received a few years ago from a woman who at that time sat on a committee which examined textbooks being used in secondary schools in California. She noticed that a current text gave an account of World War II which avoided mentioning that Germany was an aggressor in that conflict. When questioned, the publisher explained that this detail was omitted because "We are now trying to be friends with West Germany." In a similar text the statement was made, "An atom bomb was dropped on Hiroshima." There was no indication of which nation dropped the bomb. The explanation for this omission was that further information "would mar our image with the students." The truth would prevent friendship with West Germany and would make it difficult for students to respect and love their country; therefore, reasons the practical and realistic man, it is better to produce a generation of ignoramuses who will, by virtue of their innocence, be both patriotic and friendly. It is not too difficult to imagine some of the feelings Jefferson would have had about this variety of "education." These two examples may be extreme, but the fact that even one adopted textbook could be based on such an educational philosophy is sufficient to illustrate that we do not have education in Jefferson's sense. Jefferson advocated a virile, exciting, relevant, and dangerous process that would help to produce periodic cultural revolutions to keep the ruling classes on their toes, instead of allowing them to accumulate the usual fatty tissue under their scalps. ("God forbid that we should ever be twenty years without . . . a rebellion.")

It is a little frightening to compare Jefferson's forthright statements, about religion, for example, with those of recent presidents. Jefferson, mindful of the horrors of history, indicated his distaste for institutional Christianity in unmistakable language and accused the Presbyterian clergy of being the most bigoted of all, eager to burn more heretics if they still had the power to do so. Eisenhower, on the other hand, was so impressed with a suggestion by his Glasgow-born Presbyterian minister, the Reverend George Docherty, that he quickly passed it on to members of Congress. Senator Ferguson and Congressman Rabaut competed in pushing through a resolution adding "under God" to the Pledge of Allegiance to the flag. John Calvin, who submitted his mind "bound and fettered" to God and forced others to do likewise, would have been pleased, especially as the Reverend Docherty's sermon fell on Lincoln's Day, which could so easily have spawned rebellious ideas. Both Eisenhower and Johnson have entertained the Reverend Dr. Billy Graham (defended in 1949 by the Reverend Docherty against criticism by the Unitarian minister E. Powell Davies) at White House lunches; Jefferson would probably have told Dr. Graham to go jump in the Potomac, or perhaps to visit a warmer place. If one compares the honest statements of our first five presidents with the pious mouthings of our latest five, one might draw the conclusion that after a bum start we at last have men of God in the saddle—but that would be a most dubious and misleading interpretation, to say the least. We started with presidents who were sincerely and sometimes scandalously deistic, and who knew quite a lot about their religion (what recent president would, like Jefferson, cull from the New Testament the philosophy of Jesus and read it regularly?). Washington's "public image" as a truth-teller has stood the test of time and historical research remarkably well, and John Adams and Jefferson were both notoriously outspoken.[15] What are our latest presidents noted for?

History could be a great and exciting educational force if it were not censored. There are so many lessons to be learned from history, but neither children nor adults are allowed to learn them. Facts that rock the boat, that might "upset the community," are quietly deleted, and it is argued that it would do no good and only harm to include them. If Jefferson were teaching a course in history there would be plenty of boat-rocking. A high school student might come home some day and heatedly demand of his good Presbyterian parents why Calvin allowed a girl to be beheaded (for the heinous crime of striking her parents) during his reign of terror in Geneva 400 years ago. This atrocity is not exactly a secret; it is soberly reported by leading historians; but it is the sort of fact that is not taught.[16] Why disturb the children and their parents? Instead teach about old wars and political conflicts that are unintelligible (as usually taught) and are guaranteed to get no student excited enough to start any intelligent trouble (other kinds of trouble are often tolerated to an absurd extent) or do any reading on his own. By deleting all troublemaking facts, children can learn (on their own) that history has nothing to offer them that has any understandable relevance to their everyday lives or any implications for doing anything about anything; thus it can be reasonably certain that they will never read at their leisure one of those uncensored history books that would actually inform them of something exciting, relevant, and important. Even from that one atrocity in Geneva a student could learn several significant facts of life: that men can be, like those respectable councilmen who carried out Calvin's philosophy of life, pious and just on the surface, but cold-blooded killers underneath, and that other respectable men will conceal

15. It is ironic that Washington was the occasion for so many pious lies by Mason ("Parson") Weems, whose book went into eighty editions. The myth of the cherry tree was perpetuated by McGuffey's *Readers* and that of the prayer at Valley Forge was immortalized in paintings and posters. In the 1920s J. P. Morgan "patriotically" burned some letters by Washington on the ground that they were "smutty"—cf. Cunliffe (1958). As for the present author, the more I have learned about Washington the more human, admirable, and lovable he has become.

16. Most historians who mention this incident say merely "child" but Schaff (1903), p. 491, gives the sex. As Schaff was not one of the Calvin haters, whom he mentions, and as this statement appears in the fourth edition, revised, I assume it is not one of the many apocryphal stories circulated by Calvin's enemies.

and cover up their atrocities, so that the "image" of their church and their founder will not be marred, and so that people will not be "hurt." And that a man can be a kind and courageous hero in some respects, and, at the same time, a beast in others. Frightening lessons, but lessons that everyone should learn as soon as he can, for such men have always ruled the earth, and the "common" people often revere them, just as they revered Nero and mourned his deposition and death. Although "everybody" knows what rulers do, the "common" people do not know, for they are nobodies.

THE REJECTION OF THE BODY

What we feel and believe about human nature depends to a great extent upon what we feel and believe about ourselves, which in turn depends to a great extent upon our feelings and beliefs about our bodies. A man who feels his body to be unclean is certain, therefore, to have not too high an opinion of basic human nature, unless he can reject his own feeling as somehow pathological. If he accepts his feeling of bodily uncleanliness as right, and sanctifies his feeling into dogma, then he must see human beings as imprisoned, at least during their lives on earth, in filth. Such was the doctrine that developed within the Church of the Middle Ages. The body and its functions were rejected as unclean, and to emphasize its uncleanliness and unworthiness some sincere ascetics would wear the same garments for years without removing them and without bathing, so that it was said that one could detect a holy monk even before he came into view. We should remind ourselves that as usual there was no unitary trend. The vast majority of the population of the Middle Ages lived as comfortably with the body and its odors as most other savages, and were capable of a Rabelaisian enjoyment of sex that many of our "free" contemporaries would envy. Many priests and monks were no more rejecting of the body and its functions than other members of the population, just as many are not today. In official doctrine, however, those who rejected their bodies won out, and, as would be expected, the body of woman was considered even filthier than the body of man. A shining illustration of the regard for the body and its functions is provided by one Lotario de' Conti, a young man in the late twelfth century, who wrote the following:

How filthy the father; how low the mother; how repulsive the sister . . . dead, human beings give birth to flies and worms; alive, they generate worms and lice . . . consider the plants, consider the trees. They bring forth flowers and leaves and fruits. But what do *you* bring forth? Nits, lice, vermin. Trees and plants exude oil, wine, balm—and *you,* spittle, snot, urine, ordure. *They* diffuse the sweetness of all fragrance—*you,* the most abominable stink. . . . We who shrink from touching, even with the tips of our fingers, a gob of phlegm or a lump of dung, how is it that we crave for the embraces of this mere bag of night-soil? . . . [God has decreed that] the mother shall conceive in stink and nastiness.[17]

Lotario de' Conti's attitude, whether a minority attitude or not, was important, for attitudes of the ruling classes always have at least some effect. When he had matured, de' Conti enabled Mother Church to reach the pinnacle of "her" power, for he reigned as none other than Innocent III.

It is easiest to treat humans as vermin if one can be convinced that they are in fact vermin, and there is no better way to be convinced than by means of the denigration of the body. Professor Norman Brown, in his very excellent and courageous *Life Against Death,* argues that man's erect posture, placing his head, with its important sense organs, on a different level from that of his genitalia and buttocks, has much to do with the rejection of the body. A perhaps equally important factor has been that anatomical development which has made it impossible, for the vast majority of humans, to engage in an activity easily observable in the behavior of dogs, cats, and many other mammals, namely, the licking of one's ano-genital region. Like most activities of animals in their natural state, this one appears to be of greater value than the mere provision of idle pleasure and sensory gratification. Some years ago Dr. Herbert Birch performed an experiment at Swarthmore College in which hoods were placed on pregnant rats, preventing the usual ano-genital licking which is increased during pregnancy. When the young were born, none survived. The mother rats, with hoods removed, ate most of their offspring and refused to nourish those that remained, treating them in much the same way that they treated their excrement.[18]

17. Huxley (1956), pp. 151–53.
18. Birch (1956).

The fantasy of taking one's own penis into one's mouth, which sometimes appears in the dreams of those who would not tolerate such a thought while awake, is expressed in the ancient symbol of the self-begetting uroboros, the serpent with its tail in its mouth. This symbol, found on stone tablets by archaeologists, lives on in the legend of the "hoop snake," which can travel at great speed, a mythical creature still used to frighten or amuse children in various parts of the United States. That the activity symbolized is indeed frightening to some twentieth-century adults is illustrated by an incident that occurred in Texas, one of the sites of the hoop-snake myth, only a decade or so ago. A boy of about thirteen, after the assiduous study of yoga, was discovered by his parents in the actual practice of the symbolized achievement. He was carted off immediately to a psychiatrist, from whom he did not escape.

Another condition which may have played an important part in the medieval denigration of the body was the difficulty of keeping reasonably clean, as do most healthy animals of the forest. The easy acceptance of the body found among people of the South Pacific may be related to the daily availability of the ocean. Except for some fortunate few who lived along the shores of the Mediterranean the savages of Western Europe had no convenient cleansing agent available, soap being virtually unknown. As Aldous Huxley has pointed out so cogently in his essay "Hyperion to a Satyr," from which some of the foregoing observations have been taken, the theologians would have disapproved strongly of bodily cleanliness as a means of removing the "stink and nastiness" from the act of love, because the two belonged together and it was blasphemy to claim that they did not. Furthermore, the virtue of modesty forbade washing below the belt.

Ideologists are dangerously clever people; they have a talent for developing ideologies which make possible the self-righteous throat-cutting of their enemies or rivals, the two being largely synonymous to men who live for status or power. The denigration of the body and its functions was convenient for the liquidation of the enemies of those organization men who ran the Church. Anyone could be accused of some kind of "nastiness" and, during the Middle Ages especially, the accusation of almost anyone was likely to be at least a half-truth. There were many forerunners of the horror which I shall describe presently; one that is of especial interest is often referred to as the "great crime of the Middle

Ages," the liquidation of the Knights Templars by Philip the Fair, King of France, with the cooperation of Guillaume de Paris, Inquisitor of France, of the learned authorities of the University of Paris, and of Pope Clement V, who was effectively bullied into a lying cooperation (see pp. 75–76). The motives were economic and political, but in justifying their actions the theologians made use of the nastiness of the body so carefully documented over the preceding centuries. Specifically, the Templars were charged with including within their secret initiation rites the kissing of the posteriors and the pledge to provide sexual service to any brother in need; and it was charged further that the pledge was often carried out. By means of torture and threats of torture many confessions were secured, but there is abundant evidence that the Templars were innocent, even though Lea grants the probability of a small amount of posterior kissing. As he puts it, ". . . a large majority of the order consisted of serving brethren on whom the knights looked down with infinite contempt. Some such occasional command on the part of a reckless knight, to enforce the principle of absolute obedience, in admitting a plebeian to nominal fraternity and equality, would not have been foreign to the manners of the age." [19] If we examine some of the horseplay of the informal initiations of college and high school fraternities of our time, in which a blindfolded candidate may be more or less fooled about what he has done or what is demanded of him to achieve brotherhood, then Lea's speculation does not seem farfetched.

The "obscene" kiss, as it was called, had a signification beyond that of nastiness, for it formed a part of the alleged rites of the worship of the Devil in the Witches' Sabbat. The Templars, like all others accused of the obscene kiss, were said to be heretics and worshipers of Satan. There has been considerable controversy, among those few historians who have specialized in the history of witchcraft, about the actual existence, or the extent of the existence, of the Sabbat, and about the extent to which the Witch Cult had a continuous existence back into earlier centuries. Be that as it may, the denigration of the body was a convenient ideological weapon for the suppression of any unwanted opposition and the scapegoating that is essential to tyranny, for the masses, as well as the majority of the learned authorities, firmly believed in the widespread existence of the Sabbat. The ancient origins of the obscene kiss are as

19. Lea (1961), p. 705.

obscure as the origins of the expression that invites this act. The origins may be identical, and the vitality of the expression may be renewed from time to time in the practices of boys when fighting ruthlessly for dominance, playing games with penalties, or conducting initiation or shaming ceremonies away from the restraining influence of adults. The most important point is, however, that the power of the obscene kiss to frighten, horrify, or humiliate depends upon the rejection of the anal region in a way that no healthy self-respecting mammal rejects it. Perhaps some liberal proctologists, who have been ribbed unmercifully by their psychodynamically minded brethren in medicine, will agree that the rejection of the anus is one of man's more destructive achievements, contributing to psychosomatic disorders which are painful, pathetic, and sometimes fatal.

THE CENSORSHIP OF HORROR

One may travel widely in Europe today, visiting numerous museums, art galleries, antique shops, and bookstores, and talking with many natives about many subjects, including history, without seeing or hearing any evidence that the institution which dominated Europe for nearly five hundred years ever existed. There are of course arguments for ignoring past events if they are gruesome: Why waste one's life in morbid rumination? Still, not all gruesome events are ignored; for example, one can count dozens of portraits of Saint Sebastian (imagined hundreds of years after the event), and while he is often very beautiful, despite occasionally being full of too many arrows, anyone who knows the rest of the story can hardly want to be continually reminded of it (after being left for dead he was found and nursed back to health; he then loyally and trustingly returned to his Emperor, Diocletian, who this time had him beaten to death). And numerous other martyrdoms are depicted, usually less pleasantly than Saint Sebastian's. Certain gruesome events of the past are not censored, whereas others are. The Roman Catholic Church has taken care that one grim and tragic event almost two thousand years ago is not forgotten, for it is depicted on the walls of every church or cathedral one visits. The Church is of course entirely justified in reminding its members of the central historical fact of their religion. Knowing the past helps immeasurably to give meaning and understanding to the present; in fact, ignorance of the past is dangerous, as we are then more likely to repeat the same mistakes—as has been noted so often before, with so little effect.

The institution that dominated Europe for almost five hundred years was the Holy Office, better known as the Inquisition, which started in Languedoc (now southern France) about 1233, following the Albigensian crusades, and soon spread throughout most of Europe, continuing with increasing ferocity until the seventeenth century, then declining and disappearing, in most places, by the early eighteenth century. Most Americans, and probably most Europeans also, have heard only of the Spanish Inquisiton. Those cruel Spanish Catholics! To think of Spaniards as cruel fits in with stereotypes all too common in our country. In the first place, many of them are relatively dark. Then, too, they are Catholic. Finally, they enjoy bullfights. In fairness to Spain, if for no other reason, the history of the Inquisition should be more widely taught. Spain was one of the *least* of the Inquisition-ridden countries until 1480, and even after that date the worst persecutions were not in that country; they were where one might expect to find them, in Germany, France, England, and Scotland.[20] Furthermore, the Protestants, once strongly organized, were just as cruel as the Catholics; some say even more cruel, though it is difficult to make a choice in this respect.

Hatred is most easily practiced when it is called by a sweeter name, such as "love" or "kindness." A similar advantage is to be found in calling treachery "loyalty." Lying, trickery, and cheating are more palatable when named "duty to the truth." In founding and operating the Inquisition, the ideologists had a problem, for according to a long-standing maxim included in the first volume of the Codex Juris Canonici, "confession should not be extorted, but rather be brought forth of the man's own accord." Furthermore, the Church had an old motto, "the Church abhorreth blood." To a well-trained ideologist such difficulties are by no means insurmountable, and the ideologists of the thirteenth century were well trained. It was shown conclusively that heresy, as it destroyed the soul, was worse than murder, which destroyed merely that despised vessel, the body, and worse than high treason, as heresy repudiates God and Christ, not merely an earthly king. It was also shown that heresy

20. Lea (1907a), vol. 4, chap. 9; and "The Witch Persecutions in Transalpine Europe," in Lea (1942).

was so dangerous that if unchecked it might destroy Mother Church herself. If his Mother is threatened, what kind of contemptible coward would not do all in his power to protect her?

The ideologists also had at their disposal the civil authorities, the "secular arm," who could carry out both torture and execution, although in 1262 Urban IV removed the last barrier to the use of torture by the inquisitors (and their assistants) themselves by giving them authority to absolve each other of "irregularities," a nicer expression than "the use of torture." As for execution, in "abandoning the heretic to the secular arm" so well was it understood what the secular arm was to do that the Holy Office could, without danger of being misunderstood, beseech the secular arm to avoid "all bloodshed and all danger of death," making it possible for some modern historians to insist that the Church never burned anyone.

To think of the inquisitors as men who were consciously and intentionally cruel is to miss one of the most important lessons of history. There were no doubt a few who were in this category, just as there may be a few psychiatrists in this category. When one learns what these men actually did, it is tempting to say that hearing of the pleasure of Heaven mentioned previously had made them impatient, and that perhaps some skepticism led them to make sure that they would not be robbed of this pleasure. The truth, however, is much more profound, more educational, and more chilling, even though it robs one of a certain self-righteous indignation that he might otherwise feel. The inquisitors were for the most part men who consciously strove to perform their duty to God and the Church and *to be as merciful as possible.* They were also practical and realistic men, who knew that not everything could be sweetness and light and that the *truth could be understood only by a small minority.* They realized that their role was one of great importance and that the public looked to them for guidance; therefore, being practical and realistic, they realized that the public image they projected should be of considerable concern. Except for its slightly archaic language, most successful men of the twentieth century would recognize the advice of Bernard Gui, Inquisitor of Toulouse in the early fourteenth century, as practical and realistic indeed.[21]

21. See p. 73 above.

IDEOLOGY THE SLAVEHOLDER

The Frankenstein monster theme, found not only in Mary Shelley's story, has a universal appeal, because it symbolizes a tragic and frightening event that has occurred over and over again in man's history, namely, he has been destroyed by his own creations. These creations may take a material form or they may be more abstract. There has been much furor in recent years about the possibility that man may be enslaved by his own machines or destroyed by his own bombs or by his detergents, insecticides, food preservatives, and noxious fumes. The most awesomely destructive monsters, however, have been not material but abstract, those ideologies which enslave and subsequently demand blood sacrifice. Almost everyone knows the word "scapegoating" but the mechanism of scapegoating is not really well understood even by those professors who lecture on the subject—if it were understood, courses in sociology and social psychology would create much more excitement and boat-rocking than they ordinarily do. The release of hostility and aggression in scapegoating is recognized, but the equally important function of diverting the attention from the actual source of hostility is somehow largely ignored, perhaps because as one begins to see this function clearly one begins to be disturbed. Slavery is universal, but it has many deceptive forms. Slavery in the United States was not abolished in the 1860s; only one form of slavery was abolished. Slavery breeds hatred, which only in rare instances can be expressed directly against the master without very unfortunate consequences to the slave. If a slave is permitted certain pleasures and other satisfactions, then he may be a willing slave without too much pent-up aggression; otherwise either the master or someone else is likely to get seriously hurt. Slaveowners have usually known this simple truth, as have military leaders. One of the functions of severe military discipline is to create a hostile animal eager to tear the enemy apart, not only without mercy but with a self-righteous sense of duty; even so, unless servicemen are allowed to blow off steam in other ways once in a while, when opportunity permits, they may become too mean and surly to handle. The emphasis on asceticism, not only sexual but in many other realms as well, could hardly have led the clergy to be uniformly kind and loving. The worldly pleasures of those members of the clergy who did not keep their vows were necessarily tainted with hypocrisy; even the pleasures of status and power had to be hypocritical, because the priest was supposed to feel humble and unworthy. The inquisitors were chosen for their integrity, largely from the ranks of the two new and therefore still relatively uncorrupted orders, the Dominican and the Franciscan, and one can easily imagine the feelings of these men toward their more lax brethren of the cloth.

Ideology has been the master and man, its creator, has been the slave. Every society has its official ideology, permeating the language, child-rearing practices, rituals, arts, habits, attitudes, perceptions, concepts, professions, and recreations. The ideology is embodied in these processes, not merely in verbal formulations. Formulations are changed or forgotten but ideologies live on, to reappear in deceptive new formulations. Ideologists, the "wise" men of the society, spend their lives formulating and reformulating, codifying and further entrenching, alternately purifying and corrupting that which is already in the culture. They continually put old wine into new bottles, deceiving not only the masses but themselves into believing they have created something new. Their struggles to bring order out of chaos and to extricate themselves from the absurdities of the life-crushing monster are like those of a man struggling in quicksand, sinking more deeply into the mire the more he struggles. Such were the verbal gymnastics of the medieval theologians, like those of the psychoanalysts and communists of our time.

The first to fall within the awful power of the Inquisition was the population of Languedoc, following the Albigensian crusades, although Robert le Bugre was for a time active in northern France, until his insane zeal led to his own imprisonment. The Inquisition then spread rapidly over most countries of Western Europe. During the first 250 years of its existence the Holy Office persecuted heretics of all kinds—Cathari, Patarini, Waldensians, Hussites, Luciferans, Lollards, Beghards, Beguines, Brethren of the Free Spirit, many of these being overlapping or ill-defined categories. There were also plenty of Catholics among the persecuted. Certain bishops and archibishops tried to protect their flocks, protesting to the Pope that heresy was absent or negligible among their own people; such defiant ecclesiastics were themselves intimidated, defrocked, or liquidated, if necessary. Less than one hundred years after the death of Saint Francis, the Spiritual Franciscans were extinguished with a cruelty unsurpassed up to that date, by the Dominicans and by their brothers the Conventual Franciscans, who were much more practical and realistic men. The Spirituals had committed the heresy of adherence to the rules of their founder, as well as such indiscretions as their attempts to defend the lepers from persecution in 1321 and 1322.[22]

Medieval theology was an ideal ideology for tyranny. It was extremely complex, requiring years of study for its mastery, and it was worded in a learned language, Latin, known only to the educated few. It was full of vagueness and contradictions, but at the same time it contained many fine distinctions and had the appearance of great precision. There were many conflicting authorities that could be cited at one's convenience, depending upon what was to be proved. It was concerned with a Reality perceivable clearly only by those initiated into its mysteries, a Reality which might be fully in accord with what appeared on the surface (which might be perceivable even by a naive observer) or might be in complete opposition to the surface appearance. Only an expert was able to tell which of these conditions, on which life or death often depended, obtained. It was centered around puzzling and troublesome aspects of man's existence, such as sex, man's relationship to God, and man's relationship to the Devil. Finally, there was no way of mastering this difficult subject except through subjugation to teachers dedicated to the defense of orthodoxy and the stamping out of heresy. With all these advantages, coupled with the use of deceit and torture, both of which Lea assures us "were resorted to freely and without scruple, and there was ample variety to suit the idiosyncrasies of all judges and prisoners," it is not surprising that

22. I am glad, however, to be able to clear some of the early Franciscans of California of the charge against them by Robert Briffault, just in case any reader has believed it. In *The Mothers* (New York: Macmillan, 1927), vol. 2, p. 519, Briffault states, "The good Padres of the Mission of St. Francis, on the site of the present city of San Francisco, were compelled to burn alive many scores of those shamans and shamanesses before they could stamp out heathenism from among the Indians and gain their ear for the message of the Gospel." This charge apparently resulted from a faulty translation into French of the reference which Briffault cites, because upon consulting the latter the nearest statement I was able to find reads as follows: "There were priests, or sorcerers, both male and female, among them. . . . These priests wore long robes made of human hair, and were formidable rivals to the missionaries. Scores of these human-hair robes were burned by the Fathers, before their rivals were driven out of the field" (Titus Fey Cronise, *The Natural Wealth of California* [San Francisco and New York: H. H. Bancroft, 1865], p. 24).

anyone could be accused of "heresy" and that the accusation alone was sufficient to terrify many into complete submission.[23] As if these advantages were not sufficient, however, there was the added principle of great power. "A person who is off the norm in one respect is likely to be off in another respect" (see p. 123). The inquisitors were well aware of this principle and they made the most of it. Upon arriving in a given community, they called a meeting of all inhabitants and admonished them not only to report themselves and anyone else whom they had reason to believe might be heretical, but also to report any occurrence that seemed out of the ordinary in any way—any unusual manner of dress, habit, style of living, manner of speaking, belief, or morality, as any such deviation from the lives of the "righteous" might be a sign of heresy. Naturally a citizen was not to draw the fatal conclusion himself— *that was to be left strictly up to experts*—but cooperation and assistance was essential if the experts were to be able to protect the community from this deadly and satanic virus.

Until he gained more sophistication, coming only when it was too late, the average lay citizen was as eager to rid the community of "heresy' as were the inquisitors. The reason that the principle cited above is so important, however, is that, applied in conjunction with a vague category whose appropriate usage is the exclusive prerogative of an expert, *it can be used to bring a population into line in any respect whatsoever.* The average citizen realized too late that his own behavior, especially as it could be seen by others only from the outside, was "unusual" in at least one respect. If he did some observing and thinking he would see that everyone was in the same fix. Once his "unusual" behavior was reported, then he was faced with the task of satisfying the inquisitor that he was not a "heretic," and, as Lea and Coulton have shown in painstaking detail, this was a virtually impossible task unless both the mercy and the thought processes of the inquisitor (for he was usually conscientious) were favorable. The Inquisition thus frequently resulted in a terrified conformity in all possible ways, as well as in much greater secrecy or "discretion" in any behavior that might be considered unusual. Even with the modern advantages of government- and foundation-sponsored research projects, questionnaires that can be filled out by a literate population, IBM cards, computing machines, and statistical methods, it

23. Lea (1961), p. 193.

is not easy to determine what is usual or unusual, especially with respect to such matters as sex behavior and religious and moral convictions. The inquisitors, therefore, even more than the ideological experts of today, could locate the "norms" conveniently and with sincerity in their own fantasies.

THE ATTACK ON THE WITCHES

It would be surprising indeed if the awful power of the Inquisition had not been used for many purposes—political, economic, power, status, and revenge, and by laymen as well as by the inquisitors themselves. It was not until 1484, however, that the Inquisition launched its full attack upon those objects against whom the most complete indictment had accumulated over the centuries. In that year Innocent VIII proclaimed his famous Bull *Summis desiderantes,* in which he deplored the malignant power being exercised with high frequency in Teutonic lands through witchcraft, and giving the inquisitors Henry Institoris and Jacob Sprenger full authority to stamp out this evil. Although not uniformly successful in their efforts, they accomplished their most crucial objective, establishing firmly the reality of witchcraft and providing the manual which was to set nearly all of Europe ablaze with a spectacle that the twelfth-century ideologists could not have dreamed of, not even in their imagination of the pleasures of Heaven.

Tertullian had called woman "the gate by which the demon enters" and long before the fifteenth century all demonologists had agreed that vastly more women than men were involved in the use of demons to accomplish the purposes of the Devil. In the *Malleus maleficarum* ("Hammer of Witches"), which Lea called, "the most portentous monument of superstition which the world has produced," Sprenger explained this prevalence by a diatribe against women, for which, as has been noted, there was plenty of historical precedent, and he thanked God for the relative absence of this wickedness in the male sex.[24] He insisted upon the reality of the Sabbat, which by the Cap. Episcopi, a document of the ninth century (or earlier), had been generally and officially considered to be a *delusion* produced by demons. Certain learned authorities, especially Gianfrancesco Ponzinibio, tried to uphold the Cap. Episcopi

24. Lea (1961), p. 835.

but the new view prevailed and the Sabbat became accepted as a fact which it was very dangerous to deny. It is interesting that there is still controversy, among those few specialists in the history of witchcraft, about the extent to which the Sabbat was a delusion or actually took place, and about what actually transpired if in fact it did take place. Margaret Murray, an English anthropologist, maintained that it did occur and that furthermore the Witch Cult had a direct and continuous history back into prehistoric times, that it was, in fact, the Cult of the Horned God. After an unyielding controversy with the historians, who at first merely scoffed at her thesis, she achieved the triumph of being invited to write the article on witchcraft for the *Encyclopedia Britannica.* Her thesis of continuity with the ancient past is still disputed, but the claim that many of those called "witches" were practicing their religion, not just a form of sorcery or an unprovoked attack upon Christianity, is more generally accepted. It is possible that the cruelties of the Inquisition had led some of the more daring to revive older religious ideas and rituals. The many mixtures of Christianity and indigenous religions found today in Africa and Latin America support the idea that during the Middle Ages many people who considered themselves Catholic had retained elements of their older religion, and, just as today, women would be more likely to cling to the older beliefs than men.

Among the most serious charges against the witches were rendering men impotent and women barren, killing and eating children, devoting unbaptized children to the Devil, causing abortion or drying up a mother's milk, and having intercourse with the Devil or with demons serving as incubi (male) or succubi (female) as required. These charges alone give considerable support to the thesis that the witches represented the mother (the seductive mother, the prohibiting mother, the devouring mother), but there are other sources of support as well. Although they served the Devil, they rode or flew to the Sabbat under the leadership of Diana, the Roman moon goddess, connected historically with the Greek goddesses Artemis and Hecate and associated in antiquity with the Great Mother. Other goddesses or legendary figures such as Holda and Dame Habonde were named also. Lea considers it "inexplicable" that Bishop Burchard, writing in the eleventh century, added Herodias to the sinister list, but in view of the part which the infamous woman of that same name played in her daughter Salome's fatal dance, resulting in the severed head of John the Baptist (an event rivaling Saint Sebastian as a historical theme in European art museums), Bishop Burchard must be credited with an exceptionally effective political move, innocent though it may have been. The awesome powers attributed to the witches also argue for their matriarchal significance: they could raise tempests and hailstorms, cause horses to go mad, cause or cure sickness, bring plagues of locusts and caterpillars, predict the future, bewitch anyone, destroy crops and cattle, and make hidden things known. In vain it was pointed out that if witches actually had such powers it was hopeless to oppose them anyway. The helplessness of the victims contrasted so obviously with their alleged powers that the theory was invented that the witch lost her power as soon as she was apprehended by an officer of justice. By means of the principle that a person off the norm in one respect is likely to be off in another, any old woman who was unpopular, very independent, solitary, "odd," snobbish, or cranky, or who clung obstinately to the customs of her generation or to antiquated religious beliefs was highly vulnerable, especially if she owned property which could be useful to Church or State. But young women were vulnerable too, especially if they were beautiful or seductive or followed their mothers' old customs or beliefs, and men were also vulnerable, especially if they tried to protect any of the women. No one was safe, and the population became as bloodthirsty as the inquisitors, sometimes even more so, as they were convinced by the ideologists that only when the evil was cleaned up could the terror cease. Most of Europe went mad in an orgy of matricide unequalled anywhere else in time or space.

One country in which persecution for witchcraft made little headway is the only country known to most Americans to have had an inquisition at all. After 1480 the Spanish Inquisition was one of the most active and persisted much longer than elsewhere, well up into the nineteenth century. Even as late as 1927 Carmen Padin was sentenced at Segovia to imprisonment for two years, four months, and one day for having said in public, "The Virgin Mary had other children after the birth of Jesus," relying upon biblical texts as her authority.[25] The Spanish Inquisition was used for political purposes, became highly corrupt, and helped to carry out the merciless extermination of Protestants, who never gained the strength they had in other areas, and the equally merciless banish-

25. Coulton (1938), p. 308.

ment and liquidation of Jews and Moriscos. Torquemada, the Inquisitor General, distinguished himself and possibly deserves his prominent reputation although the number of executions during his term of office is now sometimes estimated at less than 2000, compared with 8800 or even 30,000 formerly attributed to him. Nevertheless, the failure of Spain to persecute witches with anything like the enthusiasm of the Anglo-Saxon countries is a striking and extraordinary historical fact which presents an important historical puzzle. Burr gives the following quotation from a letter from Lea:

> It is a very curious fact, which I have nowhere seen recognized, that in both Spain and Italy, the Holy Office took a decidedly skeptical attitude with regard to the Sabbat and the Cap. Episcopi, that preserved those lands from the madness prevailing elsewhere. I have a good many original documents that place this in a clear light and I think will prove a surprise to the demonologists.[26]

Lea documents his assertion in his usual painstaking detail, but refrains from speculating on the reasons behind this "curious fact." At the risk of sounding presumptuous (which it is too late for the present author to worry about anyway), perhaps it is partly explicable in terms of the general attitudes toward women, including mothers, in both those countries. Italian and Spanish women have been kept in ignorance and subjugation in a way that makes the average American woman bristle with indignation, but perhaps there has not been the contempt for the female role and the hatred and fear of women (and the romantic symbiotic slavery to women) found in Germany, for example, and the rejection of everything "feminine" in men. Is it easy to find Spaniards, of either sex, who hate or fear women? The relatively good record of Italy, even though the locus of popes, is also explicable in this manner. It was a learned Italian jurist, Gianfrancesco Ponzinibio, who tried to uphold the Cap. Episcopi. One of the few bright spots in the history of the Inquisition is the set of regulations laid down in Venice by the Council of Ten in 1521, even in the face of opposition by Leo X. Lea states, "had its enlightened spirit been allowed to guide the counsels of popes and princes, Europe would have been spared the most disgraceful page in the annals of civilization." [27]

26. Lea (1942), p. 3.
27. Lea (1961), p. 838.

John Knox, founder of Scottish Presbyterianism, a firm believer in witchcraft and in the inferiority of women, outdid even his admired colleague Calvin in condemning pleasure. Scotland was probably the only country where all pleasure, without any exception whatsover, was condemned as sinful. In his *Philosophy of Witchcraft* Ian Ferguson tells us that it was in that country that the witch hunts were most cruel.[28] A counterpart of *Malleus maleficarum* was written for Protestants by Benedict Carpzor, and Lea states, "Protestant and Catholic rivalled each other in the madness of the hour." [29]

THE PAINLESS TORTURE

It is possible to subject human beings to the most excruciating tortures and yet to feel completely devoid of sadism if one can simultaneously believe that the victims feel no pain. The demonologists provided a suitable rationale: the screams of the victims on the rack or at the stake were the screams of the Devil, not of the witches themselves. Only the Devil felt the pain, and one could rejoice that he felt it. If this doctrine seems antiquated or bizarre, then it is worth noting that a highly respectable dogma among some contemporary experimental psychologists could have served almost as well. These men will solemnly assure you that there is no possible way to know what another human being is feeling or sensing, in any proper sense of the word "know." They will not only assert this, but will become indignant when their dogma is challenged, and will accuse the challenger of being unscientific (heretical) and unfamiliar with the works of recent learned philosophers of science. In 1950 Dr. Clarence Graham, an eminent authority in the field of vision, who I am positive does not want to burn anyone, cautioned against asserting that subjects *see* anything in psychophysical experiments in vision, and aggressively insisted that the experimenter knows merely that "yes" and "no" responses have been given to certain stimuli under certain conditions.[30] Whether it is legitimate to say that experimenters themselves see or hear anything is not usually discussed, but at any rate Dr. Graham is by no means the only outstanding experimental psy-

28. Ferguson (1924). See also "The Witch Persecutions in Transalpine Europe," in Lea (1942).
29. Lea (1961) p. 839.
30. Graham (1950).

chologist who would have to maintain, in order to be consistent, that the most we can infer from the historical records is that the witches and heretics sometimes engaged in "screaming behavior."

Even being burned alive was not necessarily considered sufficient punishment for the sin and crime of witchcraft—tearing off the breasts (or tearing out the tongue) with hot pincers, followed by roasting *slowly* over hot coals was not rarely deemed more appropriate. When it was felt that the witch deserved more mercy, she was first strangled or beheaded, or a small sack of gunpowder was hung around her neck.[31]

If anyone doubts that the term "cold-blooded fiends" is appropriate for the inquisitors of the witchcraft persecutions, despite the benign public image which they projected in their role as learned authorities on the nature of man, then the treatment of the children of convicted witches, known at present only to a few specialists, should remove their doubts. It was usual for the children, who were assumed to have been indoctrinated with the beliefs of their parents, to be taken to the scene of the burning and flogged. An additional procedure which was sometimes followed is worth noting; the children were forced to watch. . . .

THE PERSISTENCE OF HORROR

If torture and human sacrifice belonged only to the past, we might with profit forget the Inquisition. As we shall see, however, both these horrors are still with us, in ways of which the average American is completely unaware. Lessons of the past can never be learned unless they are squarely and honestly faced. It has been to the advantage of both Protestant and Catholic rulers to erase the history of the Inquisition. Anglo-Saxon Protestant writers and publishers of textbooks have produced for populations dominated by Anglo-Saxon Protestants—hence only the Spanish Inquisition has usually been mentioned. When "witch hunts" are mentioned, on the other hand, and when the term is meant literally, the average educated American thinks of the Salem witch trials, which the honesty of the early American Puritans and also of the later inhabitants of Salem and vicinity has made it impossible to ignore. In *Yankees and God* Chard Powers Smith demonstrates that the hanging of

31. "The Witch Persecutions in Transalpine Europe," in Lea (1942).

41 witches in 62 years (including 21 in Salem in 1692), tragic though those events were, gives the New England Puritans a relatively good record compared with the more "cultured" Europeans of the day, taking into account the vast difference in population. The public confession of error by those responsible, even including a *judge,* is probably unparalleled in history.[32]

One might build a case against the inquisitors strictly on the basis of sex repression. There was an obvious fear, hatred, and contempt of women which was of obvious value to men striving to be chaste, or at least celibate, or to find excuses for their weakness. *Merveilles de l'autre monde* ("Wonders of the Other World"), a popular book by the Abbé Francois Arnoux, Canon of Riez, published in Rouen in 1622, provides a description of Hell which emphasizes both the wages of sexual sin and the pleasurable spectacle awaiting the saints in Heaven:

> In Hell the devils scream one to another; wound, flay, butcher, slaughter, murder without let or stay; thrust swiftly such a one upon the live coals, hurl such another into the furnaces or the boiling cauldrons. And the light women, these shall have in their arms a dragon most cruel, flaming with fire, or, if thou wilt, a devil in form of dragon who shall bind and enchain their feet and their legs with his serpent tail and shall clasp their whole body with his cruel talons, who shall put his beslabbered and reeking mouth upon theirs, breathing therein flames of fire and sulphur and poison and venom, who with his nose, glandered and hideous, shall breathe into theirs a breath most stinking and venomous. And, to come to an end, this dragon shall make them suffer a thousand agonies, a thousand colics and bitter twistings of the belly, and all the damned shall howl, and the devils with them: "See the wanton! See the strumpet! Let her be tortured indeed! To it, to it, ye devils! To it, ye demons! To it, ye hellish furies! See the harlot! See the trull! Hurl ye upon this whore and wreak upon her all the torments ye can!"[33]

32. Smith (1954). Some Europeans however, put up a valiant fight against the witch persecutions; among these were Giordano Bruno, Saint Vincent de Paul, the Jesuits Benoit Pereira, Adam Tanner, Paul Laymann, and Fredrich Spee, and the physicians Paracelsus, Johann Weyer, and Thomas Sydenham. The first to deny, at least in writing, the reality of witchcraft and the power of the devil was the Englishman Reginald Scot, whose *Discovery of Witchcraft* was burned by the pious demonologist James I.

33. Grillot de Givry (1958), p. 39.

There was fierce though unsystematic, persecution of homosexuals also, both as heretics and then as witches. Thus, latent heterosexuality and latent homosexuality might be elaborated as the most important psychological contributing causes to these horrors of the past. I could build such a case myself and a psychoanalyst could no doubt build an even better one. In his recent *Sex and Crime* Clinton Duffy, former warden of San Quentin and presumably a sensible man, has argued that *almost all crime,* of all varieties, is due to some kind of sex inadequacy.[34] If two wrongs could make a right, perhaps everyone, including nuns and priests, should be placed under the authority of the leading sex ideologists of our time to be helped to become "sexually adequate," whatever that phrase is supposed to mean, so that everyone would be less likely to commit a crime or to be unusually cruel. The Freudian psychoanalysts could then have even more fun than the earlier inquisitors.

The explanation I shall give does not imply turning anybody over to anybody. In what follows I shall attempt to show that the mistakes of the past are being made today and that there is danger that the situation will become worse unless certain trends are stopped and reversed. Now that the unusually learned and astonishing Montague Summers has gone to his reward (or punishment, as the case may be), I doubt that any prominent Roman Catholic will wish to revive the Holy Office, or even sing its praises. Summers, who believed (or at least said he believed) in werewolves and vampires as well as witches, was not at all intimidated by history. He referred to the *Malleus maleficarum* as a "noble treatise" and lamented that if the Inquisition had not been hampered in its work Europe would be much better off today.[35] At any rate, theologians are no longer the most powerful ideologists of our society, and it is ironic that at a time when many of our high priests are attempting to convert organized "Christianity" into the genuinely kind religion intended by its founder, the public is turning more to the rival ideologists, with their "new" ideas. The medicine man is attempting to overthrow his ancient rival, the high priest, and many high priests are unfortunately giving in without even a struggle.

34. Duffy (1965).
35. Summers (1928).

THE "MYTH" OF THE SNAKE PIT

One of the large mental hospitals operated by the State of California has had a particularly unsavory reputation for many years. Its more violent critics have called it a "snake pit." A psychiatrist told me that of five psychoanalysts who had been appointed as consultants, he was the only one who remained, the others having resigned in disgust. He added that it was only because of some sense of obligation to the patients that he had not also resigned. A visitor to this "snake pit" would receive a pleasant surprise. He would find some of the older wards a bit barren and gloomy, but even there the walls and floors would be clean, the staff cheerful, and the patients well behaved. The newer wards would seem very nice indeed. On the geriatrics wards, among the older buildings of course, he would see many old ladies sitting quite peacefully and comfortably. The wards would be free of the offensive odors which in old-fashioned asylums were ubiquitous. The patients would be clean and neat and some of them would smile or exchange a few words as the visitor passed. Snake pit, indeed! The visitor would conclude that such stories were absurd and that Thomas Szasz, a psychiatrist who has carried his fight against institutional psychiatry to the public, is a ridiculous troublemaker.[36]

America has become famous for nice odors and appearances, and justifiably so. In California even the execution chamber is comfortably deluxe. Our brand of horror is typically American, as is only natural, and is therefore not even seen as horrible by the average American; in this we are no different from other societies. Natives rarely see the horrors of their own society; if they do, they are in danger.

A story from behind the scenes will begin to enlighten the reader about the "snake pit" with smiling old ladies. An attorney who worked very actively for several years in a mental health association told me of a client who had enlisted his aid in protecting herself from our modern inquisitors. She had been given one of the most common and powerful treatments at this particular hospital, electric convulsive treatment (ECT), which is also very popular in many other hospitals, including

36. Szasz (1963, 1965).

some that are private and very expensive. Techniques vary, but the essential condition is the application of sufficient voltage (from 70 to 150 volts) to the temple for a sufficient period of time (a fraction of a second will suffice) to produce unconsciousness and convulsions. Fractures and even death were not uncommon during the development of this treatment many years ago, but the technique has now been perfected so that these two side effects are rare. A mouth gag is used for the prevention of tongue bite; strong pressure is exerted against the jaw to prevent its dislocation, etc.

In the prescribing of ECT it is customary to decide in advance that a certain number of treatments will be given. Numbers that are chosen usually vary between twenty and eighty, though fewer or more are also possible. Frequency of treatment varies usually from daily to weekly, and the treatment is often given on an outpatient as well as inpatient basis. Many conditions are treated; among these are depression, schizophrenia, and various psychoneuroses.

Attitudes of the patients themselves vary considerably. Some go almost eagerly to the shock table, whereas others, as noted in the *American Handbook of Psychiatry,* are "apprehensive." [37] That the word "apprehensive" is not too dissimilar from euphemisms used in former centuries is indicated by the term which patients themselves often use in referring to their treatment—"electrocution." The side effects (such as loss of memory for events immediately preceding the shock and often for events more remote), the thought that their brains may be permanently damaged, and the *usual impossibility of altering the number of treatments to be given* produce in many patients not "apprehension" but an emotion from which most members of our society are spared—terror. Even more significant, however, is the fact that many of the terrified patients *are afraid to show that they are afraid.*

The lawyer's client was one who was "apprehensive" about the ECT that was given to help her. Once the series was complete, however, she found that she was at least still alive, and she sat on the ward without complaint.

A conscientious physician, once he is determined to cure a patient, does not allow a relapse to go untreated. A conscientious nurse is duty bound to report the daily condition of patients to the physician. The

37. Kalinowsky (1959), p. 1502.

lawyer's client had been looking not too cheerful and the nurse had noticed this fact. It became apparent that if she continued to appear uncheerful a second series would be ordered. With some effort, she began to straighten up and to manage a smile as the nurse made her daily rounds.

It has been argued by several experts, including the justifiably renowned Dr. B. F. Skinner of Harvard, as well as various legal and penal reformers, that punishment is a very ineffective means of controlling human behavior. This assertion is a half-truth; it is impossible to achieve certain kinds of results—the kind that Dr. Skinner, who can't help being a human being, despite his inhuman theoretical convictions, wants to bring about—through punishment. For example, happiness and spontaneity cannot be brought about by the punishment of misery and robot-like behavior. Furthermore, crime cannot be appreciably decreased, in a society with our kinds of constitutional safeguards with respect to due process of law, by increasing the severity of sentences or even by doubling the police force. In a totalitarian society, however, with due process largely a matter of convenience for the authorities, punishment can be very effective in controlling *behavior,* because it generates a *fear* that is realistic and entirely justified. I do not have to rely on indirect information from lawyers about this particular hospital; numerous ex-patients have told me that there one learns rapidly to be very cooperative in doing whatever he is supposed to do and causing no trouble. Local convalescent homes (the word "convalescent" is somewhat misleading) are more than willing to accept ex-patients from this hospital, for that very reason. The patients have been "broken," as one "breaks" a horse or any other once-proud animal.

A few years ago, while employed in a mental health clinic, I interviewed a woman who had been given ECT at the hospital previously mentioned. She came to the clinic because she wanted help in making a decision, and as was customary I obtained information about previous treatment. She told of having become frightened after the series had begun—"thinking about that electricity going through my brain"—and of how she had tried to behave in a way that was acceptable and to convince the doctor that she had improved and needed no more shock. The remaining treatments had been given, anyway. This story was told without hatred; in fact, she made clear that she was not complaining about the hospital. I was curious about what had happened and obtained a written statement from the hospital authorities. The statement was entirely in accord with her account. Curiosity was not my only feeling, however. She had grown up in the South, before moving north and then coming to California. I also grew up in the South, and she was a type of woman I had encountered before, a type that often worked in homes like ours and that put the children on a pedestal, more than our own mothers did. (I believe that is why many of us throughout life act as though we are very important people, when we obviously are not.) She was a member of the only large group of people to have mastered that much-touted virtue of humility and the ability to love those who considered them to be of an "inferior" race. The official record of the hospital is as follows, with names and dates omitted:

DATE OF ADMISSION: —— 1961
TYPE OF ADMISSION: Mentally ill.
PSYCHIATRIC DIAGNOSIS: 22.3 Schizo. React., Paranoid
SUMMARY OF HISTORY: Patient had been categorized mentally
   ill, with the diagnosis of Schizophrenic Reaction. There was some
   confusing data about her admission to the hospital. She appeared
   affectively appropriate and had some insight but did appear to be
   withdrawn and at times rather blocked. However, she was a rather
   timid person, and since she was a Negro, she was seemingly more
   reserved in a ward where there were only white patients. She had been
   in —— but had returned to this state with 2 of the 3 children to
   be close to her father. She had been treated in a hospital in ——
   with compazine. Physically, she was a mildly obese Negro woman—
   otherwise physically normal.
TREATMENT AND COURSE IN HOSPITAL: Patient was
   first given thorazine, but had some reaction to this drug so it was dis-
   continued. She was given EST and after about 8 ESTs she appeared
   much better, and there was little need for further treatment. However, she was given a more complete course, in case she might have
   had the more malignant mental illness that she was thought to have
   when she came in. She showed no need for any medication other
   than thyroid, grains 1, and was given progressively increased visits,
   tolerated them exceedingly well. Her mother and the patient both felt
   that she was well, and I could find no evidence in my observations in

the last month of her hospitalization that there was any mental illness present. Therefore, she was discharged as improved.

S I G N I F I C A N T   L A B O R A T O R Y   T E S T S : Within normal limits.

D A T E O F R E L E A S E : —— 1962

T Y P E O F R E L E A S E : Discharged, Improved.

There is no indication in this record of the feelings of terror and helplessness which this patient experienced. With that added information this document is a true horror story to those familiar with hospital procedures and with ECT (EST, or electroshock therapy, is an older term). It is very similar to some of the protocols of the Inquisition. The psychiatrist who ordered this treatment was not being intentionally cruel, but neither were most of the inquisitors.

This same psychiatrist had also treated an unusually beautiful and talented young woman whom I saw later in psychotherapy. This patient had also tried to stop the ECT series, without success, and she told how terrified she had been, as she thought that her memory for several previous years was being permanently destroyed and that her brain was possibly being damaged, and how she had cried and pleaded with the doctor. I remarked that tears did not seem to express fear, but she explained that she was very afraid to express fear, because then she would be called "paranoid." She was very probably right: patients who show fear of psychiatrists are nearly always called "paranoid." The average psychiatrist resents any suggestion that patients have a right to legal protection from his help, if they do not want it.

Another ex-patient I saw in the clinic had expressed apprehension by screaming, trying to escape, trying to climb the walls, and struggling with the aides as she was led away and tied down. She had no memory of this behavior and knew of it only from other patients. She had finally escaped from the hospital.

A very convincing firsthand account of the traumas of ECT is given in *The White Shirts* by Ellen Field.[38]

There are other horrors of "nice" mental hospitals of which the uninitiated visitor would never dream. A psychiatrist from the aforementioned hospital informed a committee of the local mental health associa-

38. Field (1964).

tion that it was often discouraging to attempt to discharge a patient, because after six weeks of planning and preparation, involving considerable time and effort by more than one staff member, a telephone call from the Superintendent's office might announce, "This patient is not to be discharged," with no further explanation. The psychiatrist went on to add that this call, with its fatal message, would *not be entered in the patient's record, and that at some later date a new staff member could therefore not tell, from the record, why the patient was still in the hospital.* It may be difficult for the reader to realize that there are today human beings condemned to spend the remainder of their lives in these "enormous mausoleums," as one psychiatrist, Don Jackson, called them in a public address, for reasons which are kept hidden from the "patient" himself and also from those who are charged with his care. To someone familiar with the chain of events leading to hospitalization and with the maneuvers and evasions of relatives and others who for one reason or another do not want the "mentally ill" person around, but also do not want him to know the truth, this fact is not at all surprising. Psychiatrists are frequently asked to visit a home in the role of "friend," or to practice some other deception to prevent the family member from knowing that he is suspected of being "mentally ill." Two deputy sheriffs whose duty was to apprehend those for whom commitment petitions had already been filed in the district attorney's office (these are not "emergency" cases) informed me that it is the rule, rather than the exception, that the individual first learns that he is considered "mentally ill" when they arrive to escort him to the mental hospital. He sometimes receives treatment with drugs or even ECT before the court hearing, at which, one of these deputies remarked, certain relevant facts are concealed to protect other members of the family.

Many of the old people who are conveniently labeled "mentally ill" die within a few months after being uprooted and subjected to imprisonment within a "hospital." Many survive however; according to the November 1962 issue of *Mental Health Progress,* published by the California State Department of Mental Hygiene, three out of five remain hospitalized until death, *even though only 44.3 per cent of these need to be in mental hospitals.* The remaining 55.7 per cent, according to this publication, could be cared for in family-care and nursing homes, rest homes, general hospitals, or at home. It is strictly illegal, of course, for people who are not classified "mentally ill" to be cared for by state funds appropriated for the treatment and care of the "mentally ill." It is not, however, in accordance with the "public image" that we, the American public, wish to project, to create appropriate homes for the aged who are unwanted or who are incapable of caring for themselves.

LOVE AND SEX

We should ask under what conditions do we become cold, cynical, irrational, and hypocritical, for these are the character traits which make possible the horrors of the present just as they made possible those of the past. In attempting an answer to this question I am forced to use a dirty four-letter word, "love." I am not making a joke, unfortunately. Any word which calls forth disgust and contempt is obviously considered "dirty," and "love" qualifies not only among "scientifically oriented" behavioral scientists but among many more ordinary mortals as well. Love is considered to be an epiphenomenon based upon sex, and Freud was not the first to consider it such. In this, as in many other matters, Freud formulated and codified that which was already to be found deeply embedded within the cultures of Western civilization. In *A Psychologist Looks at Love* Theodor Reik remarked on the scarcity of psychological writing on love, compared with the voluminous literature on sex.[39] A decade later, in the mid-fifties, the situation had not improved. A psychologist who collected data on love behavior (not sex behavior) had his book-length manuscript rejected by numerous publishers. When one of these informed him that his book was well written but that the topic itself was not of sufficient interest he gave up.

By "love" I mean a certain class of conscious feelings and attitudes. One may feel love toward the object, or feel loved by the object, or both. The "object" may be one or many, concrete or abstract. In some instances love includes conscious sexual desire, in others not. *Love is more basic than conscious sexual desire.* The frightened, depressed, apathetic, or repressed adult, like the frightened or anguished child, needs love, not necessarily sex. A psychotic, like a traumatized soldier on the battlefield, often needs desperately to be held in a physical embrace which can give the feeling of being loved. Everyone needs love. A person can

39. Reik (1944).

live without sex, but he cannot live without love; without the death of at least a part of himself. All people of good sense know this, but they are usually inhibited from saying so openly.

Psychological literature on intimate peer relationships during childhood and adolescence is as scarce as that on love; yet it is in these relationships that the patterns of love for peers are crystallized, built, it is true, on the foundation of relationships within the family, concerning which the literature is almost as enormous as that on sex. Harry Stack Sullivan, one of the great thinkers of psychiatry, wrote on the chum relationship more than twenty years ago, and the fact that there has been so little follow-up on this subject is highly significant; the subject is embarrassing and threatening because it exposes the worst absurdities of Western civilization. Sullivan defines the state of love as that in which the satisfaction or security of another person becomes as significant as is one's own satisfaction or security. This state of loving one's neighbor as oneself is made possible by the sharing of experiences and the recognition of similarities, and thus if it occurs at all it ordinarily first occurs with a member of one's own sex.[40]

Physical intimacies are nearly always a part of the chum relationship between boys, especially those who are most physically active. These physical intimacies may or may not include sexual intimacies, and these, even if they occur, may be practiced with any of several different attitudes, e.g., as a humorous activity that happens to be fun or as a serious and intense part of the affectional relationship. Boys who consider their genitalia dirty or who have been taught that sex is dirty or that homosexuality is dirty will not allow the chum relationship to be contaminated in this way. The split between love and sex, insisted upon by those theologians who argue that agape should be uncontaminated by Eros, is accomplished. Girls are a kind of joke at this stage, inferior beings who will someday receive the dirty part of their bodies. Later, when a boy with this attitude toward sex falls in "love" and puts some girl on a pedestal, this fact of life may remain a kind of grotesque though necessary part of the relationship. The ladies of Victorian and post-Victorian days were cast in the role of virginal goddesses who were to allow men to "do this" to them, but were not to derive enjoyment from it themselves. The man who considers his penis dirty is likely to cast his mate

40. Sullivan (1947), p. 20.

in the role of the "good" woman who must be free of dirtiness; at the same time he will be dissatisfied and seek a "bad" woman with whom he can be more spontaneously dirty. This pattern, familiar to all madams, as well as to many "good" women, has been extremely common in America and is not rare at the present time, even among young people.

Boys who practice sex within the chum relationship—even if it is considered merely funny—are more likely to accept sex as a non-dirty activity later on in their heterosexual relationships, but of course they may have more trouble than the formerly mentioned type if their spouses consider sex "dirty."

Boys who do not practice sex within the chum relationship because sex would contaminate it may nevertheless indulge in homosexuality, with boys with whom they are less close or with boys who are considered inferior (cf. p. 81). This kind of homosexuality may be friendly and indulgent, or it may take a much more destructive form, in the ruthless exploitation of boys who can be bribed or bullied.[41] The variety of homosexuality among boys accounts for the traditional taboo of silence on this subject among gentlemen. If gentlemen could agree that homosexuality is necessarily an evil practice, then such agreement could become a popular pastime. As their backgrounds differ, especially with class mobility and the mixing of the classes, they cannot agree and thus they avoid the subject. As the official attitude in our society is one of disapproval, codified into laws that are absurdly severe (there was usually no open debate when they were passed), it is not surprising that those who disapprove are more vocal than those who do not; mental health experts and members of the clergy are no different from other men in this respect of differential noisemaking.

Within the chum or buddy relationship, with or without sex, one can learn how decent and loving a similar human being can be. When this happens, and when it is obviously a mutual happening, it becomes difficult, at least for a while, to think of oneself as a stinker and to become cynical about the basic nature of man. Those who are fortunate enough to maintain similar relationships throughout life are rarely cynics in this sense, and even those who had such a relationship only once may continue to believe in man's potentialities for love.

When a boy has his self-respect greatly damaged early in life, by being

41. Lewis (1955).

treated as though he is inferior, stupid, weak, sinful, dirty, bad, worthless, or when any expression of affection toward his father or toward other males is forbidden, then it is unlikely that he will develop a chum relationship, in Sullivan's sense. He may, however, find a comrade, with whom he can join in exploitation, turning hostility and aggression toward outsiders. He may become a member of a gang, relating intimately to each other by means of their actions against outsiders, including other gangs. Within such gangs, clear expressions of affection may be considered effeminate or absurd and therefore strictly taboo, as they may be even among more gentlemanly groups. Any boy whose closest approach to friendship is through collaboration in hostility toward outsiders is an excellent prospect for such a group later in life; he has been trained to be ruthlessly loyal. This camaraderie was a pattern encouraged by Hitler in the youth movement. It is characteristic that he discouraged any pairing off; soldiers were to pal around together in groups of three or more. Lack of personal identity and the resulting interchangeability of personnel, within the context of a certain intimacy available only to insiders, are characteristic of exploitative groups. The training in religious orders has traditionally aimed at these two characteristics, and the Dominicans and Franciscans were therefore very suitable for their jobs as inquisitors, even though they hardly thought of themselves as exploitative.

Mr. Ardrey, who refers to us as "Cain's children" because our ancestor, the killer ape *Australopithecus africanus* extinguished his peaceful vegetarian brother, *Australopithecus robustus,* argues that enmity toward outsiders is the chief, if not the only basis for amity toward insiders. The sole anecdote from his own boyhood, however, is that of fighting for fun *within the group,* in the basement of a church with a prayer meeting in progress above. As Mr. Ardrey writes like a decent type, I suspect there would be other boyhood incidents, such as the sharing of adventure, sports, and other competition within groups, and cooperative achievement not involving enmity toward outsiders, which he could cite that would not fit too well with his thesis.

The simple and obvious fact that the human female can perform sexual intercourse on demand or from a sense of duty or profit, whereas the male must have a certain minimum of sexual desire and internal freedom of impulse, has implications that are neither obvious nor simple. No matter how extreme or strong the official sex-negative practices, attitudes, laws, and ideologies within the society, there has had to be some way for most boys to develop at least this minimum desire and impulse, whereas there has been no such necessity for girls. Many boyhood practices, such as competition as to who can direct his stream the farthest, making a "railroad crossing" with another boy, putting out the campfire together, swimming nude, joking, horsing around, body-contact sports, uroboric completion, showering together without the partitions present in gymnasia for girls, a greater freedom to do things together away from the watchful eyes of adults, have all tended to accomplish at least the minimum necessary. The occurrence of nocturnal emissions, so troublesome for those monks and priests determined to achieve complete purity, has also been a powerful factor. Women, therefore, have suffered much more from the sex-negative and body-rejecting features of Western civilization than have men. On the other hand, their greater freedom to express *affection* toward each other, as well as toward men, parents, and children, has cooperated with their biological structure to make love (a class of feelings and attitudes) more available to women than to men. A study of history reveals that women have provided most of the love, while men, though talking more about love (until the last century or so) have provided most of the hate.

It is not sex repression per se, but the role of sex repression in eliminating love that helped make possible the horrors of the inquisitions, of today as well as yesterday. It was insisted that agape should have no taint of Eros, and it is hardly surprising that hatred was eventually practiced under the heading of agape, as it is today (it is also practiced under the heading of Eros, by different groups). Professor James Leuba, an experimental psychologist of the old school, showed very convincingly in his *The Psychology of Religious Mysticism* that some mystical ecstasies have very strong erotic components, by quoting descriptions of ecstatic union of nuns with the body of their divine lover.[42] Whereas Leuba referred to these passages as "embarrassing" and seemed to take a disapproving attitude toward them, I find them not only not embarrassing but inspiring. It is inspiring to read of a woman's unreserved cathexis for the male body. Nuns should be encouraged to have the best and most complete ecstasies possible, and if they seem to be too particular about their choice

42. Leuba (1925).

of a lover then man has only himself to blame, for having denigrated his body and its erotic and ecstatic functions. It is man, not woman, who made the rules and developed absurd ideologies. He then blamed woman for trying to keep his rules and for believing his absurdities, and also for cooperating in his hypocrisies.

THE PROFITS OF HYPOCRISY

Boys have been given another asset over girls in achieving pleasure in a society that officially limits pleasure, namely, thorough training in explicitly conscious deceit. This training usually occurs under the heading of "kidding" and is carried out by fathers and peers who are nearly always unaware of the real function of what they are doing, thinking of it as merely a harmless pastime. Both sexes are also trained in a kind of deceit that is much less explicit and conscious than kidding, i.e., they learn to play the cultural roles of boy, girl, man, woman, child, parent, mother, father, gang member, club or clique member, member of a certain social class, doctor, lawyer, merchant, chief, etc. In his *Presentation of Self in Everyday Life* the sociologist Erving Goffman provides a very informative and often witty description of deception of this kind, which is usually not thought of as deception at all, but simply as playing the role one is supposed to play.[43]

Man's ability to pretend, found only in very limited forms in other species, is one of his greatest assets but also one of his worst Frankenstein monsters.[44] By means of this ability man has been able to live in contradiction to his own official rules, carried over from one generation to another. Hypocrisy (a discrepancy between practice and official rules) has always been present in Western civilization, but when it reaches a certain high degree, as, for example, in the sixteenth and twentieth centuries, then some kind of adjustment has to be made.

The cynic, who, as pointed out earlier, is an excellent liar, profits greatly from hypocrisy, if he is sufficiently discreet. He lives as he pleases and exploits the confusion of those who, lacking the necessary information, cannot see things as they are. Among the naive, hypocrisy creates fear or guilt, which leads to secret confession to a priest, psychothera-

43. Goffman (1959).
44. See pp. 50–54.

pist, lawyer, accountant, etc. Hypocrisy is good for the confession businesses and for the businesses of complex dispensations and absolutions. (A committee of the California Medical Association, after investigating the aforementioned hospital, piously assured the Department of Mental Hygiene, "No objective evidence of patient maltreatment or neglect was discovered," and this assurance was promptly reported to His Excellency Edmund G. Brown, Governor of California.) The cynic hates and fears the morality of truth-telling, courage, honesty, love, and fair play; thus he emphasizes, at least in public, other standards, such as sex morality, belief in God, sex adequacy, being "true to oneself," equality, "kindness," erudition, training, degrees, honors, positions, success, or awareness of one's own motives.[45] If the realistic, practical, and successful cynic hears that professors have written learned papers showing that concepts of truth, love, and right-and-wrong are fallacious and must be replaced by more modern and scientific concepts, then he is delighted. Although he cannot follow their arguments and has no interest in trying to do so, he can agree wholeheartedly with their conclusions.

The cynic can also profit from a diminution of hypocrisy (among the masses), or at least a shift in the forms of hypocrisy, if he plays his cards right, for he can without scruple jump on whichever side appears to be winning, as he is willing to jump on any side except one which wants to bring all the relevant truth out into the open, and no side of this kind has ever existed, except on the part of a few individuals who have usually been regarded as insane or, at best, highly impractical dreamers. In being a liar, a hypocrite, a cheat, and a coward, and hating instead of loving his fellow, he destroys everything his mother believed in and tried to teach him, and thus he commits matricide. He loves women, though, at least as much as Nero or Henry VIII (who defended sex morality by defeating a move to allow the clergy of his time to marry).

Women, busy with home duties or the more routine kinds of employment outside the home, have traditionally lagged behind men in their knowledge of new formulations and rituals, as well as their knowledge of the extent of the discrepancies between the way things are and the way they are officially acknowledged to be. They have not fared well in cultural revolutions. All societies have their totem animals, i.e., animals that are first glorified and then destroyed. In our society mothers are in

45. Adams (1965).

danger of being the totem animals, as they have been in the past. When they were very young they were put on pedestals by their fathers, and sometimes by their mothers as well. Later they were put on pedestals by their suitors; later (for a time) by their husbands, then by their children. In former times the old women were loved by their grand-children and at least respected by their adult children; now they are widely separated from their grandchildren and regarded as foolish and tyrannical by their adult children and by the public at large. American mothers have usually done the *best they could with what they knew,* and they have not known more *because they have been repeatedly deceived by cynical men, by lies, and by the withholding of information.* They tend to put their affairs into the hands of men who are completely re-spectable, i.e., men who do not even know anyone who is not respectable (or at least pretend they do not know any such person). They thus fall into the hands of their worst enemies, the cynics, i.e., men who believe that man is no good, whether they wish, like the hypocritical Catholic clergy of the early sixteenth century or the do-nothing genial psychia-trists of the twentieth century, to leave things as they are, or whether they wish to force man to "behave himself," even in private, like John Calvin and his modern counterparts, or some of the more zealous ex-ponents of mental health who want to give experts more freedom to force their help upon unwilling "patients," candidates for office, and applicants for jobs. On the other hand, the "mean old ladies," often rightly suspicious of "isms," are sometimes their own worst enemies; they will often not listen to anyone who tries to tell them the truth and they often regard with horror those who want to free men and women (at least legally) to lead their private lives in accordance with their own decisions, without pretense, and to destroy the rackets of hypoc-risy. Thus old women become more and more alienated and are treated with increasing indifference, discourtesy, and cruelty.

FINALE

I have tried to show, in this long and unwieldy argu-ment, that Western civilization has repeatedly violated the strongest and probably the only universal taboo. The witchcraft inquisitions were only the most blatant and extreme example, and even today they have a much closer counterpart, within mental hospitals, than the average person would dream possible. It is not only in the obvious forms of cruelty, but in the cynical acceptance of the "necessity" or "desirability" of deception and withholding of information (of which the teaching of history is a blatant example), as well as in our failure to love our fellow humans of both sexes, that we commit matricide, and thus doom not only our own society but also, this time, all of civilization, to destruction.

9

Values and Dangers of Emotional Experiences and Their Relationship to Society and Culture

PREFACE   The following essay was written in late 1969 for inclusion in a book on encounter groups to which I had been invited by the editors to contribute a paper with this title. Although the editors thanked me for my "excellent contribution," they wrote several months later informing me that the publisher's editorial staff had found the paper unsuitable.

Now the six hundred deputies, personal appointees all of Hitler, little men with big bodies and bulging necks and cropped hair and pouched bellies and brown uniforms and heavy boots . . . leap to their feet like automatons, their right arms upstretched in the Nazi salute, and scream "Heils." . . . Hitler raises his hand for silence. . . . He says in a deep, resonant voice, "Men of the German Reichstag!" The silence is utter.

"In this historic hour, when, in the Reich's western provinces, German troops are at this minute marching into their future peacetime garrisons, we all unite in two sacred vows."

He can go no further. It is news to this "parliamentary" mob that German soldiers are already on the move into the Rhineland. All the militarism in their German blood surges to their heads. They spring, yelling and crying, to their feet. . . . Their hands are raised in slavish salute, their faces now contorted with hysteria, their mouths wide open, shouting, shouting, their eyes, burning with fanaticism, glued on the new god, the Messiah. The Messiah plays his role superbly. His head lowered as if in all humbleness, he waits patiently for silence. Then his voice, still low, but choking with emotion, utters the two vows:

"First, we swear to yield to no force whatever in restoration of the honor of our people. . . . Secondly, we pledge that now, more than ever, we shall strive for an understanding between the European peoples, especially for one with our Western Neighbor nations. . . . We have no territorial demands to make in Europe! . . . Germany will never break the peace!"

It was a long time before the cheering stopped. . . . A few generals made their way out. Behind their smiles, however, you could not help detecting a nervousness. . . . I ran into General von Blomberg. . . . His face was white, his cheeks twitching.[1]

The above excerpts illustrate some of the values as well as some of the dangers of emotion. Many of these "little men with big bodies" had no doubt experienced life as "meaningless" until Adolf Hitler filled them with passion. With strong emotion, particularly of a positive kind, the body comes to life—Shirer's use of the word "Messiah" is apt in more ways than one—and life, far from being meaningless, becomes an absorbing drama.

The search for "meaning" in life, although often thought by the searcher to be primarily a philosophical problem, is a search for feeling, and when feeling is achieved the search is believed, for a time, to have ended successfully.[2] "Ah, sweet mystery of life, at last I've found you!" Romantic passion is a frequently found answer to the search, but other emotions can be equally satisfying and convincing, or even more so. The more emotionally impoverished the individual becomes, the more

1. Shirer (1959), p. 292. Shirer is quoting from his own *Berlin Diary*.
2. Many years ago Wilhelm Reich equated "meaning" (in living) with feeling; I have been unable to locate the reference, however.

impressed he is by any feelings that he experiences, and the more likely he is to become "hooked" by whatever circumstances have brought about his resurrection. As intensity and univalence of feeling and emotion (by "univalence" I mean uncomplicated by conflicting or distracting components) usually decrease as age increases, the older the individual, the more likely he is to be impressed by the circumstances which produce a strong, univalent emotion, especially if it is a satisfying one. The aspects of the situation to which he becomes attached, however, are not necessarily those actually responsible for the feeling. In religious conversion, for example, the music, architecture, chanting, hypnotic effect of the evangelist's voice and gestures, and "group atmosphere" may actually produce the feeling, whereas the convert is encouraged to attach himself to an ideology or a goal (belief in Jesus, individual salvation, the glory of the church), and to regard the ideology or goal as both the source and the justification of his enthusiasm. In accounts of conversion experiences feelings may not even be mentioned, though they are the *sine qua non* of such experiences. For example, in the accounts of the most famous conversion in history, that of Saul (Paul), nothing is recorded about his feelings during this experience, although a "blinding light" and a vision of Jesus are mentioned. This focus upon the cognitive aspect of such experiences and the neglect of the feeling aspect is typical of many accounts. The same is true of many accounts of experiences while under the influence of LSD or similar drugs; the subject may relate, with great enthusiasm, the strange and wonderful visual or auditory effects, without mentioning the feelings and bodily sensations without which the experience would have been at best only interesting or curious.[3]

This is not of course to deny that perceptual-cognitive experiences (such as being temporarily blinded, as Saul allegedly was) can produce feelings; I am simply emphasizing that it is the feelings and bodily sensations themselves that account for the conversion to an ideology or to the wonders of drugs (or people), especially on the part of those who

3. John Wesley and other revivalists found that an effective method of conversion was first to concentrate on the horrors and the high probability of Hell, and then to show the way to salvation, thus producing among the listeners the sequence of fear followed by a feeling of safety and of being loved and cared for. This same sequence of emotions is also very effective in arousing enthusiasm for LSD, psychotherapy, encounter groups, etc., although seldom produced deliberately; it undoubtedly recapitulates infantile and early childhood experiences, on those occasions when the child has been frightened and then experienced security and love in its parent's arms.

are emotionally impoverished and who have felt "dead" for years without realizing to what extent this deadening has occurred (as it occurs so gradually) or that anything could possibly happen to bring the person back to life, even temporarily.[4]

All methods which produce emotions, whether romantic adventures, revivals, dramas, dangerous feats, rallies or demonstrations, drug sessions, psychotherapy, or encounter groups share the value of bringing the individual to life, at least temporarily, and the danger of the formation of convictions and attitudes that are self-destructive or destructive to others (e.g., the delusion that all one's problems have been solved, or that one has found the answer for everyone)—in the extreme, the loss of self to another person or to a group, movement, cause, or ideology, a phenomenon described so well by Eric Hoffer, which we see happening today on a large scale, with, fortunately, many varieties.[5]

In the previous quotation from Shirer, the latter states that the Nazis "leap to their feet like automatons." They were, however, automatons alive with feeling—at that moment. They had, in fact, become automatons as the price they paid for feeling. Group activities in unison, whether chanting, cheering, dancing, marching, or even just sitting quietly together, can precipitate strong feeling, especially among young people, and the more the activity blots out or obscures individual differences, the stronger the feeling.

The current cliché, supported sometimes even by learned authors, that our society is experiencing a revolution against rationality or reason, which has been exalted at the price of feeling, is a half-truth: the latter part of the assertion—that reason has been exalted—is nonsense. No society has ever encouraged or even allowed its members to develop and utilize rationality or reason except in very limited respects. The most important rules, customs, beliefs, attitudes, and dimensions of perception and feeling are determined overwhelmingly not by reason, but by tradition, habit, and prejudice—sanctified, codified, and protected by language, rituals, and myths. Reason has had a long, uphill fight against great odds and extremely unfair tactics, and still has a long way to go. The unrestricted use of reason *always* leads to conclusions unacceptable

4. See p. 116.
5. Hoffer (1951). The loss of self is of course not only encouraged but *demanded* by every society; Jung recognized this long ago.

(and often unintelligible) to the social structure in which one is embedded. This does not imply that rules and customs maximize or accommodate feeling and emotion. The opposite of reason is not emotion, but unreason or irrationality. Irrational or unreasonable behavior is not necessarily emotional; in fact, emotional impoverishment always leads eventually to irrational behavior, because emotions, or the memory of them, must enter at times as a determining component of behavior (and perceptions, decisions, etc.), if behavior is to be rational in terms of human welfare. In ancient Carthage aristocratic infants were sacrificed by being fed alive into the mouth of an idol representing the great god Baal-Haman, within which a huge fire blazed. The mothers were forced to watch, without showing tears or other signs of any impious emotion such as grief, horror, or rage. This ritual thus combined irrationality with an absence of anything approaching natural emotional response. As the maternal instinct is one of the strongest, this ritual was obviously one of the most effective in forcing the individual to knuckle under to the authority of the group and its ideology. *There has never been a sane society*, i.e., one which has allowed its members to be naturally human in all important respects, with due allowance for individual differences. The Carthaginians were no more cruel or irrational than most other peoples have been, or are today.

It is not the mere occurrence of atrocities, but the institutionalization and social approval of them that reveals the irrationality and cruelty of a society most clearly and directly. The high incidence of crimes of violence in the United States, for example, does not demonstrate irrationality and cruelty as clearly and directly as the legislation and the judicial and penal practices which are partly responsible for the high incidence of such crimes. An even better example is the treatment of the "mentally ill" in mental hospitals, where patients are frequently deceived, shamed, shocked, and tranquilized into lifeless docility "for their own good." [6]

One of the most important aspects of socialization of the individual is the development of "appropriate" emotions, and also the development of perceptions of appropriateness of emotions, as defined by the culture. To show an "inappropriate" emotion results in being perceived as at best immature, odd, or ill bred, and at worst as hysterical, emotionally disturbed, sociopathic, or psychotic. The "appropriate" and "normal" emo-

6. Goffman (1961), Szasz (1961); also pp. 57, 169–75 above.

tional expression of a Carthaginian mother, as she watched her infant burned alive, was a pious impassivity. A mother who showed horror or rage would presumably have been seen as emotionally disturbed, sociopathic, or insane. I have chosen this example because presumably it is one which we can all agree illustrates how absurd and unnatural cultural definitions of appropriateness or "normality " of emotion can be. Examples from our own society would lead immediately to disagreement, and that is just the point I am trying to make. The consequences of expressing emotion in our society are such that most people rarely express emotion, especially in public. Only a few decades ago it was considered appropriate, in many communities, to cry aloud at family funerals; today, in those same communities, it is considered appropriate not to cry at all. A very good discussion of the value of expressing grief and the destructiveness of suppressing such expression was given many years ago by Joshua Liebman. "We must never falsify our emotions in conformity with conventions," wrote Rabbi Liebman.[7] This advice, if followed, would revolutionize any society in a way that has never occurred, but despite the fact that Liebman's book was a phenomenal best seller, the situation has not improved.

The fear and distrust of emotion has a long history. Among the early Puritans, for example, one of the heresies considered most dangerous was that of "antinomianism," or the heresy of strong emotion and of subjective conviction (especially conviction of salvation) resulting from private experience.[8] Antinomians were believed to be more likely than the average person to engage in impulsive actions, some of which might be socially undesirable, but probably the main reason this heresy was so feared and so strongly condemned was that such heretics, being full of life and strongly motivated, were very likely to oppose established beliefs and authorities. Anne Hutchinson, for example, who was banished from Massachusetts Bay Colony as a seditionist and abandoned to "Sathan" as an antinomian heretic, had not hesitated to publicize her views and to condemn, in the strongest terms, most of the leading religious authorities of the colony (she even "told off" the court, just

7. Liebman (1946).
8. Smith (1954). Smith traces the development of Puritanism over the centuries; his book is invaluable for the student of beliefs and attitudes and is filled with fascinating hypotheses.

when it seemed to be about to let her off with a mere admonition). Antinomianism ("against-the-law-ism"), as it included a conviction of being among those predestined to Heaven, despite anything one might do, seemed to open the door to "sinning" and was therefore associated, in the thinking of the Puritans, with libertinism. The actual extent to which the conviction of salvation contributed to "sinning" is unknown—some antinomians, e.g., Mrs. Hutchinson, were of impeccable "morality"—but the greater liveliness of the body, through excitement and emotion, did lead some individuals to greater sexual activity during periods of revivalism (a form of antinomianism) both in England and in the American colonies.[9]

A more prevalent heresy, especially among the clergy, was that of Arminianism (named after Jacobus Arminius, a sixteenth-century Dutch anti-Calvinist), which in effect denied the doctrine of predestination and placed great emphasis upon free will, the use of reason, and adherence to moral rules. Legal Arminianism, the moralism of severe ministers such as Increase Mather, was the seventeenth-century form of this heresy (revived in an exaggerated and much more absurd and hypocritical form in the late nineteenth century), which is what is usually and unjustly meant by the term "Puritanism." During the eighteenth century Arminianism blossomed into scientific liberalism, which doomed orthodoxy among the intellectually elite, such as the leading Unitarians.

The majority of Puritans tried to steer a middle course between these two heresies, each of which gained ascendancy from time to time. The Great Awakening of the 1730s and '40s led by Jonathan Edwards and George Whitefield was an outbreak of antinomianism, as were many of the group meetings and conventions in the decades preceding the Civil War.[10]

The fact that from its beginning our culture has included a deeply

9. John Wesley became well aware that to arouse people emotionally without suitable follow-up might deliver them to the Devil. On this point see William Sargant (1957). Sargant's excellent book contains a wealth of observations on the use of emotion, especially fear and terror, in suggestion, including brainwashing and conversion.

10. For an account of the Chardon Street Convention, which sounds strikingly similar to some of the meetings of recent years, see Smith (1954), pp. 367–71. Smith's account of how this happy and innocent exuberance merged with Arminianism and developed into deadly hatred and violence is especially relevant to what is happening today.

rooted conceptual and attitudinal polarity between reason and emotion has considerable significance for the current social revolution and the diverse movements within it. Like most such cultural polarities, it is partly valid. Emotion, in many contexts, does make reasoning difficult or even impossible and does increase the likelihood of irrational beliefs, perceptions, and actions, especially in groups, in which irrationality can so easily receive social support. Reasoning can and does in many contexts inhibit feeling, as well as perception and new, creative perspectives or ideas. On the other hand, the attempt to make decisions (including "scientific" decisions about what exists, what one is justified in believing, or what can be done to bring about certain results) without any guidance from feelings is exceedingly dangerous, and can result in the most irrational conclusions and atrocities. As indicated near the beginning of this paper, I believe that an even stronger assertion is justified, namely, that it is impossible to reason about human affairs or to see things as they are without feelings, or at least the fresh memory of them. Although from one point of view this statement is obvious and is simply common sense, it is by no means a part of the methodology of the psychology of our time. On the contrary, psychology is taught as though feelings are at best irrelevant to the scientific researcher and usually a contaminating influence which should be eliminated. One may search our more "scientific" psychological journals and books in vain for even a hint of how the authors feel about their subject matter. The academic world has attracted many people who are uncomfortable in the presence of any expression of feeling, even in print (or perhaps I should say *especially* in print); such people usually lack strong convictions, especially about anything of obvious relevance to daily life, and are therefore considered more or less "safe" to employ as teachers of our youth, even when they have heretical opinions. Our faculties badly need scholars with passionate convictions, who are willing to admit openly to such convictions and to argue openly and fairly with those of different convictions, not with the primary aim of "winning the argument" but of increasing communication and knowledge. A passionate argument should be a form of friendly and ethical competition, as indeed it often was among some of the gentlemen of the old school.

The social suppression of emotion leads not only to widespread emotional impoverishment but to more or less volcanic eruptions as the organism attempts to come back to life. A person who is emotionally alive and *who also is free to reason* is likely to be strongly individualistic and uncontrollable. The initial phases of antinomian upheavals tend to be highly individualistic, even anarchistic; as organization develops, individualism is tolerated less and less and highly anti-individualistic mass movements evolve. We see this sequence developing at the present time. Leaders of mass movements arouse emotion but do all they can to destroy reason, and thus create docility toward the leader and ferocity toward the opposition—as with trained animals, which of course the followers of such leaders are. Fascist and Nazi writings and speeches repeatedly admonished the youth not to think, but to respond to the leader. As thinking (i.e., reasoning) is hard work, the youth were only too happy to oblige. Absurd beliefs (e.g., that the Jews were "sex perverts" and had tainted blood) are also used to destroy any tendency or ability to reason. Further, only certain emotions, and not others, are encouraged; the Nazis, for example, did not encourage the emotion of poignancy, nor of love between individuals.

On the other hand, an individual who is free to reason may be rendered controllable or ineffective by destroying or limiting his emotions. Even if he arrives at correct conclusions of importance, he is unlikely to do anything about such conclusions or even to try to communicate them if they are not welcomed. Then, too, if it is true that reasoning itself is limited if the emotions are constricted, then, since each of us lives in a somewhat different emotional space (i.e., the set of emotions which we experience in our daily lives, plus memories of emotions of the past), it follows that each of us is limited, in his own way, in his ability to reason about human affairs, though some are much more limited than others.

The current upswing of antinomianism is inevitable in a society with too tight a lid on the expression of emotion. On the other hand, there are strong trends in the opposite direction; not only is there a great amount of violence that is committed unemotionally, but unemotional (cold-blooded) violence is being presented as an *ideal.* In numerous popular films and television shows, especially westerns and science fiction, the heroes (and heroines also) kill their enemies with no more emotion than one would crush an insect, or face death not so much with heroic courage as with complete indifference, sometimes in close temporal proximity to jokes. Then, too, the search for feeling is often unsuccessful and leads only to unpleasant feelings such as anxiety and depression or to excitement and sensation alone and, in either case, to an excessive use of drugs. Equally dangerous is the self-righteous indignation which is becoming more prevalent among many groups, and which is aggravated and apparently justified whenever persecution is perceived to have occurred. Righteous indignation is one of the most satisfying and strengthening of emotions unless coupled with a conviction of impotence and hopelessness; Hitler made full use of it by endlessly harping on how Germany had been mistreated. Smith traces the development of the abolitionist movement and shows how antinomianism merged with legal Arminianism into a river of hatred and destruction, in which moderates on both sides were drowned out by extremists, or became extremists themselves. The parallels with current developments are both interesting and ominous—and discouraging, also, as there are many clear lessons from the Civil War period that have obviously never been learned, largely because they have never been publicized.

In a sane society emotional expression would be a part of everyday life, public as well as private, and would be taken for granted. Tears, for example, would be common not only at funerals but also at sad or poignant plays and films and at joyful meetings of friends and relatives, and certainly they would be no cause for embarrassment. (Latin societies are much more sane in this respect than ours.) Individual differences in emotional reactions would be regarded as natural, interesting, and valuable, and not, usually, as signs of deviance, fanaticism, pathology, or immaturity. (I don't know whether Latin societies are any saner than ours in this respect; they may be less sane.) There is no such society and we can have only a very limited notion of what it would be like to live in such a society.

Psychotherapy and encounter groups offer social contexts within which emotions and their expression are supposedly not only acceptable but also necessary, if much benefit is to be obtained. The advantages and benefits are too widely known to need repetition here. It cannot be emphasized too strongly, however, that no psychotherapist, group leader, or group member is "value free" or is "open" to or "accepting" of any emotional expression that may occur, even if we exclude physical violence. A tolerance and acceptance of a wide range of individual differences can be and often is developed, but there are always limits, and it is important to know what those limits are. It is no doubt obvious to the reader that my sympathies lie with the individual who does not have the feeling (or the lack of feeling) and the perceptions that he is "supposed" to have according to ideological or group standards, many of which are codified unwittingly into psychodynamic theory and into the perceptual dimensions in common use among "psychologically sophisticated" individuals or among members of any given group. Some group sessions, like some staffings of patients in clinics and mental hospitals, resemble vultures pecking at a dying carcass. Encounter groups, like psychotherapy, offer excellent opportunities for people to grow and develop, to be helped and loved, but also to be bullied, intimidated, systematically destroyed, or brainwashed by people who are often not even aware of the ideological frameworks within which they operate, or even that they operate within such frameworks.

For reasons indicated above, as well as additional ones, I suggest that individuals be trained to stand up against the pressures of authorities and groups by utilizing procedures of the type initiated by Solomon Asch. In Asch's experiments group pressure (through the use of "stooges") led many subjects to say (and some even to believe) that a given line matched another in length even though they could see very clearly that one of the other lines was the correct choice.[11] Although there was nothing new in the finding that an individual's judgment can be influenced by judgments of others, it was startling to see that group pressure could outweigh even immediately available and very clear perceptual data. By using procedures of this kind, with many varieties of judgment, school children could be trained to withstand pressures from their peers and from authorities. Although strengthening independence and individualism, such training would also probably result in a much greater willingness to attempt to understand and accept the feelings and perceptions of others, to appreciate individual differences, and to accept whatever rules are actually necessary to maintain social order. Training of this kind would be completely out of the question in most societies (e.g., "primitive" societies); ours has a tradition of individualism and dissent which could be aroused in support.

11. Asch (1952). An apparatus developed by Richard Crutchfield and his associates at the University of California (Berkeley) eliminated the use of "stooges" by simply giving each subject false information about the judgments of the other subjects.

Rules, Rackets, and "Mental Illness"

PREFACE Several years ago, when I complained one day to my father about the baloney in psychology, he replied, "Well, of course there's baloney in every field." My father was a lawyer, with extensive experience in both criminal and civil law, and I'm sure he did not intend to except his own profession in his blanket statement. While I was growing up, there were some very funny scenes in our home, when my mother, who was a very intelligent and perceptive woman, would imitate certain courtroom procedures she had observed. She would often take the side of the witness against the lawyer, mocking the repetitious and banal questioning that lawyers often engage in. She would become increasingly indignant and would indicate what *she* would say and do if she were ever insulted by such questioning—it was very clear that, without the use of any obscenities, she would have received a stiff sentence for contempt of court. My father would, at times, patiently explain the necessity of such procedures, but occasionally my mother would succeed in "getting his goat," i.e., in arguing in such a way that

197

he would remain unconvinced, yet baffled at how to answer. In this my mother was recapitulating what many women have done throughout the centuries, i.e., seen ridiculous aspects of the extremely complicated "games" created by men. She would also at times say, with great earnestness, "*Everyone* should study law." (She had no doubt seen the enormous advantage that such knowledge gives.) The "obvious impossibility" of this proposal made it a family joke, which she accepted good-naturedly, still insisting that, however impracticable the suggestion, she was nevertheless somehow right. Actually she was on to something very profound, at the same time that she would have been greatly disturbed by the many implications of her assertion.

In a moment of grandiose enthusiasm I announced during a workshop at Esalen two years ago that I would "destroy the entire mental health racket." This greatly amused the other participants, some of whom were mental health experts, and some wished me well in my project. But it would be unfair to destroy the mental health racket without destroying the rackets of all the other ideologists. I hope that my friends and relatives in law, mental health, religion, accounting, etc., will not take offense at the attack that follows. There have always been those who want to give genuine service to others, at reasonable fees, and others who eagerly create monopolies and accumulate fortunes for little or no work at all (or for automatic rituals which might as well be performed by robots). The grossest example of the latter is to be found in the history of indulgences, a subject that must be studied to be believed, but even among the much maligned medieval and early modern clergy there were those who shunned all rackets and rendered genuine service. Then of course there have always been those

conscientious souls who tirelessly create enormous
amounts of dull, depressing work and misery for everyone. . . .

Rules, Rackets, and "Mental Illness"

RULES OF GOOD GAMES

The assertion that life is made up of "games" seems to
me somewhat cynical and offensive; nevertheless, it will be helpful to
begin by mentioning some characteristics of the rules of good games,
especially games that have been popular for many years, and are well
standardized and widely known. One of the most obvious of these
characteristics is that the rules are *clear,* i.e., there is no question about
what the rules are. Second, the rules are clearly understood by *all the
players,* with the possible exception of those who are just learning to
play. Even the latter are helped by the other players to learn the rules,
i.e., they are told, or shown, what the rules are. The rules of most popular games, especially those played by adults, are *written down in rule
books which are accepted as official,* and are available to all players. There
are exceptions to these statements, as, for example, when children spontaneously create novel games, but they hold for the vast majority of
good games, from hopscotch or red rover to football, bridge, and chess.
Furthermore, the rules of games have been designed, or have evolved
over many years (centuries, in the case of games such as chess and
bridge), to yield *enjoyment* for all the players, losers as well as winners,
and an enormous variety of games has been created, to suit almost
every taste. For this reason, games are ordinarily played *voluntarily*—
exceptions are those occasions, at school or at parties, when one is
more or less forced to play, or when one plays a game just to accommodate others. Players ordinarily play *within the rules,* i.e., they do not
attempt to *win by cheating.* There are many people who would never
play a game (for pleasure) with anyone who is not trusted to play fairly
(within the rules), even if he has the opportunity to cheat, because *there*

would be no pleasure in the game. There are of course many games, both for children and for adults, in which it is within the rules to fool or trick the opponents in certain ways, or to do something without its being detected—naturally these tactics do not fall within the meaning of "cheating" as here intended.

Not only do players of good games refrain from cheating, but at their best, in the absence of a referee, they give the benefit of the doubt to their opponents (this used to be called by the archaic term "sportsmanship" and is incompatible with playing with the sole objective of winning). When referees are used in games, they are themselves thoroughly familiar with the rules and strive to be as unbiased as possible in all of their decisions.

Finally, although good games are played primarily for the enjoyment of playing, not just winning, the vast majority of players of good games know what it means to win and what it means to lose, i.e., they are familiar with the experiences of winning and of losing and the consequences thereof. It follows that a winner has some understanding of a loser, and vice versa.

The more banal and obvious the above remarks, the better, because the firmer the foundation they lay for what is to follow.

THE CREATION OF BAD GAMES

A bad game can be created by rules that have opposite characteristics from those listed above. A thoroughly bad game would consist entirely of such rules, although such a thoroughly bad game would not necessarily be the most destructive.

The first characteristic of a thoroughly bad game is that its rules are *not clear to at least some of the players.* The number of players to whom the rules are not clear can vary from a small percentage to *everyone;* in other words, there could be games with rules not clear to anyone, even to those who specialize in rules, such as those who make the rules and those who serve as referees and as consultants to referees.

There are several means of insuring that only a minority of players, at most, will understand the rules of a game. The crudest of such means is to keep the rules secret, except to a chosen few. A more effective method however, is to *formulate the rules in language that is vague.* The vagueness of the language will in itself attract a great number of players; it will mystify and enchant, especially if it is beautiful. Well-written poetry, embodying numerous images and musical sounds, is ideal for enchanting rules of this kind. Unintelligibility has enormous snob appeal —even to some who think themselves free of status motivation—and anyone who achieves the reputation of understanding such formulations will acquire disciples who will listen to him for hours or years without any desire to challenge him, because they much prefer mystification to enlightenment (though sometimes paying lip service to the latter) and they frequently regard clarity as dull and vulgar.

Even if the rules are clear to those who originally formulate them in vague language, they can be passed on to succeeding generations, and can in this way eventually become unclear to everyone. This is especially likely if the original formulations are lost or destroyed.

Another way of preventing most players from understanding the rules is to word them precisely and clearly enough, but *in a language which most players cannot read, or understand even if spoken.* A subtle modification of this method is to use the unknown language only for certain *key words and phrases,* without an understanding of which the remainder is necessarily unintelligible. This method has the advantage of sounding extremely *learned,* and can impress those not easily taken in by vague poetry.

Still another method for insuring that rules will not be understood is to make them exceedingly *numerous and complex,* and to scatter them throughout a vast literature, available only in a relatively few libraries, even if one has the time and ability to study it.

In a good game the procedures for interpreting and enforcing the rules, the penalties for their violations, and the procedures for inflicting penalties are as clear and as clearly formulated as the rules themselves, and are usually considered part of the latter and included within the same rule books. Further, the time required for decisions of referees, infliction of penalties, etc. is sufficiently short to allow the game to proceed without undue boredom and desire to stop the game.

In a thoroughly bad game the interpretations of rules and the procedures for interpreting and enforcing the rules, the penalties for violations, and the procedures for inflicting penalties are even less clear than the rules themselves, and are at best formulated only incompletely, in a literature that is even more extensive and more scattered than that of the rules. A person can spend a lifetime studying the rules, or interpretations of the rules, of a thoroughly bad game and still not master his subject matter. Further, the game itself, and especially the procedures for inflicting penalties, are so long and drawn out that a large percentage of players, even of those who at some time wanted to play the game, want out.

Those who know the rules and procedures, at least within human limitations, do not, as in a good game, help other players to understand the rules and procedures. Instead, they take advantage of the ignorance of most players, which is encouraged and perpetuated and claimed to be inevitable and unavoidable, with great profit to themselves.

A thoroughly bad game will not be designed for the enjoyment of as many players as possible but for the misery or discomfort of as many as possible, preferably everyone. It will not usually be played voluntarily, in the sense in which good games are played voluntarily; players are either forced to play, or play "voluntarily" only in the sense that they choose the bad game in preference to others that appear to be even worse, or to an extremely severe penalty for not playing at all.

In a thoroughly bad game many of the players will cheat (i.e., intentionally violate the rules) as often as they believe they can get away with violations, to avoid as much misery or discomfort as possible, or to win, insofar as anyone wins. Cheating will be frequently justified on various grounds: that one didn't want to play, anyway; that everyone cheats, unless he is a coward, a misguided fool, or some kind of strange mystic; that it is impossible to win without cheating; that the official rules are not the "real" rules; or that one's cheating is not selfishly for oneself, but for others. Because of the nature of the rules and the way the thoroughly bad game is played, it is also much easier than in a good game to cheat and believe at the same time that one is not cheating—as in the childish act of lying while crossing one's fingers behind one's back. Even if one does not deliberately cheat, however, he will still violate rules, because of their number and complexity and his ignorance of them, and he will thus be vulnerable to penalties at any time that the referees wish to charge him with violations.

As for referees, in a thoroughly bad game their decisions are made to their own advantage, if they are themselves players, and if they are not players they arc at best "unbiased" only in the sense of selling their services to the highest bidder.

Finally, in a thoroughly bad game, although the sole objective is to win and to avoid losing at any cost, few, if any, players know what it means to win and to lose, i.e., few if any experience both winning and losing. Most players, in fact, do not experience either very clearly, nor do they know whether they are in the process of winning or losing. Even on his deathbed a person may not know whether he has won or lost a thoroughly bad game. Further, even the concept of winning or of losing may be extremely vague and ill-defined; to put it another way, in a thoroughly bad game everyone loses, though many do not know it.

LAWS AS RULES OF PSEUDODRAMAS

Lawmakers do not generally think of themselves as setting rules for games; instead, they see their work as creating and/or formulating whatever rules must be made by the government to maintain an orderly, productive, equitable, and satisfactory society. Nevertheless, laws lead to various forms of human behavior and experience which resemble games or dramas in that they entail roles which people take or are assigned, frequently with much conscious and deliberate pretense, somewhat similar to acting on a stage. The differences are great enough however, that "drama" is as objectionable and misleading as "game." For want of a commonly accepted term, therefore, I will call these human behaviors and experiences that are shaped and conditioned by laws "pseudodramas." Unwise laws lead to very bad pseudodramas, having many of the characteristics of thoroughly bad games described in the foregoing. The example of Prohibition will make these remarks clear. Despite more than half a million arrests and more than three hundred thousand convictions during a ten-year period, the Eighteenth Amendment and the Volstead Act were notoriously unsuccessful in their ostensible purpose, but it would be false and misleading to say that they had no important effects.[1] The effects were, in fact, widespread and pervasive and illustrate the *enormous power of laws, even "ineffective"*

1. During 1969 there were about sixty thousand arrests in California alone for illegal possession of drugs, usually marijuana. The inequities are probably even greater than during Prohibition.

ones. The pseudodramas thus created were not lacking in drama—going blind from drinking wood alcohol, being shot by a rival gangster for invading his territory, or losing the respect of one's children when the latter observe their parents' hypocrisy are not lacking in dramatic elements. Even the pretense ("acting") which resulted from Prohibition was not always a genuine attempt to fool others, but was similar to the pretense of an actor on stage, whose audience knows that he is attempting to play a role, not necessarily to be himself. Sometimes the audience was made up of authorities (police, district attorneys, judges, mayors) who had to be allowed to pretend that they did not know what was being carried on, or by whom and where. Pretense, therefore, was sometimes for the purpose of allowing others to pretend—it can be seen how complex such pseudodramas became and how confused the players could become, especially if the authorities themselves were profiting in some way from the numerous rackets that developed. These real-life dramas are called "pseudodramas" to distinguish them from the clean-cut action on stage, by actors who know what they are doing, before an audience of people who know that they are there to enjoy the play. The term has the additional advantage of sounding appropriately *absurd,* as the phenomena referred to are indeed absurd, involving enormous irrationalities and unnecessary suffering and deprivation for everyone.

The fact that the Eighteenth Amendment could become known as simply "Prohibition" in itself indicates that the population was generally ignorant of the principles I am trying to explain. There had been plenty of other prohibitions, some of which created pseudodramas compared with which those created by Prohibition were trifles. The prohibition of adultery, for example, while failing in its ostensible purpose, has created pseudodramas for thousands of years, victimizing large numbers of those who did not violate this prohibition themselves, especially spouses (usually wives) of adulterers and those unjustly accused.

THE PERSISTENCE OF RULES

It is very difficult to change the rules of good games, especially those popular for long periods, or to persuade an adult who likes one game to switch to one he might like even better. It is much more difficult, however, to change the rules of bad pseudodramas, regardless of how destructive they are, but for very different reasons, of much greater subtlety and complexity. (In bad pseudodramas everything, including human psychodynamic processes, becomes extremely complex, even to the point that players find it extremely difficult to understand anything that is simple.) A game, however good, is only a game, whereas a pseudodrama is part of real life, usually deeply ingrained into the culture and having a long and supposedly (mythically) honorable background. Changing an official rule does effectively change a good game, whereas even if a law can be changed the bad pseudodrama is not necessarily vitally affected (the threat of social ostracism, for example, can be as effective as the threat of jail, or even more so). But there is much more to the difference than this: rules of good games have been made with the purpose of maximizing enjoyment, whereas rules of bad pseudodramas, especially those rules concerned with the most important aspects of life—love, work, knowledge—have been made with very different purposes from those of maximizing human enjoyment, satisfaction, or fulfillment. It is often asserted that the rules against sin had salvation, i.e., the attainment of Heaven, as their purpose (at least ostensibly), but it is more accurate to say that their ostensible purpose was to help people to avoid Hell, which was emphatically and repeatedly asserted to be the destination of the vast majority. The concept of Hell was much clearer and more vivid and colorful than the concept of Heaven, and this is readily understandable since most pleasures were considered more or less sinful (too much laughter, for example, was a sin, though only venial according to most authorities) and to think of pleasures that were suitable for angels was difficult—as mentioned previously, one of the few that the theologians could agree upon was the spectacle of inferior beings writhing in Hell. There was no such vagueness and ignorance about Hell, whose fires were described as hundreds or thousands of times hotter and more painful than those of Earth, but which included also painful freezing ice, rendings of the flesh, terrible odors, hideous ravenous and rapacious demons, etc. That this sort of destiny awaits some, especially those guilty of sins of the flesh, is not an entirely dead theology; soon after Errol Flynn's death in 1959, Dr. Graham, addressing an audience estimated at twenty thousand in Indianapolis, said that he wished that the late actor could preach the sermon, as the latter would say, "Repent, repent." Dr. Graham has had a great deal to say about sex (including the assertion that we are afflicted with a sex madness, with which assertion I am in complete agreement) on his path to success, and has been greatly honored by presidents and the general public for his wisdom in such matters, whereas when Dr. Leo Koch, who was assistant professor of biology at the University of Illinois, said, in 1960, "A mutually satisfactory sexual experience would eliminate the need for many hours of frustrating petting and lead to much happier and longer lasting marriages among our younger men and women," he was promptly fired, President Henry called his statement a "grave breach of academic responsibility," and the Board of Trustees overruled a protest by more than two hundred faculty members.[2]

To recapitulate, the rules were not so much aimed at the achievement of happiness, even in the hereafter, as at the avoidance of a terrifyingly clear misery that was extremely likely to be one's fate, and that could be avoided only by a fortunate few who exercised the greatest diligence and vigilance, accompanied preferably by as much suffering in this life as they could bear. Whereas it is commonly argued that the belief in a "life after death" was a great comfort to those of the "age of faith," actually it seems more reasonable to say that it would have been an enormous relief to a great many, *especially to those who strove most sincerely to live what they believed to be the right kind of life and who, therefore, were most deserving of some happiness,* to believe that death was the end, and that during this life one was entitled to some simple pleasures and relief from continual discomfort, such as, in the case of certain saints, the removal of a hair shirt (later, certain metal appliances) and a bath now and then, so that their holiness did not make their presence so difficult for others to bear.

It might appear superficially that if rules tend to produce widespread misery, then the masses should be eager for changes in the rules, and the conservatism of the masses has therefore seemed puzzling and maddening to many reformers. The answer lies in the fact that within the terrible pseudodramas created by rules that are not even aimed toward

---

2. *Palo Alto Times*, September 22, 1960. Dr. Koch's recommendation is similar to that made by Bertrand Russell in *Marriage and Morals*, which years later led to the cancellation of his appointment as visiting lecturer at the City College of New York. The whole shabby and maddening story is told in *The Bertrand Russell Case*, edited by John Dewey and Horace Kallen (New York: Viking, 1941), a book which is peculiarly difficult to obtain.

human happiness or fulfillment, it is very difficult to work out a way of living that is even *tolerable*. As man is an intelligent and ingenious animal, even the masses (mistakenly considered "dumb" by many educated and upper-class people) can amazingly often find a tolerable way of life. A change in rules, expecially when initiated and made by others, and when made with the same purposes as the old, creates new pseudo-dramas that are equally bad, if not worse, and in any case entails the difficult process of finding a new tolerable solution, meaning one preferable to suicide (which no doubt would have been much more common during the age of faith if it had not been widely taught and believed that suicide would send anybody straight to Hell).[3]

The conservatism (in the sense of refusing to initiate or support changes in rules) of the ruling classes, although partly explainable on the same basis, has other reasons of the greatest importance. When rules make satisfaction in living difficult, then of course they will be broken repeatedly by those who can do so without suffering too much from the consequences. Those who are in the most advantageous position in this respect are the ruling classes themselves, who are often said to "make their own rules," both collectively and individually. The greater toleration of individual differences within the ruling classes, which is sensible and socially agreeable, is not so much a matter of enlightened respect for natural variation as it is simply a necessary acknowledgment that it is very difficult to force rules upon a rich, powerful, or "high-spirited" person, even if you are rich, powerful, or "high-spirited" yourself. On the other hand, the *open* violation of rules, such as the former practice of many monarchs of not only having mistresses openly, but of bestowing the title of duke upon the "royal bastards," as they were literally and accurately called, of having people jailed or executed openly on the basis of personal whim, of appointing relatives or favorites to lucrative offices when they were still children, and of taxing unmercifully, so that the ruling classes could live more luxuriously, has largely disappeared and been replaced with practices that are far more discreet and therefore even less honorable. This is not to say that there have not been members of the ruling classes who have lived according to the official rules much more strictly than the common people, and that there

---

3. Cook Islanders are said to have had difficulty in grasping the concept of suicide, and thought it incredible.

are not members of these classes today who strive to live so that their lives, private as well as public, can be "an open book." Almost needless to add, such people have not necessarily been kind to their weaker fellows, of any class.

If there is one lesson to be learned from the lives of the Great (and most history is unfortunately about the lives of the Great, the lives of other individuals having been considered of no importance to record, except in fragments such as when they caused some kind of trouble) it is that any escape from bad pseudodramas is more apparent than real. Calvin is a good example of one who has a "winning" role in a bad pseudodrama. He triumphed over his enemies and died in complete control of his city and his church. His influence was enormous and enduring; he has a secure place in history texts. No one who studies his life would want to live it, except possibly someone determined to suffer.

THE OFFICIAL IDEOLOGISTS
AND THEIR HELPMATES

Another class of especial significance which is in a favorable position to violate rules is made up of those who are given the responsibility for the enforcement of rules, including the determination of whether violations have occurred and the determination of what the rules actually are—i.e., the interpretations of rules, whenever necessary. With very few exceptions, *these are the only people who know what the rules are,* and they form a tiny minority of the population, partly overlapping the ruling classes. An even smaller class, only partly included within the first, is made up of those who claim to understand not only the rules, but also the presumed *bases* of the rules, i.e., the nature of man and whatever aspects of the world are relevant to the rules, and whose claim is recognized by the society, or some significant portion of it. These are what might be called the *official ideologists.* (The term "ideologist" is more broadly applicable to anyone who has a theory of the nature of man individually and socially.)

These two latter classes are not only in a favorable position to violate rules themselves, but to profit enormously, in money, power, and status, from the rackets generated by rules, and usually, the worse the pseudodramas created by the rules, the more profitable are the rackets which result. The ideal rule, for the creation of rackets, would be one that would be frequently and universally violated, very difficult to understand fully, based upon an ideology that would require many years of study to master, and enforced by procedures with which only the small class referred to above can possibly be familiar. The Eighteenth Amendment, though failing to meet some of these criteria, was nevertheless a close enough approximation to create enormous rackets. Much nearer the ideal, however, was the set of rules developed by the theologians (the official ideologists) of the Middle Ages. Although to the primitive Christians of the first two or three centuries it was reasonably clear whether they were or were not violating rules and what rules they were or were not violating, by the thirteenth century it was clear only that everyone was violating rules (sinning) but whether any given act or thought was or was not a sin usually had to be left strictly up to experts (the first class mentioned above) and it was highly presumptuous (and dangerous) to question any of their decisions. It was even more presumptuous and dangerous to question the justification of the rules provided by the official ideologists. The fact that the official ideologists disagreed among themselves, and the fact that they frequently pointed out, in the most scathing terms, the gross ignorance (of the rules and the procedures associated with them) and unfitness of the majority of members of the first class (the clergy) did not by any means interfere with the enormous rackets which were so profitable, and which expanded with each succeeding century.[4]

SECRETS OF THE RULING CLASSES

Although some monarchs were so bold as to make dukes of their royal bastards, there were plenty of violations by the ruling classes that were discreetly kept to themselves, or at least almost to themselves. Now one of the ways of rising to power is to learn such secrets, i.e., violations of rules that the ruling classes would prefer remain unknown to their powerful enemies or rivals and also to their subjects—or, as we say today, "the general public." If one is sufficiently ruthless, unethical, and daring, then blackmail is an obvious possibility, but it is unnecessary to be so crude as that. Merely having the power to use

4. Lea (1896). This is the most impressive work of scholarship I have ever encountered.

such information against someone is usually sufficient to obtain plenty of royal favors, provided, of course, it is known (by the guilty party) that one has such information. The best way to insure that the information be accurate and that the guilty party knows that one has the information is to get him to *tell on himself, directly to the potential blackmailer.* Even if one's integrity is such that he can be completely trusted to keep such information to himself, he can still exercise enormous influence over the guilty party, especially as the latter will tell more and more, as he feels safer and safer, and will often idolize the one to whom he confesses for his superhuman integrity, which he recognizes (if he has much experience) as extremely rare, and for his amazing and godlike understanding and tolerance of transgressions of the official rules. The Jesuits specialized in being confessors to the ruling classes, and their rise to power, as well as their development of sophisticated and modern views of sin (probabilism and casuistry) are largely understandable on this basis.[5] Within the field of "mental health" the nearest counterparts of the Jesuits are some of the well-known Freudian analysts.

RACKETEERS AND REFORMERS

History, regardless of what theory of history is considered (and there are many), has no beginning and no end. It is like a long and endlessly intricate series of novels, with the same characters appearing over and over, often in the most unexpected contexts, seen from a variety of perspectives, and with new characters entering the scene constantly, as if the plot were not already much too complex for any reader to grasp and much too fantastic to be at all credible. History is like *The Alexandria Quartet,* multiplied backward and forward thousands of times by hundreds of authors with unlimited imaginations, interwoven with generous doses of science fiction and of satire that goes "much too far." Uncensored history is largely unbelievable unless validated by the most thorough and painstaking scholarship, which historians, possibly more than any other learned group, should be given credit for achieving. Even if H. C. Lea were the only scholar that the field of history had produced,

---

5. Lea (1896). Anyone interested in ethics will find it extremely rewarding to study the history of tutiorism, probabiliorism, and probabilism. Many of the arguments are surprisingly modern.

the achievements of the field would be extremely impressive, as Lea, who had no assistants except copyists of rare books and manuscripts in several parts of the world, was like a whole team of scholars, miraculously coordinated together in a way that scholars never are.[6] Lea's *History of Auricular Confession and Indulgences,* three volumes packed with historical facts and references to source materials, tells a story which, if presented as fiction, could easily be accused of going much too far and therefore reducing what would otherwise be very competent and savage satire to *absurdity.* The pseudodramas described by Lea meet all the criteria of thoroughly bad games listed above, and they are fully as absurd as anything dreamed up by Jonathan Swift. Taken in conjunction with Lea's other works they form an unanswerable indictment not just of Christianity (so called) but of all Western civilization. There are additional aspects of Lea's historical accounts, however, to which I wish to call special attention. One is the existence of a minority of individuals, in all ages, who have hated rackets and have done their best to destroy them. These reformers have usually had an uphill fight and have usually lost. They have not necessarily been kind or freedom-loving—Savonarola (a "loser") and Calvin (a "winner") are prime examples of reformers who wanted to treat everyone with impartial severity—but all have tried to reduce an inequitable chaos. Another aspect is the existence of individuals who have tried to allow others to have some freedom and pleasure in life, despite the hateful rules. Lea speaks with indignation of priests during the Middle Ages who refused to inform certain of their flock that fornication was a sin and even seemed to be fascinated with such innocence. Even adultery was sometimes countenanced in the same way, and for the same reason. Some of these priests must have seen the absurdity of the rules governing sexual behavior and the absurdity and injustice of the prevalent hypocrisy, and protected their flocks in the only way they could, because to oppose the official rules openly and explicitly

6. Even though I have been aware for many years that the most learned people are not necessarily in universities, still I had assumed, until reading Bradley's biography (1931) of Lea that Lea was a professor. To my amazement I learned that he was a highly successful businessman, who made a fortune in the publishing business, and wrote his major works after retirement! In his spare time he performed numerous civic duties, wrote pamphlets for the Union League (which he helped organize), was consulted by presidents, led a reform movement in Philadelphia, and engaged in numerous philanthropies, in which he took a personal not merely a financial interest.

was virtual suicide, especially if anyone paid any attention to such open opposition. There were also missionaries (especially Jesuit) who refused to enlighten their converts about sexual sin and to make them clothe their bodies—these also were severely criticized, disciplined, or removed by the more rigid moralists within the Church. The same secret leniency was sometimes practiced with respect to heresy. Numerous other priests partly nullified or modified rules by granting absolution more readily for some sins than for others, not necessarily in accordance with the complex instructions they were supposed to follow (which most of them did not understand, in any case).

There were numerous priests, in other words, who were not reformers in the sense of trying to change official rules—perhaps because they saw the situation as hopeless—but who tried to help others as much as possible within the absurd and destructive social structure in which they and their flock were embedded. They participated in the lucrative rackets of confession and indulgences, but only because they saw no alternative.

EXPERTS OLD AND NEW

The parallels between practices and attitudes within the mental health professions and those within the clergy of the Middle Ages and later are revealed by Lea's work to be remarkably closer than they are thought to be even by most of those who, like me, have alluded to such a comparison, or who have pointed out that "mental illness" is the modern equivalent of "sin." Even though I was specifically looking for and expecting such parallels, I was amazed by what I encountered. A full exposition would require a large volume; here I shall confine myself to a few salient points.

The chief parallel is that between the absurd presumptuousness of the clergy in claiming exclusive jurisdiction over concepts of right and wrong and the equally absurd presumptuousness of those mental health experts (including some social scientists who have involved themselves in this field) who claim exclusive jurisdiction over concepts of "normality" and "abnormality" or "mental (or emotional) health" and "mental (or emotional) disturbances" or "character disorders or defects." Neither all members of the clergy nor all mental health experts have made this claim, but it has almost always been made, in one form or another, by *organizations,* as well as by the more prominent and ambitious members of these professions. These claims of the clergy and of mental health experts are absurd and presumptuous for similar reasons. If we examine the behavior of human beings in their natural habitats in the same manner as we would examine the behavior of any other species, then we soon see something that explodes any claim of exclusive jurisdiction over these basic aspects of human behavior, by any class of experts, however learned and experienced they may become. That "something" that we see is that *the vast majority of people know a great deal about human behavior, i.e., the behavior of those with whom they deal in their everyday lives.* Most of this knowledge is so "overlearned" that it is not even thought of as knowledge, and therefore we do not ordinarily attempt any formulation of it. If the average person attempts to formulate all that he knows about human behavior he will find that such a formulation is extremely difficult (the first sentence he writes may, on further reflection, be seen to be false), banal (since it will be largely "what everybody else knows too"), and endless (requiring a series of large volumes). Intermingled, however, with the valid knowledge of human behavior that is common to almost all members of a given social structure are delusions, superstitions, stereotypes, and enormous blind spots, such that the individual sometimes cannot perceive that which is clearly before his eyes. The "experts" in human behavior begin their professional careers with about the same knowledge and the same delusions as others. They are then exposed to an enormous body of "knowledge," including a vast literature only a tiny fraction of which they can even read, let alone master. Many of them fall into a trap that is repeatedly set along the way, namely, they become convinced that *we know very little of importance about human behavior.* Many Ph.D.s in psychology solemnly affirm this statement and piously add that there is an urgent need for more research—the most socially acceptable doctrine among scientists of all kinds (usually accompanied by a request for money). There is an even more extreme doctrine, however, common among psychologists, that *nothing of real importance about human behavior can be proved.* This doctrine is developed and supported by what is called "methodology," and is a variation of the old philosophical statement, considered extremely profound: "All I know is that I know nothing." Another popular doctrine is that *there are no new important discoveries to be made in psychology*—all those that are of importance having already been made by Freud, etc.[7] All these doctrines are false and are as absurd as any to be found among medieval theologians, some of whom held similar beliefs. The expert becomes trapped by such doctrines when he submits to much more stringent rules about making any assertions than those imposed upon laymen, concerning the same matters. He must "prove" what he has to say (as "prove" is defined by the methodologists of his profession), whereas laymen are free to use any observations and any reasons they can muster (as well as emotional appeals to prejudice, ignorance, and superstition, if they are ignorant or ruthless enough to do so). The expert is not only typically without conviction (which has usually been destroyed even if he had any to begin with) but has been trained to regard conviction and especially *enthusiasm* with suspicion; he thus condemns those among his colleagues who display conviction about anything of sweeping importance (except, of course, conviction about skeptical doctrines and the urgent need for more research) and leaves "laymen" alone, as though they are beneath his notice. This attitude contributes to the result of having the community and the nation ruled by ignorant and ruthless people, with "forceful personalities" and an equally forceful determination to avoid learning anything of basic importance which they don't already know.

At the same time, however, and somewhat paradoxically, experts attempt to establish a role that enables them to make decisions and pronouncements and engage in certain practices *without having to give any convincing justification to laymen,* on the grounds that the justification is intelligible only to experts. A justification in terms of the specialized knowledge of experts is of course intelligible only to experts, especially if it is worded in a language known only to the latter, or filled with references to a vast and complex literature. The next step, which can be taken more or less simultaneously, is to establish a *monopoly* over such a one-sided role. These steps are usually taken in good faith, i.e., they seem both to experts and to laymen to be a natural and inevitable result of the establishment of a body of knowledge and

7. I remember when I firmly believed this doctrine. It now seems very strange.

techniques and of adequate training centers. *This view is a snare and a delusion* and if the majority of people fall into it the experts of human behavior will rise to power (as they are already doing) in the same way that the clergy rose to power, with comparably disastrous results. The study of human behavior and experience is not one of the newest but on the contrary the *oldest* science, and *there are no laymen in the study of human behavior and experience.* This is not so say that those who have been professionally concerned with human behavior and experience for many years do not know anything of importance that the average "layman" does not know, or cannot work with other people on their problems in ways that the average "layman" cannot; on the contrary, most experts know many things of importance which they are very careful *not* to tell "laymen," apparently under the delusion that they would be torn to pieces on the spot. Many "laymen," however, are in the same position —and refrain from telling others for exactly the same reason; furthermore, everyone, with the possible exception of very young children and the severely mentally deficient, is in an advantageous position to be the world's leading expert on one person, namely, *himself,* because he is the only person to whom his own experience is directly available.[8] But we all—expert and "layman" alike—have our delusions, superstitions, and blind spots, even about ourselves (even after one or more "enlightenments"), varying from one person to another in an astonishing and bewildering manner, and we err in both directions about the knowledge of others—sometimes assuming that they are ignorant about matters concerning which they are far better informed than we are, and simultaneously assuming that they can see what is right before their eyes, or hear what is clearly and literally being said to them, or what they are saying themselves (one of the most effective techniques in psychotherapy is simply to have someone repeat several times what he has just said and to focus on it, instead of rushing on to something else).

8. People have been duped into believing they don't know much about themselves in the same way that they were formerly duped into believing they were terrible sinners. "I don't know myself" or "I don't know who I am" are the modern counterparts of "I am a terrible sinner," and are highly regarded by groups of believers. To claim to know oneself is as presumptuous as it was to claim to be without sin; it is best that this claim be made for oneself by others. Those who are thought by groups of believers to have attained self-knowledge are like those who were thought by believers to be without sin; a very few of them may be saints, and a great many of them are people whom it is wise to avoid.

MODEST PROPOSALS

During the past decade there have been increasingly ambitious proposals to subject certain groups of people (for instance school children, candidates for political office, employees in certain industries or government offices) to screening procedures (tests, interviews, etc.) in order to weed out those with "mental illness" or "personality disturbances or defects," or to prescribe remedial action (such as counseling or psychotherapy). These proposals continue to be made despite the criticisms and heated controversies (including extended hearings in Congress) that have arisen around the testing programs that have already been in use for some time in government, industry, and education. One of the most recent proposals is by Dr. Arnold Hutschnecker, a psychiatrist who was formerly an internist and who, in the latter capacity, treated Mr. Nixon while he was Vice President. Dr. Hutschnecker proposed that psychological tests be administered to all six- to eight-year-olds in the United States to *determine their future potential for criminal behavior*. President Nixon asked the Department of Health, Education, and Welfare to study Dr. Hutschnecker's proposal.[9]

Dr. Hutschnecker's proposal was widely denounced by both experts and laymen and was not recommended by HEW. It is ironic, however, that only a few days following all the widespread unfavorable publicity, a much more sweeping proposal was announced by James Allen, Jr., United States Commissioner of Education (HEW), and this second proposal has apparently aroused little if any public opposition.

> Children would be brought by their parents to a central diagnostic center at age two and a half where they would be given physical and educational examinations to determine their individual needs.
>
> "The purpose of the center would be to find out everything possible about the child and his background that would be useful in planning an individualized learning program for him," Allen said.
>
> This information would be fed into a central computer, analyzed, and transmitted to a team of professionals whose job it would be to write a detailed prescription for the child and, if necessary, for the home and family as well.

9. *San Francisco Chronicle,* April 6, 1970, p. 1.

The "prescriptions" for the child would be filled by the Board of Education and the City Health Department or family doctor. Those for the family would be filled by whatever agency in the community has jurisdiction over the services needed. . . . Continuing evaluations would be made every few weeks until the child was six, after which semi-annual evaluations would be conducted by progress evaluation teams, again aided by the child's permanent computerized record.

"Prescriptions would, of course, be altered as necessary, depending upon the child's progress under his individualized learning and development plan," he said. "The parents would, of course, be consulted every step of the way."

Allen said that every child, from two and a half to six, would spend part of his time in a Good Start Center, "where he would learn how to work and play with children of various backgrounds." [10]

Although it is stated that the parents will be consulted, there is no indication of the extent to which the program itself will be on a voluntary basis, either for the child or the parents, as though that is a matter of no special importance.

When the Fourth Council of Lateran in 1215 decreed that all Catholics *must* confess at least once per year, they instituted a screening process whereby *in theory* each individual would be carefully examined by an expert, who would determine the kinds and degrees of sin of which he was guilty, prescribe the remedy (penance, those forms of which were supposed to help prevent further sinning of the same kind being called, interestingly enough, "medicinal"), and, whenever appropriate, pronounce the supplicant to be free of sin (absolution). The theories governing the screening process were even at that time so complex that the layman had to rely completely upon the expert (priest) to know whether he was or was not in a state of mortal sin (and therefore would or would not go to Hell if he died at that moment). During the thirteenth and succeeding centuries theology became even more complex and the layman's position, therefore, more and more helpless. It is true that the vast majority of the clergy, according to contemporary accounts, were about as ignorant of theology and of the procedures they were supposed to be following as the laymen—some much more ignorant—but they

10. *San Francisco Chronicle,* April 15, 1970, p. 5.

were backed by the authorities of the Church and their ignorance could be more or less hidden or at least prevented from causing too many scandals, which were a constant threat and greatly feared by the high-ranking officials of the Church (just as scandals are greatly feared today by executives in government, education, and industry).

The psychological theories upon which the determination of "criminal potential" would be based, if Dr. Hutschnecker's proposal were adopted, are as complex and as beyond the understanding of laymen as medieval theology. This becomes obvious when we consider that Dr. Hutschnecker has recommended the Rorschach Test as especially worthy of consideration for such screening. A layman would find himself completely helpless in attempting to refute the charge that his child shows evidence of "criminal potential" on the Rorschach. His only recourse would be to find either another Rorschach expert who would disagree with the first or else an expert who would deny the validity of using the Rorschach in this way (a weak defense, however well justified, if the usage were sanctioned by HEW). In taking this recourse he would moreover be considered ungrateful, uncooperative, and negligent in his duty as a parent, if not actually "mentally ill," "disturbed," or guilty of some "criminal potential" himself (the latter would undoubtedly often be the case).

Under Dr. Allen's proposal, the parents would be even more helpless, as this proposal gives a carte blanche to the experts to make whatever determinations seem suitable, by whatever means seem appropriate.

To many experts—probably the majority—the helplessness of the "layman" in opposing the expert is inevitable and therefore must be accepted. In their view, there is no more reason to expect a "layman" to be able to argue rationally with an expert in detecting "criminal potential," or any other psychological dimension, than to expect him to be able to argue rationally with a mathematician or an atomic physicist or an expert in the psychophysiology of vision about complex problems within these fields. The "new" science of personality theory, measurement, and change has, after many years of struggling development, reached the exalted position of these "older" sciences, with respect to expert versus layman. As stated previously, this view is a snare and a delusion and is analogous to the idea that only a theologian could possibly understand questions of right and wrong. Quite aside from the limitations and inadequacies of the Rorschach Test for the proposed usage, the fact that "crime" is defined by laws implies that Dr. Hutschnecker is apparently proposing the stamping out of any tendencies to violate the rules laid down by authorities (or by society). This is of course the traditional, Old Testament view of child rearing so effectively revived by Calvin, and is one of the main reasons the world has been in such a hell of a mess, because instead of a rational respect for authority and the recognition of its necessity, within limitations, it builds up a fear, hatred, and contempt of authority which must be continually repressed and therefore becomes explosive. Perhaps Dr. Hutschnecker is referring to behavior such as hurting and taking advantage of other children; in this case, I would suggest "meanness" as a much better term than "criminal potential." It would certainly be worth-while to eliminate meanness, if this could be done without the kind of tyrannical method proposed, and without eliminating a healthy aggressiveness and thus destroying one of our oldest and best American traditions of refusing to knuckle under to authorities when we believe they are wrong about something of importance.

INCOMPETENCE AND INJUSTICE AMONG HIGHLY TRAINED EXPERTS

During my training in clinical psychology I heard a resident in psychiatry say, apropos a psychiatrist who was one of the most highly trained experts in the hospital, "Dr. ―― has no business working in a mental hospital; he should be out digging ditches somewhere." Although even as a novice I had seen that some of the remarks made by this expert about patients were so ridiculous as to be embarrassing, still I thought the resident's remark was unduly harsh. Later, however, I decided that the remark was not harsh enough, in view of the consequences to other human beings of having such a man in such a position. Yet if it had been possible to create a different social structure, in which even a lowly resident (or patient, or psychiatric technician) could confront a high and mighty authority *openly*, with the general assumption by all present that there are no laymen in human behavior and that human behavior is so complex that neither expert nor "layman" need feel humiliated at being shown to be grossly wrong about some important matter, whether about a given person (including himself) or about people in general, this particular expert would have had much to offer, and I'm sure he could have more than held his own on many points. The same kind of situation exists, of course, in government, industry, the armed forces, education, etc., but in mental hospitals and clinics it is particularly disastrous. There is some progress being made, in some places, but progress is very slow, as it goes against long-standing authoritarian traditions and against status motivation which, probably because of the closing of other avenues of satisfaction (not primarily by the individual but by the rules of the social structure in which he is embedded), is apparently the dominant motivation in our society. Status is the most destructive motive there is; it is as strong among learned authorities as among movie stars, whom the former erroneously look down upon. Movie stars do not usually claim to be oriented primarily toward such lofty aims as the development and dissemination of knowledge, or the helping of other people. The same relative lack of hypocrisy is found among businessmen, another group inappropriately considered inferior by academicians. Even politicians, hypocritical though they often are, usually admit that they want to be in control, and openly campaign for power.

Szasz has exposed the absurdity and hideous injustice of the treatment of "mental illness" by some experts. In *Psychiatric Justice* he presents trials that are astoundingly analogous to trials for witchcraft. In one of these, especially, it is no exaggeration to say that the patient's attorney made fools of the hospital psychiatrists who claimed that the patient was "in such a state of idiocy, imbecility, or insanity as to be unable to understand the charges against him, the procedures, or of aiding in his defense." Yet the judge, after six weeks for deliberation, ruled *against the patient*.[11] Anyone with any sense of fair play who reads this case will wonder why. My own hypothesis is that the judge realized the implications of ruling in favor of the patient, namely, that these psychiatrists, in positions of great responsibility and with experience of hundreds of cases (whereas Szasz had been involved in only a very few court cases), *did not know what they were doing, at least in this particular*

11. Szasz (1965). I am referring to the case of Mr. Louis Perroni (a fictitious name). As Szasz points out, everyone claims to be *for* the patient, and that is one of the basic troubles. The inquisitors were *for* the heretics and witches, doing their best to save their souls.

case, and could not see the obvious even when it was pointed out to them. Unfortunately, this is the correct conclusion, horrifying and incredible though it may seem to many laymen (it will not seem at all incredible to many experts, especially the younger ones, and unfortunately they are generally already too accustomed to this conclusion to be horrified by it). The solution is not simply more training and more experts and higher salaries for psychiatric technicians—it did not help the witches and heretics when the number of inquisitors was doubled, and when they were more highly trained and experienced in their methods.

IN DEFENSE OF THE M'NAGHTEN RULE

It is of course partly with tongue in cheek that I defend the much discredited M'Naghten Rule—that one who commits a serious crime which is *malum in se* (wrong in itself, not just against the law) is "insane" if he did not know that what he was doing was wrong. But only partly. The most effective, determined, dangerous, and destructive people tend to be extremely *moralistic* in the wrong direction, i.e., a direction that destroys human lives and takes the joy out of living for those who remain. By "moralistic" I mean someone who has certain emotions, the chief of which are *righteous indignation* and *guilt,* and who has a sense of obligation (of "ought"). This definition should make clear that I am not suggesting that being moralistic is a bad thing in itself; on the contrary, a person who is not at all moralistic is also dangerous and destructive, especially when trusted with responsibility, and is properly called "demoralized." When too many people become demoralized the country is in for plenty of trouble.[12] Righteous indignation,

12. The following passage from Hamilton (1942) is of great interest in this connection:

"As the idea of Zeus became loftier, two august forms sat beside him in Olympus: THEMIS, which means the Right, or Divine Justice, and DIKE, which is Human Justice. But they never became real personalities. The same was true of two personified emotions esteemed highest of all feelings in Homer and Hesiod: NEMESIS, usually translated as Righteous Anger, and AIDOS, a difficult word to translate, but in common use among the Greeks. It means reverence and the shame that holds men back from wrongdoing, but it also means the feeling a prosperous man should have in the presence of the unfortunate—not compassion, but a sense that the difference between him and those poor wretches is not deserved.

"It does not seem, however, that either Nemesis or Aidos had their home with the gods. Hesiod says that only when men have finally become completely wicked will Nemesis and Aidos, their beautiful faces veiled in white raiment, leave the wide-wayed earth and depart to the company of the immortals" (pp. 40–41).

unless accompanied by a conviction of impotence, is an energizer which makes one ready and willing to put up a fight (literal or figurative), and someone who has this emotion at his disposal has a great advantage over one who does not.[13] Hitler was an extreme moralist, repeatedly energized by righteous indignation about the way Germany had been treated and energizing others with his inspiring oratorical fury. Germans were demoralized and Hitler moralized them. Even in the final days and hours of his life Hitler apparently believed that his cause and methods had been highly moral. Philip II of Spain, generally considered one of the cruelest monarchs of all time, was extremely moralistic, doing his utmost to do his duty, i.e., to protect and extend the "true faith," and he was regarded by many long after his death as the model of a Catholic ruler. Calvin was an extreme moralist, as were many of the inquisitors. Some of the "witches" were deluded in believing that they had actually attended the Sabbat and were thus "mentally ill," but the inquisitors, who were deluded in a more socially acceptable and much more dangerous manner, are the ones whom the M'Naghten Rule would identify as "insane."

In a fascinating paper on ethical values, Lea argued against Lord Acton's view that historical figures should be judged by the same moral standards by which one judges his contemporaries.[14] Lea cited Philip II as an example of someone who should be given at least credit for being moral in his own terms, which were shared by many others of his time. Lea's emphasis upon taking the historical context into account is valid (and for this reason, among others, Calvin should be placed several notches above Hitler), but Lord Acton still had a point, which Lea indirectly acknowledged by speaking of a "slow and uneven progress upward" in morality over the centuries. Lea's point is that the moral standards themselves were faulty and inferior—that certain acts which were thought and felt by almost everyone, not just cruel rulers, to be moral were clearly immoral. By the M'Naghten Rule, therefore, the populations of Western Europe (and many other parts of the world as well) have been, with few exceptions, "insane." This is very similar to the point I tried to make by the assertion in the paper on psychosis that

13. It is probably at least partly for this reason that women have tended to gain the upper hand in marital relationships in the United States.
14. "Ethical Values in History," in Lea (1942).

people have been "mean and crazy." It is impossible to appreciate this point fully unless one reconstructs, in his imagination, many historical scenes and realizes the highly inappropriate emotions which the actors were experiencing.[15]

If the M'Naghten Rule is generalized a bit, to consider anyone "insane" if he has a completely unreasonable *scale* of morality, then the insanity of Western civilization becomes even more obvious, because for many centuries sexual "sins" and crimes were officially on a par with homicide (just as they are today in the statutes of most of our states) and, as homicide was so continually practiced by pious monarchs and encouraged and blessed by the "Christian" organizations in formal ceremonies and printed documents, sexual acts eventually aroused much more horror, righteous indignation, and revulsion than murder, just as they apparently do today on the part of a large proportion of our population. The placing of heresy (which in practice boiled down to disobedience to ecclessiastical authority) on a par with homicide (and much worse than homicide, after about the twelfth century) points to the same conclusion.

From the little that is known about Jesus, he was apparently a relatively sane man, using the generalized M'Naghten Rule as a standard.

RULES AND MORALITY

Morality is concerned with what people ought and ought not to do, just as rules are. For centuries "sin" and "crime" were synonymous and our legal codes today grew largely out of moral (and immoral) concepts and attitudes, and moral (and immoral) concepts and attitudes continue to modify legal codes. The distinction between morality and adherence to a legal code is not necessarily easily perceived, even by very sophisticated people. In the highly popular and critically acclaimed motion picture *Gigi*, for example, the heroine and her lover (a confirmed bachelor) direct their lawyers to draw up a legal contract

---

15. If we could observe historical scenes as they actually happened, then we would be able to see and hear immediately the cruelty and irrationality of whole societies (except for young children). The making of documentary films will eventually lead to this result. Even now, not only some of the old documentaries but some of the old features give immediate insights into the irrationalities of the time at which they were made.

prior to their living together. This is presented in such a way as to make such a contract seem extremely ridiculous, mercenary, and unromantic. When the lover, just on the eve of consummation of this arrangement, asks the heroine to marry him, the girl's mother and Maurice Chevalier and the audience all say "Thank Heaven," and there is the usual happy ending, with the usual marital bliss ahead. But probably very few members of the audience stop to think that "getting married" meant that they would now enter into a legal contract, writtten not by themselves or their own lawyers, in terms which they would understand and to which they could honestly agree, but one defined by the legal code and judicial decisions of France, made without any reference to them or their individual desires, scattered throughout an enormous literature, in a language they could not understand—understandable, in fact, only to a lawyer or a judge. Unless Gigi and her lover were very different from the average American couple, they would have only the haziest notions of the legal contract they were entering into. We may wonder, as we read history, why populations accepted so much obvious tyranny as right and just, but it is hard to find any more tyrannical acts of a government than the legal regulation of the most important personal relationship without any allowance for differences in the type of legal contract desired and without even insuring that the legal contract thus imposed is understood by those directly concerned. Furthermore, the State can change all the contracts, suddenly and all at once, without even consulting the parties concerned. Hopefully this will someday be regarded as a curious barbarity, and people will wonder why we could not see it as such.

The perception of the absurdity of the legal institution of marriage, as it now exists (of which the divorce rackets form only one aspect, though an enormous one in itself), leads to a much more important and inclusive one: that it is even more absurd and unjust to subject a population to rules and procedures without teaching the people what the rules and procedures are, and *what their bases are,* than it would be to force people into a game and expect them to play it without knowing what the rules and procedures are (their bases do not usually need to be taught, as games have been devised for enjoyment, as stated previously). We are so used to the idea that only lawyers and judges can have this kind of knowledge that we do not see the absurdity and injustice of the helplessness of the layman. The "barbarians" of northern Europe of the early Middle Ages would be much more likely to see this than we are, just as the early Christians would have seen immediately the injustice and absurdity of the helplessness of the layman vis-à-vis the priest of the late Middle Ages. The rackets of lawyers (minimum fees for divorce, probate, etc.), accountants, and mental health experts are all comparable to the rackets of the clergy of earlier times. There will always be plenty of "sin," "mental illness," "crime", litigation, and confusion, with plenty of business for racketeers, unless people are taught rules, procedures, and bases, and are stimulated and allowed to contribute to creative solutions to the problems of living, with due and unprecedented allowances for individual differences.

Appendix and Bibliography

A Note on "The Necessity of Phenomenology"

I have already told how I was sometimes seen as "anxious and defensive" when actually I had been angry and what I would regretfully call "offensive." The same kind of people who make such misinterpretations also tend to make other interpretations, behind one's back, in terms of unconscious motivation, levels of communication, etc., and to those who think in this way conscious contents are often of so little importance that there is no need even to attempt to ascertain them. Some of the laymen who are "psychologically sophisticated" are (as in religious cultism) even more extreme than the experts. It struck me as extremely ironic that those who are most prone to label others "paranoid" are the most paranoid people I have ever encountered, in the sense of seeing and hearing "hidden meanings" in what others do and say. I want to emphasize that in making this general assertion I am not thinking of any specific individual; the people who surrounded me were by no means consistent in this way, and I was very fortunate to be associated with experts who placed considerable emphasis upon clear, direct, and out-in-the-open communication, e.g., Don Jackson and Virginia Satir. I still remember with gratitude Don's telling me, during a phone conversation, "Joe, you're talking like a damned nut." But all of us who have been trained in the field of "mental health," including those who, like myself, are not psychoanalytically trained or even particularly analytically oriented, know more than enough to be able to make very damaging interpretations, which appear at least on the surface to be quite plausible, of any behavior that we happen not to like for one reason or another, and all too often to convince ourselves that our interpretation is sincere and fair. Many laymen are in the same position, especially if they have undergone quite a bit of psychotherapy. Another way of putting this is that each of us has knowledge of some ideology which permits us to believe that any behavior of which we disapprove in some way is a sign of heresy ("mental illness" or "emotional disturbance" or "character disorder" or "low level of development" or "lack of self-knowledge"). I realized, with appropriate horror and disgust, that I had sometimes been guilty of this kind of injustice myself, and I still have to remind myself that it is a continuing and never-ending possibility, especially to the extent that I become cold and indifferent toward someone, which I certainly do at times.

At any rate, although I had for many years disagreed strongly with the philosophy of science that dominated academic psychology, and had published a few heretical papers,[1] the *potential destructiveness of any psychology that puts little or no emphasis upon conscious events struck me with greatly renewed force.* It was with great excitement, therefore, that I conceived an argument based upon mathematical logic (which I had studied years before as a graduate student) which hopefully would defeat the behaviorist–logical positivist–operationist position (which is congruent with any psychoanalytic psychology that de-emphasizes conscious events), which is still the dominant, though unacknowledged, ideology in departments of psychology.

My excitement reached such a pitch that I was deluded into thinking I had contributed a milestone in the history of science. Even in my inflated condition I felt an imperative need for confirmation from at least one mathematical logician and made a trip to Berkeley to see one whom I had known in graduate school, only to find that he was no longer working in the foundations of mathematics and, though friendly and cordial, was much too busy to go into my argument. I was becoming somewhat desperate (not too unusual a symptom among those who think they see something important that others do not see) when I learned that John Myhill was at nearby Stanford. A paper by Myhill

1. Adams (1953, 1955, 1957); Adams and Brown (1953).

which I had read several years before had actually been the starting point of my argument,[2] and thus it was perhaps not too surprising that he told me that I was essentially correct in that portion of the paper. I told Myhill later that he had "saved my sanity." I dittoed about fifty copies and sent them to a number of distinguished psychologists, physicists, philosophers, and logicians, most of whom I had known while at Princeton. Many were kind enough to reply, some very favorably. A friend to whom I had sent a copy showed it to Gödel, who commented that the conclusions which I draw from his theorem are suggested by it but are not strict consequences of it, but that there are strict consequences of his theorem which are in some way similar. His generous offer to discuss this with me in case I were in the vicinity of Princeton reinforced my conviction that these ideas were of earth-shaking importance (of the many famous scientists and scholars in the city of Princeton during my years of graduate study there, Gödel was probably the most inaccessible of all—I had never even had a glimpse of him).

The paper was submitted to the Psychological Review in 1960 and was rejected, with lengthy comments by the anonymous referee. The editor invited me to revise it, but after a few attempts (following my hospitalization and discharge, which occurred while the paper was being considered) the task seemed hopeless and pointless. The paper had already been revised twice, and to expand it into a thorough exposition would require a huge tome which no one would read even if I were able to write it.

Originally this paper, together with the referee's comments, were to be printed in this appendix, partly for humor and partly with the hope of snaring some experimental psychologists into reading it. Everyone who has seen the book manuscript, however, has urged that "The Necessity of Phenomenology" be omitted, as much too technical even for an appendix, and I have at last reluctantly admitted the wisdom of this advice.

---

2. In the early 1930s Kurt Gödel proved a theorem (the "incompleteness" theorem) which caused a revolution in the field of mathematical logic. Myhill's arguments took Gödel's theorem as a point of departure.

Bibliography

Adams, J. K. 1953. "Concepts As Operators." *Psychological Review,* vol. 60, pp. 241–51.
_____. 1955. "Expressive Aspects of Scientific Language." In *On Expressive Language,* ed. H. Werner. Worcester, Mass.: Clark University Press.
_____. 1957. "Laboratory Studies of Behavior Without Awareness." *Psychological Bulletin,* vol. 54, pp. 383–405.
_____. 1961. "Differentiation and Dedifferentiation in Healthy Functioning." *Journal of Humanistic Psychology,* vol. 1, no. 2, pp. 30–38.
_____. 1963a. "The Overemphasis on Sex in Western Civilization." *Journal of Humanistic Psychology,* vol. 3, no. 1, pp. 54–75.
_____. 1963b. "Psychosis: 'Experimental' and Real." *Psychedelic Review,* vol. 1, pp. 121–44.
_____. 1964. "Deception and Intrigue in So-Called 'Mental Illness.' " *Journal of Humanistic Psychology,* vol. 4, no. 1, pp. 27–38.
_____. 1965. "The Neglected Psychology of Cowardice." *Journal of Humanistic Psychology,* vol. 5, no. 1, pp. 57–69.
_____, and Adams, P. A. 1961. "Realism in Confidence Judgments." *Psychological Review,* vol. 68, pp. 33–45.
Adams, J. K., and Brown, D. R. 1953. "Values, Word Frequencies, and Perception." *Psychological Review,* vol. 60, pp. 50–54.
Adler, Polly. 1953. *A House Is Not a Home.* New York: Rinehart.
Ardrey, Robert. 1961. *African Genesis.* New York: Atheneum.
Asch, S. 1952. *Social Psychology.* New York: Prentice-Hall.

233

Bailey, D. S. 1959. *Sexual Relation in Christian Thought.* New York: Harper.

Bateson, G., et al. 1956. "Toward a Theory of Schizophrenia." *Behavioral Science,* vol. 1, pp. 251–64.

Bazelon, D. L. 1960. "Crime and Insanity." In *The Mentally Ill Offender: A Symposium.* Sacramento, Calif.: Department of Mental Hygiene.

Beers, C. W. 1921. *A Mind That Found Itself.* New York: Doubleday.

Birch, H. G. 1956. "Sources of Order in the Maternal Behavior of Animals." *American Journal of Orthopsychiatry,* vol. 26, pp. 279–84.

Boisen, A. T. 1936. *The Exploration of the Inner World.* Chicago: Willett, Clark.

Bradley, E. S. 1931. *Henry Charles Lea.* Philadelphia: University of Pennsylvania Press.

Brinton, Crane. 1959. *A History of Western Morals.* New York: Harcourt, Brace.

Bugental, J. F. T.1962a. Precognitions of a Fossil. *Journal of Humanistic Psychology,* vol. 2, no. 2, pp. 38–46.

—————. 1962b. "Self-Fragmentation As a Resistance to Self-Actualization." *Review of Existential Psychology and Psychiatry,* vol. 2, pp. 241–48.

Cameron, N. 1959. "Paranoid Conditions and Patients." In *American Handbook of Psychiatry,* ed. S. Arieti, vol. 1. New York: Basic Books.

Carnap, Rudolph. 1947. *Meaning and Necessity.* Chicago: University of Chicago Press.

Chandler, A. L., and Hartman, M. A. 1960. "Lysergic Acid Diethylamide (LSD-25) As a Facilitating Agent in Psychotherapy." *AMA Archives of General Psychiatry,* vol. 2, pp. 286–99.

Clarke, A. C. 1961. "The Evolutionary Cycle from Man to Machine." *Industrial Research,* vol. 3, no. 5, pp. 30–35.

Cohen, S. 1960. "Notes on the Hallucinogenic State." *International Record of Medicine,* vol. 173, pp. 380–87.

Coulton, G. G. 1938. *Inquisition and Liberty.* New York: Macmillan. Boston: Beacon Press, 1959.

Cunliffe, Marcus. 1958. *George Washington, Man and Monument.* Boston: Little, Brown.

Cuppy, Will. 1950. *The Decline and Fall of Practically Everybody,* ed. Fred Feldkamp. New York: Holt.

Dobbs, Z., et al. 1962. *Keynes at Harvard,* rev. ed. New York: Veritas Foundation.

Dollard, J., and Miller, N. 1950. *Personality and Psychotherapy.* New York: McGraw-Hill.

Duffy, C. T., with Hirshberg, Al. 1965. *Sex and Crime.* New York: Doubleday.

Durant, Will. 1944. *The Story of Civilization,* vol. 3, *Caesar and Christ.* New York: Simon & Schuster.

————. 1950. *The Story of Civilization,* vol. 4, *The Age of Faith.* New York: Simon & Schuster.

————. 1957. *The Story of Civilization,* vol. 6, *The Reformation.* New York: Simon & Schuster.

Ferguson, Ian. 1924. *The Philosophy of Witchcraft.* London: G. G. Harrap.

Field, Ellen. 1964. *The White Shirts.* Los Angeles: Tasmania Press.

Ford, C. S., and Beach, F. A. 1951. *Patterns of Sexual Behavior.* New York: Harper.

Fromm, Erich. 1941. *Escape from Freedom.* New York: Farrar & Rinehart.

Geyl, Pieter. 1958. *Debates with Historians,* rev. ed. New York: Meridian Books.

Goffman, Erving. 1959. *The Presentation of Self in Everyday Life.* Garden City, N.Y.: Doubleday.

————. 1961. *Asylums.* Garden City, N.Y.: Doubleday.

Graham, C. H. 1950. "Behavior, Perception, and the Psychophysical Methods." *Psychological Review,* vol. 57, pp. 108–20.

Grillot de Givry, Emile. 1931. *A Pictorial Anthology of Witchcraft, Magic, and Alchemy,* trans. J. Courtenay Locke. Boston: Houghton Mifflin. New York: University Books, 1958.

Gross, M. L. 1962. *The Brain Watchers.* New York: Random House.

Hamilton, Edith. 1942. *Mythology.* Boston: Little, Brown.

Harkness, G. 1931. *John Calvin.* New York: Holt.

Hebb, D. O. 1949. *The Organization of Behavior.* New York: John Wiley.

Hoffer, Eric. 1951. *The True Believer.* New York: Harper.

Huxley, Aldous. 1956. *Tomorrow and Tomorrow and Tomorrow.* New York: Harper.

Jahoda, M. 1958. *Current Concepts of Positive Mental Health.* New York: Basic Books.

Jourdain, P. E. B. 1918. *The Philosophy of Mr. B*rtr*nd R*ss*ll.* London: Allen & Unwin.

Jung, Carl. 1928. *Two Essays on Analytical Psychology.* New York: Dodd, Mead. New York: Meridian Books, 1956.

Kalinowsky, L. B. 1959. "Convulsive Shock Treatment." In *American Handbook of Psychiatry,* ed. S. Arieti, vol. 2. New York: Basic Books.

Kelly, G. A. 1955. *The Psychology of Personal Constructs.* New York: Norton.

Kennedy, John F. 1956. *Profiles in Courage.* New York: Harper.

Kesey, Ken. 1962. *One Flew Over the Cuckoo's Nest.* New York: Viking.

Köhler, W. 1938. *The Place of Value in a World of Facts.* New York: Liveright.

Koffka, K. 1935. *Principles of Gestalt Psychology.* New York: Harcourt, Brace.

Korzybski, A. 1948. *Science and Sanity,* 3rd ed. Lakeville, Conn.: International Non-Aristotelian Library.

Krech, D., and Crutchfield, R.S. 1948. *Theory and Problems of Social Psychology.* New York: McGraw-Hill.

La Barre, W. 1954. *The Human Animal.* Chicago: University of Chicago Press.

Lea, H. C. 1866. *Superstition and Force.* Philadelphia: Henry C. Lea. Westport, Conn.: Greenwood Press, 1968.

————. 1896. *A History of Auricular Confession and Indulgences in the Latin Church.* Philadelphia: Lea Bros. & Co. Westport, Conn.: Greenwood Press, 1968.

————. 1907a. *A History of the Inquisition of Spain.* New York: Macmillan. New York: AMS Press, 1966.

————. 1907b. *History of Sacerdotal Celibacy in the Christian Church,* 3rd ed., rev. London: Williams & Norgate. New Hyde Park, N.Y.: University Books, 1966.

————. 1939. *Materials Toward a History of Witchcraft,* ed. A. C. Howland, with Intro. by G. L. Burr. Philadelphia: University of Pennsylvania Press. New York: Thomas Yoseloff, 1957.

————. 1942. *Minor Historical Writings and Other Essays,* ed. A. C. Howland, with Intro. by G. L. Burr. Philadelphia: University of Pennsylvania Press.

————. 1961. *The Inquisition of the Middle Ages.* New York: Macmillan. (Abridged version of a 3-vol. work first published 1887–88.)

Lemert, E. M. 1962. "Paranoia and the Dynamics of Exclusion." *Sociometry,* vol. 25, pp. 2–20.

Leuba, J. H. 1925. *The Psychology of Religious Mysticism.* New York: Harcourt, Brace.

Lewis, C. S. 1955. *Surprised by Joy.* London: G. Bles.

Liebman, J. L. 1946. *Peace of Mind.* New York: Simon & Schuster.

Mackenzie, C. 1962. *Certain Aspects of Moral Courage.* New York: Doubleday.

McReynolds, P. 1960. "Anxiety, Perception, and Schizophrenia." In *The Etiology of Schizophrenia,* ed. D. D. Jackson. New York: Basic Books.

Maisel, A. Q. 1962. "The Tragedy of Sane People Who Get 'Put Away.'" *Reader's Digest,* February, pp. 98–102.

May, R. 1961. "The Meaning of the Oedipus Myth." *Review of Existential Psychology and Psychiatry,* vol. 1, pp. 44–52.

Miller, George A., Galanter, Eugene, and Pribam, Karl H. 1960. *Plans and the Structure of Behavior.* New York: Holt.

Mills, C. W. 1956. *The Power Elite.* New York: Oxford University Press.

————. 1963. *Power, Politics, and People.* New York: Ballantine.

Mowrer, O. H., and Solomon, L. N. 1954. "Contiguity vs. Drive-Reduction in Conditioned Fear: The Proximity and Abruptness of Drive-Reduction." *American Journal of Psychology,* vol. 67, pp. 15–25.

Murray, M. A. 1933. *The God of the Witches.* London: Sampson Low, Marston.

Myhill, J. 1952. "Some Philosophical Implications of Mathematical Logic." *Review of Metaphysics,* vol. 6, pp. 165–98.

————. 1960. "Some Remarks on the Notion of Proof." *Journal of Philosophy,* vol. 57, pp. 461–71.

Ness, A. 1938. " 'Truth' As Conceived by Those Who Are Not Professional Philosophers." *Skrifter Utgitt av Det. Norske Videnskaps-Akademi i Oslo, II Hist.-Filos. Klasse,* no. 4.

"New Theory of Schizophrenia, A." *Journal of Abnormal and Social Psychology,* vol. 57 (1958), pp. 226–36.

O'Brien, B. 1958. *Operators and Things.* Cambridge, Mass.: Arlington Books.

Osmond, H. 1957. "A Review of the Clinical Effects of Psychotomimetic Agents." *Annals of the New York Academy of Science,* vol. 66, pp. 418–43.

————, and Hoffer, A. 1958. "The Case of Mr. Kovish." *Journal of Mental Science,* vol. 104, pp. 302–25.

Perls, F., Hefferline, R., and Goodman, P. 1951. *Gestalt Therapy.* New York: Julian Press.

Plato. 1963. "A Touchstone for Courage." *Psychedelic Review,* vol. 1, no. 1, pp. 43–46.

Ploscowe, M. 1951. *Sex and the Law.* New York: Prentice-Hall.

Reich, Wilhelm. 1946a. *The Mass Psychology of Fascism.* New York: Orgone Institute Press.

————. 1946b. *The Sexual Revolution.* New York: Orgone Institute Press.

————. 1949. *Character Analysis.* New York: Orgone Institute Press.

Reik, Theodor. 1944. *A Psychologist Looks at Love.* New York: Farrar & Rinehart.

Rosen, J. N. 1953. *Direct Analysis.* New York: Grune & Stratton.

Sarbin, T. R. 1954. "Role Theory." In *Handbook of Social Psychology,* ed. G. Lindzey. Cambridge, Mass.: Addison-Wesley.

Sargant, William. 1957. *Battle for the Mind*. New York: Doubleday.

Schachtel, E. 1947. "On Memory and Childhood Amnesia." *Psychiatry*, vol. 10, pp. 1–26.

Schaff, Philip. 1903. *Modern Christianity. The Swiss Reformation*, 4th ed., rev. New York: Scribner's.

Shirer, W. L. 1960. *The Rise and Fall of the Third Reich*. New York: Simon & Schuster.

Skinner, B. F. 1957. *Verbal Behavior*. New York: Appleton-Century-Crofts.

Smith, C. P. 1954. *Yankees and God*. New York: Hermitage House.

Stevens, S. S. 1951. "Mathematics, Measurement, and Psychophysics." In *Handbook of Experimental Psychology*, ed. S. S. Stevens. New York: John Wiley.

Sullivan, H. S. 1947. *Conceptions of Modern Psychiatry*. Washington, D.C.: William Alanson White Psychiatric Foundation.

————. 1962. *Schizophrenia as a Human Process*. New York: Norton.

Summers, Montague. 1928. Intro. to *Malleus maleficarum* by H. Kramer and J. Sprenger (first published c. 1489). London: John Rodker.

Szasz, T. S. 1960. "The Myth of Mental Illness." *American Psychologist*, vol. 15, pp. 113–18.

————. 1961. *The Myth of Mental Illness*. New York: Paul B. Hoeber.

————. 1963. *Law, Liberty, and Psychiatry*. New York: Macmillan.

————. 1965. *Psychiatric Justice*. New York: Macmillan.

Taylor, G. R. 1954. *Sex in History*. New York: Vanguard.

Terrill, J., Savage, D., and Jackson, D. D. 1962. "LSD, Transcendence and the New Beginning." *Journal of Nervous and Mental Disease*, vol. 135, pp. 425–39.

Watts, A. W. 1961. *Psychotherapy East and West*. New York: Pantheon.

Werner, H. 1948. *Comparative Psychology of Mental Development*. Chicago: Follett.

Whitaker, C. A., and Malone, T. P. 1953. *The Roots of Psychotherapy*. New York, Blakiston.

Wilder, Thornton N. 1938. *Our Town*. New York: Coward-McCann.

Wright, Thomas. 1957. "The Worship of the Generative Powers During the Middle Ages of Western Europe." In *Sexual Symbolism*, by R. P. Knight and T. Wright. New York: Julian Press.